# Hampshire
# Within Living Memory

# WITHIN LIVING MEMORY SERIES

*Other Counties in this series include*:

# Hampshire
# Within Living
# Memory

Compiled by the Hampshire Federation
of Women's Institutes from notes sent by
Institutes in the County

Published jointly by
Countryside Books, Newbury
and the HFWI, Winchester

COUNTRYSIDE BOOKS
3 Catherine Road
Newbury, Berkshire

ISBN 1 85306 290 1

The cover photograph of strawberry bedding
in the 1920s is courtesy of Curdridge WI

Designed by Mon Mohan
Produced through MRM Associates Ltd, Reading
Printed in England by J.W. Arrowsmith Ltd, Bristol.

# Contents

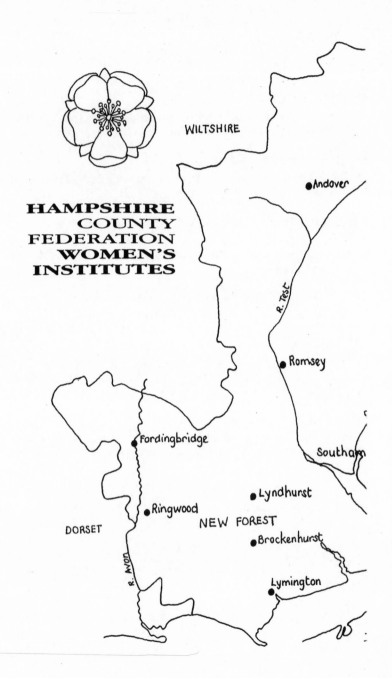

HAMPSHIRE
COUNTY
FEDERATION
WOMEN'S
INSTITUTES

WILTSHIRE

Andover

R. Test

Romsey

Fordingbridge

Southam

Lyndhurst

DORSET

Ringwood

NEW FOREST

Brockenhurst

R. Avon

Lymington

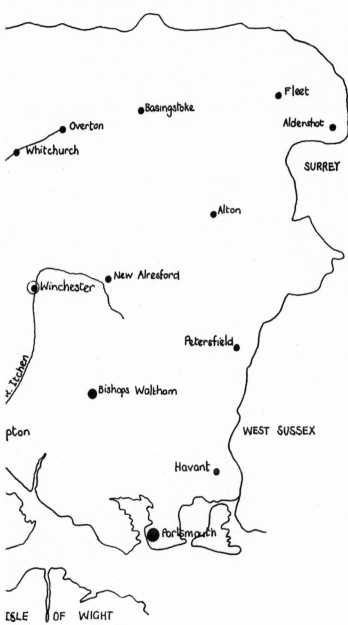

BERKSHIRE

Fleet

Basingstoke

Aldershot

Overton

SURREY

Whitchurch

Alton

New Alresford

Winchester

Petersfield

R. Itchen

Bishops Waltham

pton

WEST SUSSEX

Havant

Portsmouth

ISLE OF WIGHT

# Acknowledgements

Hampshire Federation of Women's Institutes would like to thank all WI members, their friends and families, who supplied material for this project through their local Institutes, and everyone who has in any way contributed. A great deal of time and effort has gone into researching the facts and we are most grateful. Wellow History Society and the Odiham Society Magazine have also been kind enough to allow us to use some of their material.

Unfortunately we were not able to include extracts from every submission; to do so would have meant some duplication of content, and of course we had to take into account the total amount of space available in the book. But all the contributions, without exception, were of value in deciding the shape and content of the book and we are grateful for them all.

Particular thanks go to Rosemary Taylor of Brockenhurst WI who did the drawings at the beginning of each section.

Co-ordinating this book has been a delightful experience with over 100 WIs enthusiastically contributing their memories of life in Hampshire.

Barbara Wells
Co-ordinator

# Foreword

Hampshire, being a large county, is full of contrast. There are the wonderful expanses of open countryside of the New Forest in the south west and the downland of the north and east; the central valleys of the clear running rivers Itchen and Test and the varied coastline. This variety is reflected in the diversity of cities like Winchester, Southampton and Portsmouth, each with a unique history, and areas of industry such as Basingstoke and Eastleigh.

It is easy to think when passing through our old market towns and picturesque villages that nothing has ever changed. Of course, this has never been true but perhaps in this century the pace of change has been particularly dramatic. Many contributors to this book have been surprised that anyone should be interested in their experiences. For usually their lives were no different from their friends and neighbours and therefore 'normal'. However, when all the contributions are read a rich pattern arises which causes the reader to recall something they had long forgotten or surprises them with something they never knew.

I have been struck by the large number of people who experienced an upbringing with few resources and possessions and yet felt they were very lucky in the way they grew up and that it was a time of great happiness. To the generation growing up since 1960 with apparently endless supplies of fuel and water, the convenience of modern technology, an increase in car ownership and foreign travel and the influx of foreign foods, the difference in the lives of their forebears in comparatively recent times will be fascinating.

# List of Contributing Institutes

Abbots Ann, Andover Afternoon, Ashurst, Avon, Basing Afternoon, Basingstoke Evening, Basset, Bedhampton, Bighton, Bishops Waltham Afternoon, Bishops Waltham Evening, Bishopstoke, Bitterne, Boldre, Boyatt Wood Eastleigh, Braishfield, Bramdean & Hinton Ampner, Bramshaw, Brockenhurst, Burghclere & Newtown, Buriton, Burley, Bursledon, Catherington, Chandlers Ford, Charlton, Cheriton, Church Crookham, Cliddesden, Compton & Shawford, Cowplain, Crowe Hill, Curdridge, Denmead Afternoon, Denvilles, Dibden Purlieu, East Woodhay, Easton, Everton & Lymore, Fair Oak, Fareham Park, Farlington, Farringdon, Fleet, Fordingbridge, Forty Acres, Four Marks, Greatham, Hale, Hamble-le-Rice, Hammer Vale, Hartley Wintney, Highclere, Hordle, Horndean, Hyde & Frogham, Hyden, Kempshott, Kingsley, Langley, Laverstoke, Lee-on-the Solent, Lindford, Liphook, Littleton & Harestock, Lockswood, Longstock & Leckford, Lovedean, Lymington, Lyndhurst, Marchwood, Mattingley, Meonstoke, Exton & Corhampton, Micheldever, Milton Green, Nether Wallop, Odiham, Old Alresford, Old Basing, Overton, Padnell Park, Passfield & District, Pennington, Ropley, Rotherwick, Sandleheath, Sheet, Shirley, Solent Afternoon, Solent Evening, South Wonston, Stakes, Stroud Afternoon, Sway, The Worldhams, The Worthys, Titchfield Abbey, Twyford, Upper Clatford, Vernham Dean & Linkenholt, Waltham Chase, Warsash, Waterside, Wellow Owls, West Meon, Wield, Winchester City, Winton, Wonston & Sutton Scotney.

# TOWN & COUNTRY

# SOME TOWNS AND VILLAGES REMEMBERED

**Villages where we all knew each other and doors were never locked, cattle and sheep driven through the centre of town, the excitement of market day, a way of life that was slower and more peaceful – these are just some of the memories of Hampshire's towns and villages since the turn of the century.**

## A PORTSMOUTH CHILDHOOD

'My father Cecil was born into a Portsmouth family on the 24th September, 1896. The city's main employer, the Royal Dockyard, was then changing from wooden to iron and steel ships, having a monopoly on craftworkers and depressing outside wages. Cecil's father had two occupations, a shipwright by day, and running a typical Portsmouth beerhouse, in his own home, by night. Although his own father in particular was strict, and in spite of the poverty and poor housing of those times, Cecil never mentioned any unhappy childhood days.

In those years it must have been a lot more fun being a boy – able to go swimming for example; my father was amazed when he first saw *a woman* actually swimming off the beach at Southsea. Brother Horace, who lost an eye whilst young, being equipped with an expensive hand-painted glass eye, on this same beach managed to break three eyes, a disaster at ten shillings and sixpence each.

The harbour made a great playground, especially Flathouse Quay, where huge timber logs, chained together, would be seasoned for years in the brine. One day after church (the boys sang in the choir of St Thomas) while running across the logs they managed to fall in the water. Once home, they smuggled their best suits into the bedroom tin trunk – horror the next Sunday, the suits were still damp and going mouldy. They didn't sit down for a week.

Luckily, a good education from Portsmouth grammar school equipped the boys well for life – the dockyard annually creamed off the brightest pupils in fiercely contested exams. Cecil's ancestors having been shipwrights for about 150 years, he felt it time for a change. Joining the Army, his regiment was shortly afterwards sent to India – just for two years. They arrived home ten years later.

Families didn't go away for holidays in his childhood; as a summer treat all the mothers and children would go across the harbour to Stokes Bay, ladies and babies in the horse-drawn bus from a ferry pontoon, older children running alongside – fares for all made the outing too expensive.

The low lying city streets flooded regularly, more sport. The boys would hang on the backs of carriages and carts, until some publicly minded citizen would shout, "Whip behind you, guvnor". The driver, with a dextrous flick of his long whip over the shoulder, would try to catch them before they jumped off.

When quite young, on Saturday nights, the children were entrusted with an important task. Off to famous lamplit Charlotte Street, to hang about until no more customers were in sight, when the stall vendors, having no refrigeration, disposed of meat cheaply, say a penny a joint. Local bakers then charged one penny to cook your Sunday meat in their oven. There were many "take-away" shops, serving pease pudding, jellied eels, stews etc, collected in your own basin. Public houses had separate "jug and bottle" entrances, the ladies going there with their bead-edged lace doyley-covered jugs for draught beer to take home; a night in sitting chatting with their friends, whilst mending clothes and looking after the inevitable children.'

'After the First World War there were many men who did not return. Some were too badly injured to work, and in any case work was not easy to find. In the late 1920s "Pompey" as the Navy called it, was a very busy town full of "Jolly Jack Tars" in their bell bottom trousers and round caps with the ship's name on the ribbon. Fishermen would come to our house with fresh fish in their baskets. My mother, being a Cockney, always bought the eels, which were very lively and wriggled off the table until she stunned them.

I remember an early Navy Day when floats came round the town with sailors, some in fancy dress, collecting money for charity.

There was plenty to be done on a day out. Picnics on Southsea's long stretch of beach, or if it was very windy we would eat our sandwiches in the big grassy hollow on the common, which now of course is the Rock Gardens. Another day out was a trip on the Horndean Light Railway which started at Cosham, went over Portsdown Hill, through all the little villages (one of which is now the town of Waterlooville) ending at Horndean.

At one time there were four theatres in Portsmouth. For sixpence one could sit very high in the "Gods" joining in the singing, occasionally booing, but enjoying a couple of hours' happy entertainment. By the 1930s cinemas were springing up all over Ports-

13

mouth. We wallowed in American romance and tried to look like film stars. Most cinemas had a Wurlitzer organ which, during the interval, rose up from the floor while the organist played.

One of the sights of Portsmouth was the dockyard turning out each evening. Thousands of men on bicycles stopped the traffic on all routes around the yard.'

## HAMBLEDON

'Hambledon from whichever way you approach it, on foot over the hills or by road, is beautiful, the most outstanding feature being the church, dating back to Saxon times and situated on the north side of the valley.

At the start of the 20th century the way of life was still very Victorian but that was soon to change with the First World War. Many of the houses and cottages were well built and some of the larger houses stood in their own grounds, but none of them had the "mod cons" we expect today regarding water, drainage, sanitation, light and heat. Roads were grit with ditches at the side, travel was on foot, by horse and carriage, or by bicycle which had replaced the penny farthing bike.

Even so the village was well endowed with shops and businesses to supply most local needs. There were two breweries, a laundry, seven public houses, two butchers, three bakeries, four grocers, two draperies, four sweet shops, a chemist, two harnessmakers, two blacksmiths, two carpenters and undertakers and many other craftsmen, builders etc. One doctor, Dr Roe, looked after Hambledon and Denmead and did his rounds on a pushbike, and we had a nurse and midwife. Other than the usual children's ailments, diphtheria was very bad and several small children died; adult ailments included consumption, pneumonia and influenza.

Village life was very active with many clubs and societies. Musically there was a choral society, a church choir, a brass band trained and conducted by a Royal Marines bandmaster, a string dance orchestra, and many played the piano and other instruments. The school gave concerts and a pantomime at Christmas. In the summer there were many functions with May Day and the maypole dancing, flower shows etc. In winter came Hallowe'en, bonfire night, and carol singing with the band around the houses at Christmas.

A roller skating rink, men's and ladies' cycle club, men's and ladies' cricket club and tennis club, men's and boys' football teams, a Guide company, Mothers' Union and Women's Institute were other interests. The Hambledon Hunt met three times a week in the area, the fox killing many lambs and poultry in the district. Both church and chapel were well attended and the school gave children a good basic education. Discipline was strict and we were taught to be patriotic to King and Country. An exam was held each year which enabled the two top boys and girls to go to a county boarding school.

Another highlight was the local race meeting held once a year on the racecourse and people came from far and near to it, mainly in horse-drawn vehicles. Cars were only just beginning to come on the scene.'

## WEST MEON

'I chatted to an old lady aged 85 who was born in the village and lived here for most of her life. She told me about life in 1914 when there were just rough roads and no pavements. There were six shops, a blacksmith, a boot repairer and a tailor. The three pubs were the Red Lion, the New Inn, and the White Horse.

The large rectory is now West Meon House. The rector had a big family "all doing their share in the village". There was also a curate. The rector was in charge of Woodlands chapel as well as West Meon church, and he went about his duties in a horse and carriage driven by a coachman. The services at Woodlands were held in the afternoon on a Sunday. Sunday school at West Meon was held in the school every Sunday morning and from there the children went into the church for the service. The boys sat on one side of the font and the girls on the other side! The children were allowed to leave before the sermon. The bellringers practised every week and they had an annual dinner in one of the Jubilee Cottages.

In those days there were no cars, but there was an active railway running six trains a day up to Alton and down to Fareham.

West Meon school had five teachers. There was no drinking water at the school and the pupils had to cross the road to Knaps Yard where Mrs Walter Read provided them with their drinking water. Warnford had its own school, but when the children were seven years old they went on to West Meon school, and they walked between Warnford and West Meon.

At the Queen Victoria Institute a dance was held every Monday night and the cost was sixpence – the music was provided by a piano and a violin. Also weekly a whist drive was held. The Men's Club was there too and housed a large billiard table.

There were many farms making cheese and butter and rearing sheep. Mill House was a working mill run by a miller and a thresher. The river Meon turned the water wheel to provide the power to grind the grain. Walter Read's building yard employed about 30 men.

There were two horses, one was used for the waggon and the other for the trap. When the children left school at 14 years of age, some of them became apprentices at the yard.

The council houses were not built until after the Second World War and where Long Priors is today, there was a pond which froze over in winter and the children used to skate on it. Lippen Cottages are now built where a row of old fashioned cottages owned by Daniel Coats (cotton manufacturer) stood.

The Cricket Club was at Westbury and the shooting range, which was used by both ladies and gentlemen, was behind the Drill Hall.'

## WINCHESTER

'In the 1930s school sessions began and ended with prayers and I am sure I was not the only one in my school to add to these on a Monday, "Please let me get home before the cows come!"

Mondays were market days in Winchester and the cattle and sheep were herded through the streets. They started off confused and ended their journey frantic, afraid and panicky. The route was via North Walls and Middle Brook Street and my school exit led to the former and my way home along the latter.

With luck, but rarely, the cattle would not be in sight and if I ran fast enough I could reach home without incident. However, if even the tip of an ear was visible I could not outrun the herded animals who were shouted at and whacked hard with stout sticks as well as having the increasing downward slope of the hill in their favour. They came in batches of between 20 and 40 – cows, calves and steers. If I was overtaken it was a very frightening experience for a five year old and my two boltholes were either behind the iron railings of Trinity church grounds or in one of the many doorways which opened onto the pavement. The doorsteps afforded little protection, especially as the animals were so confused they were not aware of any other being. In fact they often tried to turn back and moved in a circular motion when the herdsmen tried to turn them back. They would clamber over each other and unintentionally gore one another.

The reason for this behaviour was the slaughterhouse, on the site of the present Brooks Shopping Centre. This was not the modern abattoir – pole axing was still carried out and the beasts became aware of their fate as they neared this place. There was a safer but longer route I could take, which brought me past the slaughterhouse within minutes of the cattle's arrival and while they were being killed. Their bellowing was pitiful and blood would be streaming under the huge double wooden doors, over the cobbled drive and running into the

16

*The blacksmith's shop at Bradley, with young Reg Pearson shoeing the horse. The smithy was of great importance in the days when horses were used for work and for transport.*

gutters and overwhelming the drains – an unattractive alternative!

This may sound barbaric but life was different then, the whole of this area of Winchester was alive, vital and colourful. There was the nearby Tudor Inn where the farmers and butchers sealed their business deals. The dusty atmosphere around the corn merchant's, that made one catch one's breath; the smell of chocolate from the factory next to Woolworths. A hack stable where the horses slipped on the cobbles on frosty days; a doss house and a barber shop with the longest striped pole imaginable. There was a stamp dealer, eye glass always in place, who sat behind a dark window in a dark room (we girls thought the boys very brave when they entered his abode to buy stamps). Pubs abounded, as did big families. I remember Ben Newsam who sold all manner of secondhand goods and whose garden railings were old iron bed-heads, placed shoulder to shoulder; the rag and bone merchants who would pay a penny for a rabbit skin; Mr Sharpe who sold "home-made ice-cream" which looked and tasted like custard, and the Italian family who produced superb soft ice-cream. The old lady with the tiny shop, who sold sweets by the farthingsworth and lemonade in bottles with marbles in the neck. Andrews faggot and peas shop, with scrubbed wooden tables and benches – the pet monkey that could be seen on hot summer days, running around the top of the high walls of his owner's garden. I recall the beautifully kept heavy horses adorned with leather and brass. Smells, sights and sounds abounded only a stone's throw from the High Street. Today this area is all neat, clean and tidy but perhaps there is less character than in the "Brooks" of my childhood.

My mother-in-law, who is now in her late eighties and has always lived in Winchester, tells me she remembers as a child walking with her father along the Itchen Navigation to a river keeper's tiny cottage on the opposite bank. Here she rang a bell and in response a basket was sent over by pulley from the cottage. In the basket was a small package of home-made sweets, for which she paid by putting money into the basket and returning it by pulley over the river to the cottage.'

## HYDE AND FROGHAM

'Homes in the area did not have running water, relying on wells which during very hot weather ran dry and then water had to be fetched by bucket from other wells in the area which always had fresh pure water, and still have up to the present day.

Electricity was not connected until the 1930s. Paraffin and coal were delivered and wood and gorse stumps were used for fires and fuelling coppers.

A smallholder recalls that work was planned around Ringwood market. Mother did the washing on Mondays, and made butter on Tuesdays which her husband took to market on Wednesdays with strawberries (in season), eggs and vegetables and perhaps a calf in the cart and a heifer trailing behind. The whole acreage had to be productive, grass for hay cut with a scythe, a patch of mangolds, parsnips and turnips for the cows, and carrots, some for the pony in the winter. Thursday was baking day; flour was bought at the mill in Ringwood and would last two or three weeks, the baking would be sufficient for a week. It was baked in a brick oven fired by brushwood from layered hedges. Friday was shopping day and Saturday cleaning and preparation for Sunday when no work was done apart from feeding the animals. Men would often seek other work outside their own plot, reed gathering being an example.

Bracken and fern was used for animal bedding. Cutting was not allowed before 15th September and a ticket was necessary from the woodman which cost three shillings and sixpence a load. After 26th September it cost three shillings. If green it was poisonous to the animals. The area was well supplied in that there was a travelling knife and saw sharpener and a rag and bone man, with resident wheelwright, baker, confectioner and butcher. There was a local policeman and roadman. The Co-op shop was available for basic needs and smelt strongly of cheese and dried fish.

The village received many evacuees during the Second World War, some of whom stayed on in the area. One house catered for 13 evacuees at one time. The local Home Guard had two look-out posts. Odd bombs fell in the area and two American aircraft collided and the fall out destroyed a local house. The Royal Tank Corps was stationed in the area, adding colourful interest for the children. Land girls were used on the farms, one farm supplying the daily school milk ration.

There was an abundance of blackberries which were harvested by the children, villagers and gipsies and sent to the market. Holly was picked and sent by train to Covent Garden and holly wreaths were sold in the village.

There was a brickworks, some of the bricks being used in the building of a nearby chapel and, it is thought, at the village school.

A rifle club flourished, with one member making and firing his own rifle. The village hall had to be bricked at one end to prevent bullets going through the neighbouring fence. Hyde Band was in existence and dances were held in the hall, as well as whist drives.'

## SHEET

'I was born in Sheet in 1899, becoming a member of a family of 13 children, which was an appropriate number for a mother who was the midwife of the village. She would disappear into the night in her black cape, clasping her black bag, to attend either a delivery or a despatch. My mother was a tower of strength to the villagers, often attending minor ailments for less money than the doctor would charge.

In those days, Sheet had its own parish council with no connection with Petersfield. It was a happy close-knit community where people gathered on the green where my father, who was the church verger, planted the first sapling. John Bonham Carter planted the existing horse-chestnut. He expressly chose a conkerless tree so that windows nearby would not get broken! Big flints were piled on the green for "Peg" Tom to crack for road repairs. Cattle also congregated on the green having been driven from Chichester on their way to Alresford. The drover would stop for some food and beer.

As well as performances by the Sheet Choral Society, there were the "Troupers" who visited the sick and put on concerts and pantomimes. Every August Petersfield and Sheet Sunday schools would join forces for an outing to Hayling Island by train. The train had to be split at Havant being too heavy for Hayling Island bridge. On our return to Petersfield station, we were met by horse-drawn waggons and we would sing all the way home, especially loudly under the Midhurst Bridge.

Sewerage and the supply of water was primitive in the early years. We had an uncovered main drain in Sheet and most people had their own wells with the addition of a couple of standpipes in the village. In the early 1930s when Sheet could not afford the sewerage rates, Petersfield took over the parish and things were never the same.'

## SOUTH WARNBOROUGH

'When I was a girl in the 1920s and early 1930s we lived on the A32 and my parents kept the village shop, bakery and post office. The main road was a most exciting place for children and we saw some wonderful never to be forgotten scenes.

Each year during the summer holidays the Army from Aldershot marched to manoeuvres on Salisbury Plain. The sun shone and the bands played rousing music and all the village people turned out to see this colourful spectacle. There seemed to be thousands of soldiers on the march. There were the infantry and mounted battalions on beautifully groomed horses. Their soup kitchens were drawn by horses and an appetising smell of onions wafted on the slight breeze as the smoke puffed out through the chimney. The most colourful were the Scottish regiments with their bagpipes skirling and all varieties of kilts swinging as they marched. Sometimes a section would halt on the village green and they would produce their mess tins and queue up for their meal. Some of the soldiers would dash into our little shop and the noise of their hobnail boots scraping on our brick floor was like a stampede. They would buy five Woodbines in a flat green paper packet for twopence or a packet of Wrigleys PK chewing gum for a penny.

The Cross Tree was the gathering place in the village. Wooden seats were built around the tree and its trunk provided a back rest. Villagers would gather on warm Sunday summer evenings to watch the few cars and charabancs coming back from a day at the sea. Some of their faces were very red from the sun and sea breezes. But everybody used to wave happily to each other although they were complete strangers. Quite a few gipsy caravans passed through the village. The gipsies would be on their way to a local farm where they would be employed hoeing the crops in the fields. They also went hop picking a few miles away in Bentley or at Church Crookham

*The Stores at South Warnborough in the 1920s. This quiet scene would be transformed when the Army marched through from Aldershot!*

where there were acres of hop fields in those days. The gipsy women always looked at the clothes lines and asked for baby or children's clothes when it was obvious there were children in the household.'

## KINGSCLERE

'It was then just a large village with two main streets, George Street and Swan Street in which most of the shops and works were. There was a large church built of stone with flint facing, with a leaded roof and six bells in a square tower. Of the two schools one, the Litten, used to be part infants with two female teachers, after which the boys went on to the other part to be taught by two male teachers, one the church organist, the other the choirmaster. The girls went to a school in North Street with two mistresses. They were both C of E schools with Sunday schools so on Sunday the church was the focal point.

A small stream supported four mills although I only remember two of them working, but they employed quite a few men. The two smithies were always busy with shoeing horses from the surrounding farms and repairs to harrows etc, while the tent and rope works in George Street employed several people. The racing stables on the Winchester Road was another source of work and with the number of large houses employing staff both inside and out, most of the villagers did not have far to go, which was just as well as there was not much transport in those days. A horse-drawn van used to go to

Newbury twice a week, otherwise it was by bicycle if you owned one, although the two garages usually had some for hire.

With two bakeries, two grocers and two butcher's shops, two boot repairers, one tailor, a drapery store, an animal feed store, a coal merchant and a post office, with several other shops selling sweets and greengrocery while two had a mixture of goods from nails to postcards, all in all we were well catered for.

Many people had some garden or an allotment which was a great help in supplying their vegetables. The Dell Hill and Hook were part of Hyams charity and when the rent was paid at Michaelmas there was a small loaf and a piece of cheese with a glass of beer, while the money went towards buying sheets and blankets for the needy. Another old custom was the ringing of the curfew bell at 8 pm during the winter months. There was a legend that someone was lost in fog on the downs and was guided home by the bell and left a legacy to keep it going.

I do not remember a lot about the First World War except for the soldiers marching through the village with their bands, horse and mule limbers and mobile kitchens. One of the houses was turned into a convalescent home for wounded soldiers. Many men went to war and families had to manage as best they could but most got by, everyone was equal and helped one another.

After the war motor cars began to get more popular and a family started a bus service to Newbury, the nearest town.'

## BICKTON

'Bickton is a riverside hamlet near to Fordingbridge. Today it boasts a trout farm and farm shop and its houses are occupied mainly by professional and retired couples. During my childhood there in the 1930s ponies wandered through the village (and learnt to unlatch gates) and there was plenty of activity in the small community.

As well as the carpenter's shop there was a wheel-binder and blacksmith and, until a short time before, one resident sold oil for lighting, cooking and heating. He also dried rabbit skins in his shed; unfortunately for the next door cottage the latter side line attracted rats!

The trade with which I was most familiar was that followed by my grandfather, the blacksmith, whose forge was adjacent to our cottage. He had to be prepared, if necessary in the early hours, to shoe the horses drawing loads to and from Bickton Mill where was produced a famous brand of baby food. (Eels were trapped in the millstream by the men working there.) I remember, at the age of four, being lifted on to a box so that I could pump the blacksmith's bellows.

22

Many villagers worked on the farms and there were enough young men living here to form a Bickton football team.

Households were almost self-sufficient. Hard work in the large gardens provided vegetables and most kept a pig, chickens and ducks – the latter could be seen early in the day waddling in procession to the water meadows and returning in the evening, each going unerringly to the right house.

At pig-killing time neighbours helped each other – both with the work and in consuming the more perishable items before the sides of bacon were smoked in the wide chimneys. My grandmother made beer and wines while my grandfather enjoyed the cider he made himself. Eggs were preserved in isinglass and beans in salt. At harvest-time rabbits were added to the menu, village youngsters waiting with sticks round the ever-decreasing circle of corn left by the binder to waylay their prey.

Homes were anything but labour-saving. Before the advent of piped water the pump in the kitchen had to be primed and the "little house" in the garden kept clean and neat. Until electricity came, oil lamps were filled and trimmed.

No bus passes or taxis then – from the age of five the children walked the mile to and from Fordingbridge school, carrying their lunch-time sandwiches. On their return they could buy sweets from the shop in the front room of one cottage with its small stock of groceries and other "everyday" items.

How unhurried and secure those pre-war days seem to us now.'

AROUND SOUTHAMPTON

'Early memories of Southampton during the 1930s are the very large numbers of unemployed waiting at the gates of J.I. Thornycroft's Woolston yard in the hope of being offered work. Starting work at the age of 14 usually meant a wage of around ten shillings a week (15 shillings if you were lucky!). Woolworths paid about 16 shillings in 1939. There were very few jobs open to girls at this time – mainly in shops, offices or workrooms, or if you were clever a bank or library. Work in Southampton was mainly in the shipyard, the docks or railways.

A shopping trip to town was a treat, going via the floating bridge and walking over the iron railway bridge to Edwin Jones at Houndwell which was bombed in 1940. In 1933 there were horse-drawn hearses still to be seen and up until the 1950s milk was delivered by horse and cart. One of the characters in Sholing before the war was the fishmonger who called with his horse and cart, who used to say of his kippers, "They eat like a piece of 'am, ma'am."

Christmas was a time we all looked forward to; when everybody was more relaxed and maybe took a glass of port or ale. Wine was unheard of in the working-class family. The diet was very plain in the 1930s; usually a meat joint on Sunday which appeared in various guises throughout the week – cold meat and bubble and squeak on Mondays with twopennyworth of piccalilli bought from the corner shop in a basin, and perhaps shepherd's pie on Tuesday, etc. Before the war Southampton's East Street was crowded on Saturday evenings with people jostling for meat being sold off cheaply by the market traders because they did not have cold storage facilities. Other shopping was from David Greig, where they had a large block of butter in the window carved into a thistle, or the Home & Colonial in Victoria Road, Woolston, and we used to be able to buy a delicious lardy cake from Johnsons in Portsmouth Road for a shilling. During the war and after, one didn't need a lot of money to buy a week's rations. I remember spending ten shillings for two of us in 1948 when first married!

The 1935 Royal Jubilee was celebrated in Swift Road, Woolston, with a street tea party, with bunting decorating the road and each child receiving a commemoration mug and medal from the town council.

Empire Day was a great occasion and at Middle Road infants school, Sholing, children were dressed to represent a country in the Empire. At Merry Oak senior school pupils were dressed in either red, white or blue and assembled on the playing field to form the Union Jack.

One very important event in the year was the St George's Day parade at Netley. Scouts, Guides, Cubs and Brownies, accompanied by the Boys' Brigade band would march through Netley for a service in the grounds of Netley Abbey – a very beautiful setting for such a service. It was, of course, quite a social gathering.

St Mary's Scholing Sunday school treat was a train ride from Sholing station to Lyndhurst Road station, with games and tea in the New Forest, or perhaps a trip to Twyford Down. Sholing church also had a thriving Young Men's Club who met every Saturday in the Institute to play table tennis, billiards, etc.

Saturday morning visits to the Ritz cinema in Bitterne, in the ninepennies, were also fun, waiting to see what had happened to our hero from the previous week.

During the summer holidays we would walk to the Weston shore passing the rolling mills and the seaweed hut, made of seaweed and used by fishermen to store their gear. Once a year, however, we would take the train to Pokesdown station and from there walk to Boscombe beach with a picnic, buckets and spades, etc (probably

24

in our best clothes!). That, and a visit to grandparents in London, would be our "holiday" each year.

Teenagers living in the Woolston area during the 1940s were fortunate indeed to belong to the Manor Road Methodist youth club run by the minister, Revd H. Biggin, assisted by Mr Lamerton who kept the sports and cycle shop in Bridge Road. Travelling by train to Hamble youth club for a dance, members would be quite unperturbed by the air raids and the anti-aircraft guns firing overhead on Hamble Halt station! The club had a good football team and also a number of members sang in the Methodist choir, returning from a cycle trip to Lee-on-Solent on many a Sunday to sing at the evening service.

Working in Southampton docks during wartime one was able to see the ships and parts of the Mulberry Harbour assembled for the D-Day landings and to experience the eerie emptiness on the morning after they had sailed. For days before the roads had been lined with army trucks waiting for the "off". Boys and girls of 16 and over had to join the ARP, the National Fire Service or the Home Guard. Night watches were kept by the fire service on the roof of the Broadway cinema in Portswood where incendiary bombs were tracked from a glass-windowed shed! Working in the docks and being in the ARP I was assigned once a week to the underground telephone exchange for the night – I don't remember having to do anything but received a subsistence allowance for having a night's sleep!'

ECCHINSWELL AND SYDMONTON

'In the 1920s and before, most of the land and large houses round about, i.e. Sydmonton Court, were owned and leased out by one family and most people worked locally. The large houses, for example, employed a butler, housekeeper, parlourmaid, five or six housemaids, footman, hallboy and pantry maid. All wore uniforms of some sort, the men often with brass buttons and the females with caps. There would also be a cook, kitchenmaid, scullery maid, kitchen boy, ladies' maid, valet, head gardener, five or six gardeners, three gamekeepers, two estate carpenters, foresters, laundry maids, grooms, nanny and nursemaid.

The village school had around 90 children between five and 14 years old, with a head teacher and assistant and a young woman for the infants. Some children walked up to six miles to school and home again after. They had to carry their lunch. School started at 9 am and finished at 4 pm, and was heated by a water boiler. Teachers usually lived in the school house and there were two schoolrooms and an earth toilet outside. The school choir once won a competition and were taken to the nearest town, to the cinema (silent film). The Sunday school treat once a year would be on farm waggons pulled by horses, to Beacon Hill with a picnic and lemon sherbet and ginger beer. The Sunday school teachers and the vicar would go with them.

There were three shops in the village then. One shop had a bakery and made bread and cakes and delivered by horse and two-wheel cart three times a week. Local milk was sold by the scoopful into jugs and bowls. The bread was made from local flour, ground at the village mill (still working). Only three people were wealthy enough to have cars.

There were occasional dances at the school, and lantern slide shows at the church once a week during Lent. There was a village carrier and he had an ex-army lorry and took orders in the morning for shopping from the town and delivered the items later in the day. He owned a 14 seater bus which used to go to town on a Saturday at 6 pm and leave to return at 9 pm. He also delivered coal in the army lorry.

Most of the men were farm workers and worked from dawn to dusk and their wives used to help with the harvest and haymaking. No tractors then. The pub was very popular with the men after work and they played shove halfpenny and darts. Each farm would have its own harvest supper for the workmen, having bread and cheese and draught beer and pickles. No wives!

In 1924 lorries took people to Newbury where they got on the

26

steam trains to go to the Wembley Exhibition. That was the only outing some people had in their lives. By the late 1920s three buses would go with the choir and some others to the seaside just once in a year, leaving at 8 am and getting there around noon.

There was no village hall, so any social events were held in the winter in the village school. Most villagers walked to Kingsclere flower show each August, about four miles each way.

There was a local blacksmith and a local undertaker and coffins were made in the village and were pushed to the church for the funeral on a bier, if local, or carried on a horse-drawn cart from further away.

Farmworkers' homes were bound to their jobs and if they lost the job they lost the house and had to try and find another or be put out on the street. Most of the small cottages have been bought up and turned into expensive houses now.

The cottages often had a well in the garden which was their water for drinking and washing etc. If they were lucky they had an outside tap. People used to keep a few chickens if possible and some of them a pig. They used to snare rabbits too to make a tasty stew and usually they grew all their own fruit and vegetables. Wives all made their own curtains and rag rugs and usually knitted all the socks, jumpers and gloves for the family. Men quite often mended the shoes of the family. There was very little waste in those days.'


ENHAM ALAMEIN

'At the turn of the century there were only three large houses and a cluster of small cottages in what is now Enham Alamein. All the inhabitants worked in the big houses or on the surrounding farmland. The houses were mostly thatched with paraffin lamps or candles for lighting, and a large kitchen range for heating and cooking which had to be cleaned out, blackleaded and relit every morning. Water came from the well, and there were earth closets and a cesspit in the back garden. There were no fridges or freezers but Enham Place had a large, underground ice room which years later became a secret play area for children.

The whole area, including the three houses, the cottages, plus 1,000 acres of arable land was sold in 1918 by John Hughes Earle for £30,000 to a consortium of businessmen who wished to establish a rehabilitation and resettlement centre for disabled ex-servicemen and their families. In 1919 Enham Place was demolished and Enham Village Centre was opened by the Minister of Education and 150 men began training. The doctor had his surgery at the White House and Littlecote became a hostel for the less seriously handicapped men.

A crescent of houses was built in 1924/26, named after people or charities that helped to sponsor them; these were lit by electricity at sixpence a unit. Near the St George's chapel were eight houses in a rectangle and all except one, which later became a museum, were demolished to make a village green. More modern houses were built in the 1950s with bathrooms, gas cookers and stoves that heated the water.

The disabled were taught to make chicken runs, barrows, sheds and all types of baskets, progressing to home and office furniture and engineering. From 1939 they made glider wings, ammunition boxes and patched barrage balloons, and also built two large concrete water tanks for fire fighting.

In the Seaford Rally Club and the Lansdale Wilson Institute after it was opened by the Prince of Wales in 1926, there were threepenny dances, whist drives and concerts, the disabled as actors. These were happy days, especially the excitement of the Christmas pantomime.

The village children soon accepted that most men in the village were minus a limb, blind, disfigured or ill as a result of the war. Then tuberculosis patients came; fortunately fresh country air and fresh food helped them to recuperate and return to more normal life. More war veterans came after 1939. A few bombs were dropped in the area causing damage but no serious injuries. On VE Day a young lad decided to climb the metal rungs inside the factory chimney despite smoke and hot gases and fly a Union Jack from the top. It was very foolhardy but there was no reprimand, everybody was so relieved the war was over. In gratitude for the British Forces freeing El Alamein, the Egyptian Government gave £225,000 to build houses, a school, a pub and a church (the money ran out so the school and pub were never built). The village was renamed Enham Alamein and the gates from the three Services Clubs in Cairo were hung at the entrances to the factory, White House and Phipps House where patients have their own bedsits with collective feeding and constant care.

In the early years the bicycle was very popular, but as the population increased a bus ran once a week – sixpence return to Andover four miles away, and two years later every day. Originally the driver would shop for those unable to go and bring back orange juice, baby food, or medicines. If he finished quickly he would look after small children in his bus while Mum rushed unhampered to finish her shopping.

Most houses had big gardens so everybody grew their own vegetables and fruit, or collected dandelion and nettle leaves as money was scarce. Milk from a special herd was delivered to the houses in a 17 gallon churn and sold by the jug. Bread baked by wood faggots at Woodhouse bakery was also delivered daily. A butcher and a fishmonger called once a week. By 1950 Enham, Woodhouse and Little London had their own small general store.

The summer house at Enham Place was used for a while as a shepherd's hut, then moved brick by brick to the village green, where it was re-erected exactly as before, apart from the chimney, as a bus shelter.'


BOLDRE

'Towards the end of the Great War, about 1917 when North London was not considered safe, I was sent to live with my grandparents who lived in Boldre. Their house, Forest Corner, was on the main Brockenhurst–Lymington road, at the corner of the turning to Sway. How well I remember the latter because looking towards Set Thorns some two miles away, I could follow the few cars enveloped in the large cloud of dust they created. In the summer cars were usually open and Granny and Mother had to wear their hats secured by a veil tied at the back. When this was removed it left an intriguing pattern on their noses, which much to their annoyance, I found very funny.

In those early days there were no buses so we travelled everywhere by governess trap. Grandfather always offered walkers a lift, with the remark that bad riding was better than good walking. When he died a few years later, Mother used to go for the day and was always lucky in being offered a lift, then by car.

Going back to the early 1920s, we took the trap to meet our visitors at Brockenhurst station and do our shopping either there or in Lymington. Most of the inns had stabling and we would leave the pony at one in Lymington when we took the paddle steamer to Yarmouth or Totland Bay. The crab or lobster tea was the special treat on the return. I seem to remember such teas at the Black House at Mudeford where we used to stay with relations, whose garden was on the water's edge. Kingfishers were very common at that time and sad to relate they were often caught by the cats and ended up in those fashionable glass cases. Another trip in the trap was to Thorns Beach where we collected winkles.

Riding round the forest on my Dartmoor pony I got to know the area well. At that time there were many red squirrels around and I always hoped to see an otter on the Lymington river when I passed the bridge leading to Boldre church. So much is written about conservation these days it may be surprising to know that all those years ago, people were prosecuted for digging up the gentians in the forest.

*The well at 26 East Stratton in the late 1940s – 'mod cons' were slow in coming to many villages.*

The pony was also used to pull the heavy lawn mower, and for this he had a special set of four leather shoes. In due course he was replaced by a motor mower which was sometimes difficult to start, fortunately at that time Stanley Salmon opened his garage opposite. It must have been one of the earliest.

Our house was right on the edge of the forest and coaches (then called charabancs) were beginning to appear on sightseeing trips from Bournemouth. As they passed I heard the guide announce, "We are now entering the New Forest which is 62,746 acres." We were privileged in having forest rights which allowed us to graze a number of our horses and ponies. These were rounded up each year for branding and occasionally strayed on to private land and were pounded. We always hastened to collect them otherwise we should have been charged for their keep.

Some interesting people lived in the area. There was a couple who lived at Batramsley. Mr Baxter had fought in the Boer War and was one of the soldiers who helped to bring the body of the Crown Prince Imperial back to England; for this his mother the Empress Eugenie gave Mr Baxter a life pension. Lady Crawford had the unusual hobby of ivory carving and had a special room set aside because of the amount of dust created. A large chest contained the tusks. We occasionally went to tea with Mr and Mrs Adams who lived in a cottage on the Hincheslea House estate where he was head gardener for Miss Lovell. He was a clever Scotsman for not only was he in charge of all the bedding hot houses and the piggery but also the dairy and we could hear the noise of the churn whilst we were having tea, and what teas to remember! Golden butter and lots of whipped cream with home-made jam, bread and scones. Nowadays one wonders how he had time for hobbies but he proudly showed us his latest piece of wood carving. We also had some music as he liked to be accompanied when he played the violin. He was in the local dance band and recalled with pride that at one of the parties in Brockenhurst, Winston Churchill's mother came up to him and said, "Adams, I never knew you played the fiddle."

Every six or more years several cords of wood were delivered; this was followed by a man with a machine and saw who worked for several days ensuring we had logs for winters ahead.

The southern area of the forest has changed very little. Brockenhurst station and the village are much as I remember them, except that the forge has gone. Balmer Lawn has grown much larger. A postcard of 1903 shows it was just a large country house bearing the name, in large lettering, "The Holt Family Hotel".

In the First World War there was a prisoner of war camp on Setley Plain and another reminder of that period was in a field half a mile from Brockenhurst on the Lymington road, where a number of temporary buildings served as a hospital for Indian soldiers. In a corner of this a pyre was used for the cremation of those who gave their lives for this country.

On the edge of the forest there were a number of gravel pits, the bright colour of the gravel contrasting with the heather. Now they are filled with gorse, heather and trees and no longer visible. The same has happened to all the ponds that our ducks enjoyed; all so overgrown that only small puddles can be found.

In the late 1920s a bus service was started between Southampton and Bournemouth and as it passed our door it was a great advantage. Up to that time our well had supplied us with all the water needed, not even going dry in the exceptionally hot summer of 1911, but the arrival of both mains water and gas was another step forward at that time.'

## SOUTH WONSTON

'At the beginning of the century, life in the village was very basic with few amenities. There were only a few make-shift bungalows and houses along a muddy cart track, on plots which the residents had bought from a local farmer, Henry William Blake, at £10 an acre. The plots were paced out by the farmer, who also marked the boundaries with a plough. Such a haphazard method caused quite a headache for the local conveyancer who came from Winchester to settle any disputes, as the lines were not always straight!

Water in the village was always a problem, every drop had to be carefully conserved in rain-butts. At the stables, several water tanks were sunk into the ground to serve the horses of officers and men from the Royal Flying Corps at nearby Worthy Down. One poor serviceman fell into one such tank one night, when the ground was very icy. His hat was apparently found floating on top the following morning – his ghost is said to haunt parts of the village to this day. Luckily a 200 foot well was finished around 1920, which finally alleviated the situation.

Everyone lived a very contented and rural existence. There was no electricity, so lighting was provided by paraffin lamps or candles, and only the post office had a telephone. The doctor came on his horse from Sutton Scotney, the next village. Most of the people living here worked on farms, or at the air base – the women worked at the watercress beds, bunching the cress, or else they took in dressmaking. It seems that female volunteers were always needed in the fields to pick up stones and flints (of a specific size) which were taken to a collection point, measured, then taken away to fill in potholes in the local lanes, which were always kept immaculate by the local workmen.

The schoolchildren left their bikes at the first bungalow in the lane when they caught the bus to school. This house would look as if it was made of cycles stacked six high under the eaves! The bus which went along the main road was a lifeline connecting the village to the market and the shops in Winchester. In bad weather, most people would wear their wellingtons and leave them in the hedge for the long muddy walk home along the lane. There were two baker's vans delivering locally, one from the Co-op in Winchester and the other from the family bakery in Sutton Scotney. All the local farms sold milk by the jug from their back door. Villagers would also brew their own wine, such as dandelion, parsnip or raisin with elderflower. The corrugated iron hut which served as the village hall was used for sing-songs, pantomimes and whist drives; people enjoyed making their own entertainment.

The arrival of the Royal Flying Corps during the First World War brought the railway past South Wonston, providing work locally and the arrangement of a halt on the Didcot–Newbury–Southampton line. This encouraged people to come out from the town and settle locally. Unfortunately, the line was dismantled in the Beeching cuts of 1962, having provided a welcome link with Winchester for many years.

In 1926 an Army regiment of 2,800 men came to camp at South Wonston on manoeuvres. For this occasion a large water tower had to be put up at Worthy Down to service the camp, and which is still standing today. The day before D-Day, an exciting rumour spread around the village that if we went down to the main road (to the corner called Three Corner Firs) we would see something special – and we did. A convoy of staff cars carrying George VI, Churchill, Montgomery and Eisenhower and their Chiefs of Staff, all passed by on their way to rally the troops, before crossing over the Channel to France.

Life in South Wonston sounds tough in the old days. However, people had a wonderful sense of togetherness, everyone knew each other; it was a very happy community living here in those days.'

MONK SHERBORNE

'I was brought up during the 1950s in Monk Sherborne and went to school in Basingstoke. From the age of five I caught the bus in the village each morning. The bus stop was outside the New Inn (now the Mole). The landlady was a Mrs Brown. The bus went to the Barge in Basingstoke where I changed and caught another bus to the end of Cliddesdon Road and school.

In Basingstoke at the bottom of Wote Street were two cinemas, the Waldorf (where I regularly attended "minors") and on the opposite side the Savoy. Langhams was a good department store on the corner of London Road and Church Street with lots of oak fittings. The Haymarket Theatre was there, though not as grand as now. Near the Haymarket there was a wet fish shop. Leaving the Barge each evening on the bus we would go under the railway arch passing Eli Lilley and Lansing Bagnall. There was little else between here and Park Prewett entrance and then another gap before the village of Sherborne St John with Rex Dixon's shop and the watercress bed near the turning to Monk Sherborne.

At home there was a tradition of cold meat for Sunday breakfast – ham, home-made brawn and sometimes a Bath chap. When I was very young I remember taking a jug out to get milk from a churn on a horse-drawn cart. Mr George Cooper was the postman and came from Charter Alley; he always had a cup of tea at our house at about 5.30 am. We had a petrol generator for electricity, which often went wrong and we went back to oil lamps. The hot water lost so much heat between the tank and the bathroom that in winter we often

33

preferred a tin bath on the coconut matting, in front of the kitchen Ideal boiler.

There was always a summer fête as I remember, usually held in Mrs Fehr's field. We usually attended Monk Sherborne church which still had oil lamps then and the rood screen separated the nave and chancel (it has since been moved). For weddings the church gates were always locked to allow plenty of time to use all the confetti. We always went to the priory church at Pamber for Mothering Sunday and we were given a bunch of violets for our mothers.

For the Coronation (1953) a big party was held in the village hall and each child was given a silver spoon. We didn't have television then but I was invited to watch the Coronation on the one at the Guys' at Rookery Cottage. We also sometimes watched *The Lone Ranger* and *Rin Tin Tin*. We always collected small baskets full of primroses from the copse on the way to Charter Alley in the spring. Ragged robins grew in the field by our house.

As children much of our play took place at "The Dell" at the top of Kiln Lane. It is about two miles from the village, a deep hollow, water at the bottom with newts, surrounded by mature trees. There were jays and foxes here and a lot of fun to be had. I knew when to go home as my mother called me from the garden and then the dog would howl and we could hear the howling. Our dog would often sit in the middle of the road outside the house and the bus would come along, toot and wait for him to move.

There were two shops in the village, a general store and the post office store where you could get ice-creams and lollies. Batteries could be bought from a house opposite the post office. Rookery Farm had a milking parlour (the cows had names then) and one of the farms had a four or six bay parlour out in the fields. Tractors, Massey Fergusons, were in use but a shire horse was still kept on Rookery Farm. I remember the old milk cooling system and churns being put out for collection.

My grandfather Dr Daly lived in Little London where he had his main surgery and dispensary. He held a surgery in our dining-room twice a week; he would arrange for the dispensing, or prescriptions could be taken to Jukes the chemist in Wote Street in Basingstoke.

Mr Ruckston bred horses, including Arabs. He had a collection of carts and carriages and we were sometimes given outings in them. I was once taken to the point to point in Hackwood Park, Basingstoke, I remember going with two shillings and coming home with over six shillings by betting on his horses. I felt very rich at the time but it didn't lead me to a gambling life!'

## LIFE AT KINGS WORTHY HOUSE

'My father retired from the Army in 1936 and we came to live at Kings Worthy Court, a large house with eleven bedrooms, three bathrooms and four reception rooms, surrounded by 13 acres comprising a very large garden, two paddocks, a tennis court, and a wonderful complex of thatched barns around a courtyard.

To run this house we employed a cook, a kitchenmaid, a house-maid, a parlourmaid, a nanny, a valet/chauffeur (my father's former batman), a gardener and two boys and a daily who "did the rough".

Bedlinen and uniforms were sent to a laundry in Winchester, my sister's and my clothes were washed by Nanny and my parents' personal laundry went to a laundress in the village. If some item was needed urgently our afternoon walk with Nanny went via the laundress's cottage on the main road opposite the Cart and Horses.

When our shoes needed repairing our walk took us to a pretty cottage in a beautiful garden in Mill Lane, Abbots Worthy. There, in a workshop behind the cottage, worked the cobbler, a badly wounded veteran of the First World War.

Sometimes in summer when we were walking on the river path below Abbots Worthy House (then in red-brick Elizabethan style) the owner, the Countess of Northbrook, would invite us in to see her wonderful garden, miniature cliffs, sparkling rills and tiny waterfalls glowing with flowers; if we were very lucky we were invited to tea as well.

When I had to attend Southampton eye hospital to correct a dreadful squint we took the train from little Kings Worthy station (long vanished). Visiting the dentist in Winchester meant walking in along the main road with Nanny. If we had been good we had toasted tea cakes and hot chocolate at the Palace Pantry, by the Buttercross, or visited a marvellous two-storey toy shop, the London Bazaar, in the High Street, and then we returned via North Walls Park and the Nun's Walk, along the river.

My parents had a car, an Armstrong Siddley. My mother could not drive, so the chauffeur took her shopping.

We did not go to school but had lessons in the nursery from a charming lady, Miss Ings, who lived in a diminutive house by the church. During the war we were in Wales. Our house became the headquarters of Hampshire Fire Brigade and they built an enormous bomb-proof shelter on the front drive.

We returned in 1946. My sister and I went to boarding school, Nanny who had done everything for us during the war went to look after a cousin's babies and after a succession of unsatisfactory foreign and Irish maids, my mother found herself battling to "keep up appearances" with just two excellent dailies.'

# CHURCH AND CHAPEL

Sunday was a day of rest for most families, and of church services and Sunday school. Sunday schools were particularly popular for the summer and Christmas treats they provided for the children, perhaps the only outing or party some of them ever had. No wonder we look back on the Sundays of the past with nostalgia.

## CHURCH ON SUNDAY

'My father was a church organist and played in various churches in and around Basingstoke. During the 1930s when I was born, he worked for my grandparents in one of their tobacconist shops and was not highly paid. However, we were allowed to share their car, and so most Sundays everyone went to church together.

The first church I can remember was Sherfield church; I was christened there and attended morning and evening services. The congregation was very mixed, among the wealthier families were the Wills tobacco family who lived next to the church and a solicitor with his family who lived not too far down the road. Nannies from both those families looked after the children and Mother was determined I should not let her down so if I turned round to look or swung my legs she immediately gave me a sharp tap on the leg. I can still remember how cold and hard the seats were, and how I would get pins and needles in my legs as they could not reach the floor. I liked it best when I went with Dad on my own when I could sit on the organ stool with him. There were also local people, and the schoolmaster always read the lesson. The vicar must have had private means as we were all invited for tea one Sunday to talk with the Bishop of Winchester; the grown ups sat around and were served by a maid. I sat on the rug with Sam the dog and caused some amusement when I asked the maid to hold my tea plate while I drank my milk so that Sam would not eat my cake.

Easter was a time when everyone had new clothes and wore them whatever the weather. The outfit was complete, from lighter weight vests to dress coat and shoes, and usually a straw poke bonnet which Mother would trim with silk spring flowers. I do not suppose the weather was always warm but that did not seem to matter, Easter was the time to show off your finery and so we did.

My great aunt was a very well known lady for her home-made

sweet stall at the church garden parties, which were held in the vicarage gardens each year, and for her fine contralto voice in the choir. Churches played a big part in the life of the community and everyone seemed to have their own part to play. There was a simplicity about it which seems to be absent today, too many people seeking too many answers instead of just wanting to be a part of a community and helping one another.'

## THE GOSPEL HALL

'As a family we attended the Gospel Hall at Liphook, which was a 15 minute walk away. Mother was the organist. The organ was an American-type pedal organ and I always had to sit in front with her. There were three services on Sunday – best clothes compulsory. Second best clothes were acceptable for Bible readings on Tuesday evenings, and the women's and children's meetings on Thursdays. Women always wore hats. Each year we had a Christmas Sunday school tea, followed by games and a programme of recitations and singing performed for the parents. A book prize was awarded at the end. Summer outings never varied – Hayling Island by private coach. It was the only time many of us ever saw the sea.'

## BACON AND GREENS

'Each summer the Sunday school and choir at South Warnborough had an outing to the seaside. The Sunday school had a tea party booked at a seaside café, but the choir had an extra meal – lunch today, dinner then. The rest of us sat on the beach and ate our sandwiches and when the first choirboy came back my mother asked him what they had had to eat. "Bacon and greens," he said. "What a funny meal," said my mother and when my brother came back she said, "What a funny meal to give you!" "Funny?" said my brother. "We had ham and salad." Forever after in our house ham and salad was always called "bacon and greens". Even when my mother did the annual cricket lunch for the next village we always referred to it as "Bacon and Greens Dinner".

After the old rector retired we had a retired army padre as our rector. He was very fiery and used to thump the pulpit when referring to "those damned Huns" during the war. Some of the villagers thought it very disrespectful in church. We younger ones thought it added a bit of spice to Sunday.

My brother was in the choir and one day the rector called to see my mother. He looked very stern and said that he had reprimanded her son together with all the choir. My mother said, "Oh dear, sir, what have they done?" He said, "As I walked up the church path to take choir practice I could hear the organ being played so I stopped to listen. The choirboys were in the aisle doing the Lambeth Walk and your son was playing the organ for them."

"I told them off very severely," he said. "I told them about the money lenders in the temple, and they were very subdued during choir practice," he added, smiling and winking at my mother. He was really very approachable and down to earth. He introduced two buglers from his regiment to play the last post and reveille at our annual Remembrance Service in the church in November. The sound of the bugles echoed through the church as we remembered the dead of the Great War and as we prayed for those men who were now fighting in the 1939–45 war.'


## THE SUNDAY SCHOOL TORTOISE

'The parish of Farlington, which includes Drayton, had no church hall until long after the Second World War, so all social activities took place in the Drayton Institute. This was built on land bequeathed by Mr Futcher who also made possible the founding of the Futcher School of Recovery in his former home.

When I was in Sunday school my mother played the Institute

piano for us, mostly the Carey Bonner hymns and songs which we also learned in day school. The late Mrs Dannan was a much loved Sunday school superintendent who started the afternoon with a hymn, a few prayers and a Bible story. Afterwards we split up into our classes for more work on the story then returned for the final prayers and hymn.

Later, Sunday school was held at the Church of the Resurrection which was newly built. Now the rector took the service and the same little classes spread around the church and up into the tower room.

At one time Friday nights were devoted to the Guild of Love which was a sewing bee held in the tower room; the object was to make clothes for poor children in other countries. I was hopeless at needlework then and I don't remember actually making anything so I expect they just gave me a few simple seams to hem. For most of us the highlight was the break for sweets which we could buy from a small canteen. Mr and Mrs Dannan ran a sweet shop in Portsmouth so we always had a good selection. I particularly remember little boats made of something like nougat with liquorice funnels.

When I was about ten they started a Sunday school at the parish church of St Andrew (most of the congregation went to whichever church had the most convenient service times). On a hot summer afternoon my friend and I, dressed in silk frocks with gloves and hats to match, were halfway along Evelegh Road when we found a tortoise which I recognised as a runaway from next door. It never once occurred to us to go back home with him so we carefully lifted him onto our two prayerbooks and carried him with us. My friend scuttled quickly into her seat while I marched up to the rector, the Revd Cecil Booth, and asked him to look after it for us during Sunday school. He was somewhat taken aback but recovered and put the tortoise in a coal bucket from which we later retrieved him, all dusty. As soon as we got home we dashed into the next door garden and put him down with his mate who went up to him and gave him a good inspection. They were really pleased to see each other again, and of course the little boy who owned them was delighted. The tortoise had managed to crawl about a quarter of a mile in three or four days.

In 1933 Drayton Methodist church was built and that gave us an extra hall which could be hired, but still our Sunday school nativity plays, parties and Brownies took place in the Institute. Just before the war the Guides moved up to Solent Road school which was much nearer for me. Going down to the Institute used to seem miles to little legs, especially on nights when the frost was so hard that all the trees and hedges had leaves covered with ice which jingled in the wind.'

*Sunday school Anniversary at the Methodist church in Church Street, Basingstoke in 1932. Straw hats were essential wear for all female participants!*

## THE METHODIST CHURCH

'Back in the 1920s and 1930s the pace of life was slow. Apart from country walks, evening games and sing-songs families looked to the church for recreational as well as spiritual needs. My family were Wesleyan Methodists and we attended a thriving Methodist church in Church Street, Basingstoke, sadly demolished in the 1960s to make way for the "new town". I first gazed at its vastness as a toddler of three. It subsequently became a place of happy and sad memories.

The "ritual" would begin Saturday evening when shoes were polished and best clothes laid out in readiness for Sunday. These were put on after Sunday breakfast and were not taken off until bedtime. An apron was put on at mealtimes. No outdoor games would be played in your Sunday best, no button sewed on if one came off – to sew or read a Sunday newspaper was never allowed – and, of course, no sweets!

Most people walked to church and the bells rang urging you to hurry along. No lady or child entered church without a hat, the men also sported buttonholes and carried walking sticks. Sunday school at ten o'clock was followed by worship at eleven, afternoon school at two o'clock, and church again at six-thirty.

Fond of music, I remember the great Charles Wesley hymns and every June after much practice the Sunday school Anniversary would take place. The church was packed, such was its popularity. If you had a singing voice you were picked to sing a solo verse, and as a reward were invited to take tea with the minister and superintendent. The great organ, the hub of the church, was given over to a yearly concert and the late Sandy McPherson played for us in 1937.

Another highlight was the summer outing. We were taken by charabanc to a country venue for races, cricket and games. Prizes were one penny for a first and a halfpenny for coming second. Tea consisted of lemonade and slab cake, and on the homeward journey small packets of sweets were given.

As we approached our teens we were allowed to watch lantern slides, one penny a show, once a week, but we also had to attend Bible classes and sit scripture exams. I still have a necklace and several certificates I won.

Ministers were more boisterous in their sermons than today but as a small child I would sleep on my father's shoulder after being given a cough sweet, which had seen better days, from the depths of his pocket. A long day for one so young but those years gave me a great foundation for the war years which followed.

Today as I gaze at a commemorative plaque set in the pavement where the church once stood I wonder why such buildings were demolished, but I treasure the two concrete crosses that came from the roof of that church and which now adorn my garden. I have only to look out of my kitchen window at them to relive my memories.'


CAREFREE DAYS

'The greatest change in our way of life in the last 70 years must surely be how we spend our Sundays. From my early years at Eastleigh, Sunday school and church dominated our lives. From as young as four years, dressed in our best clothes, in care of older siblings we would set off to spend an hour listening to simple Biblical stories, learning of the love of Jesus and singing hymns written especially for young voices. Often we would be given pretty little cards to take home to our mothers.

At seven years we were regarded as old enough to attend the first half of the church service, being ushered out before the sermon, which even the older children found dull and dreary. Boys at seven could join the church choir. They were dressed in black cassocks, white surplices with frilled neck ruffles, making them look quite angelic and far from true. The organist who was also choirmaster, from his loft high above the choir stalls was quite capable of throwing a hymn book down at any disrupting boy and his aim was always good! Not being allowed to play outside on Sundays it was no hardship to return to school for the afternoon session.

We had our rewards of course, for at Christmas a party held in the church hut was very much looked forward to. I still remember the Christmas tree which reached almost to the roof, lit with tiny candles and on top the beautiful fairy doll which appeared every year. How I longed for her to be mine! Around the bottom of the tree would be two heaps of presents. Games like ludo, draughts and snakes and ladders for the boys, tea sets, celluloid dolls and skipping ropes for the girls come to mind. Not forgetting the orange, apple and bag of sweets to take home.

The summer treat was another popular event. I remember how we watched the evening sky for the "Red sky at night – shepherd's delight" which would mean the weather would be fine for our trip to the seaside. Mustering in the school playground adjoining the church, we would march the short distance to the railway station, excitement mounting as the train steamed in on the Portsmouth platform. This would take us as far as "Fort Brockhurst" where changing to the branch line a smaller train would take us the short distance to our destination, Lee-on-Solent, our playground for the day, supervised by the Sunday school superintendent and his wife, some senior girls and a few mothers who came along to help. I wonder why the sun always seemed to shine in those far off days? I feel privileged to have grown up in those happy carefree years when boredom was not a word in our vocabulary.'

INFANTS SUNDAY SCHOOL

'The Infants Sunday School, as it used to be called, was held in St Mary's hall at Overton every Sunday morning and we had about 60 children in the 1940s and 1950s. *Ring Bells* was always our first hymn and the smallest child was soon able to join in the chorus "Bim bom bells" with appropriate hand actions. One of the highlights of the year was the Christmas party and nativity play which the children acted to their parents and families at the end of the party. The angels looked angelic in their white robes with tinsel in their hair; the shepherds could never keep their head-dresses on, and the kings had great difficulty in presenting their gifts and bowing their heads! Inevitably just as the curtain was about to rise someone needed to go to the toilet . . . and then another . . . and another!

Another great Sunday school occasion was the tea party and games on the rectory lawn on a Saturday afternoon in the summer (if wet it was held in St Mary's hall). Remembrance Sunday was another occasion I remember. All the Sunday school children used to stand outside St Mary's hall to watch the band and parade go by on their way to church. We had to finish Sunday school sharp on time so that the children could go out again and watch the band return after the service. Directly they heard the beat of the drum their excitement contained no bounds. "Miss, the band's coming," and there would be a mad dash for the door!

During the war the parade still happened but there was no band, instead Mr Bill Bower walked in front playing his whistle pipe. It wasn't quite the same.'

# GETTING ABOUT

**The early cars caused a stir when they first appeared on the roads, and even in the 1930s cars were still comparatively rare. Before that we walked or went by horse power or bicycle. Buses soon proved a godsend to isolated village folk, and the steam trains still have a place in our hearts.**

## EARLY TRANSPORT AT CRONDALL

'The first mode of transport that I can remember in 1914 and 1915 was by horse and van, a business carried on by Mr Fulford. He was the carrier between Crondall and Farnham, using a large black cob called Tom and a covered-in van.

Normally he went to Farnham station three times a week, collecting parcels on the way. He would call in the village shops on the way to see if there was anything for him to pick up at Kinghams, the wholesale grocer's in Farnham. If any local people needed him to deliver a parcel or put anything on rail, they displayed a card in the window with a large letter F on it. Apart from the usual load of parcels and boxes, he had room for about four adults sitting on a form just inside the van, but these seats had to be booked in advance. Of course this was before there was any bus service.

Both Mr Fulford and Tom saw service in the First World War. After Mr Fulford was called up for the army, Tom was commandeered by the army and went to France, where he was wounded in the head and had shrapnel removed. Both survived the war and both came together again, so Tom and his master were able to carry on going to Farnham for several more years.

As well as Tom, Mr Fulford also had a small pony called Jack and a small brown trap with a step and door at the back, which he let out to people who liked to drive themselves. Jack got into the habit of wanting to walk rather than trot. Mr Fulford said it was the old ladies that used to hire – some of them would get out and walk up the hill or allow him to eat the grass beside the road.

For people who were a little better off there was another firm, Barnard Bros, who had two horse carriages and a waggonette that could be hired.

The carriages were very smart affairs – well sprung with leather upholstery and large enough for four passengers, with the coachman sitting high up in front on an open seat. These vehicles were hired mostly for weddings, or for mourning coaches following a horse-drawn hearse.

As for the waggonnette, that was very different – it was pulled by two horses and up to about a dozen passengers could be carried, but not in the same comfort. The passengers sat on two seats facing each other behind the driver, who sat up high with perhaps another passenger beside him. This conveyance was hired sometimes for wedding parties within a few miles of Crondall, and to transport the local football team to away matches.

Soon after the war people started to own their own cars and a bus service running between Basingstoke and Aldershot was started by the Aldershot & District Traction Company. From then on a taxi could be ordered from Barnard Bros, who bought two Ford cars then referred to as "Tin Lizzies". The carrier business gradually folded up and the poor old horses never returned.'


THE FIRST CARS

'I can remember when it was quite an event for a motor car to pass through the village of Overton. In fact, when the bang and splutter of the car could be heard descending Overton Hill it would be greeted at Lampole, Post Office and Bridge Street corners by a group of people who had quickly gathered to watch and cheer it on its way. It usually broke down further on, on Rotten Hill. My first ride in a car was in a Morris Cowley owned by the rector, the Revd John Carpenter-Turner.'

'It was only after the Second World War that most people were able to afford a car. On bank holidays and Sundays in summer, townsfolk who had cars came out to the New Forest and villagers would sit on the local green to watch the evening traffic slowly going home.'

## BY BIKE

'My mother and I went everywhere and carried everything on our bikes. The journey to school was travelled by Mother on her bike, and me on my fairy cycle. With her hand on my shoulder, Mummy would give me the extra push just to keep me going and to arrive there that day! In the rain, it was umbrellas up, heads down against the rain and cycle very quickly.

There were days when only my mother had her bike. Then it was a matter of "sharing" the three miles home. I would ride on about three telegraph poles away, hop off, park the bike and walk on up the road, leaving shopping and bags still attached to the machine. Meanwhile, Mummy would walk on towards the parked bike, hop on, and pedal off, past the walker, with waving and "Hello's" and on to the next parking pole. She would park the beast of burden, and walk on towards home. By this time, I had almost reached the bike and it was my turn to hop on, and pedal off down the road, past Mummy and on to the next stop. This system of travelling continued until we reached home. It meant that it was only half a walk, great fun, and the shopping got home!'

## HORSES AND STEAM

'In the early 1930s I was one of a family of nine children living at Waltham Chase. Father was a market gardener. Our produce was collected on Monday, Wednesday and Friday for markets the following days. I remember Father telling me of his very first trip as driver of the horse-drawn cart. He was a little concerned that he might not remember the way, but in the event the horse took him straight there and even pulled into the exact market pitch! He also told me how two horses would go as far as Hoad's Hill at Wickham and once the horse had pulled the cart to the top, they would change them over so as to give the first horse a rest.

My brother remembers the steam-driven vehicles owned by the local contractor, Fred Dyke. The fire basket under the boiler was quite visible and sometimes lumps of red hot ash would fall on the road. They were chain-driven to the back wheels, which were solid.'

## THE FIRST BUSES

'After the First World War there were no buses and only infrequent trains at Four Marks, so one either walked, cycled or went by pony and trap. When buses did arrive it cost fourpence to ride to Alton, four miles away. Deacon and Pine had a horse dray which could be hired, but the horse was nearly blind and you had to get out and walk up hills.'

'Buses used to run from Boldre to Lymington, but there were no timetables. The driver often did shopping for people who did not want to go to town themselves. It was the usual practice for mums to send their children to hold up the bus if they were not quite ready to go.'

## 'HAYLING BILLY'

'Havant, being a railway junction, was well served with trains from Portsmouth to London, and Portsmouth to Brighton.

But could anyone who lived in the Havant area during the 1920s and 1930s forget dear old "Hayling Billy"? – the train with the little engine and its two little carriages, which chugged to and from Hayling Island. Mother was always a "last-minuter", and we would race along the platform to the bay where the Hayling Billy was waiting. Often the guard would hold up the train while we scrambled aboard, but sometimes we were just *too* late, and saw the train disappearing round the corner. An hour to wait!

On fine days during the summer the train was always crowded, but coming back to Havant it was packed, with passengers standing shoulder to shoulder, even in the guard's van. Sometimes, I think, an extra carriage was put on, but the bridge over the water at Langstone was not considered strong enough to take too much weight. I was always glad when the bridge was crossed.

Another useful local train was the motor-train from Chichester to Portsmouth, stopping at every halt. Quite often on a Saturday, we would walk along to Bedhampton Halt and take the train to Portsmouth, fare ninepence, children half price.

After strolling around the shops in Commercial Road, we would end up in Charlotte Street in the early evening, when fish and meat would be sold off cheaply, practically given away. Not much refrigeration in those days. The longer one could wait, the cheaper the meat became, and lots of people bought their Sunday joints then.

Our special treat was usually a large haddock on the bone which cost sixpence which we would take home for high tea.'

# HOUSE & HOME

# THE HOUSES WE LIVED IN

From Tudor farmhouses to city terraces, from an old clock tower to an old poor house, from homes built from corrugated iron to one built from ship's timbers – the homes we lived in were varied and full of character. We all shared the lack of basic amenities though, and for most of us the coming of 'mod cons' was a welcome departure from 'the good old days'.

## A TUDOR FARMHOUSE

'Home for me was a Tudor farmhouse, five miles from Winchester. It had been renovated in the 18th century but, apart from that, it had changed little from the time it was built as a hunting lodge during the reign of Elizabeth I. Mains water and electricity didn't come to the village until 1950, so oil lamps were used for lighting and we went to bed by candlelight. A hurricane lamp was used during the winter for work on the farm.

Water was brought to the village in about 1911, pumped to a reservoir behind the village hall from Twyford waterworks. A few houses had water laid on from the reservoir but most people had to collect it in buckets from the village taps. As a result it was used abstemiously.

Each bedroom had a washstand with its set of matching china, usually decorated with flowers, consisting of washbasin, large cold water jug, soapdish, chamberpot, and sometimes a toothbrush holder. Bath night was on Friday, when a tin bath was placed in front of the fire and filled with hot water. There was no indoor plumbing and the lavatory was at the bottom of the garden, hidden behind a yew tree. Not much fun paying a visit there on a cold, wet night.

Cooking was done on a paraffin stove or on the open fire. The saucepans and the kettle were of heavy black iron. The kettle hung on a crane which swung out over the fire. It seemed to be permanently on the boil to provide endless cups of tea. The fireplace was a deep inglenook with a salt box on one side and a built-in wooden seat on the other. These were never used during my childhood but to a child's imagination they gave the appearance of cosiness. The house was cold (no central heating then) and on a cold winter's night one

48

would sit by the fire, burning one's legs but freezing at the back.

The house had been lived in by my family from the mid 18th century, so the furniture was a motley collection of items from that time on. How I wish I had more of them now!'

## THE TIED COTTAGE

'I married a farm worker in 1938 and moved to Tichborne, where we shared a cottage with another farm worker and his wife. Two years later, with our son, we moved to another, more isolated cottage, the tenant of which was the shepherd. This cottage had two rooms upstairs and two downstairs plus a scullery. Water was pumped from the well, oil lamps and candles provided light and there was the usual dry closet down the garden. The shepherd, remembered as the "filthiest old devil who wouldn't change his clothes", occupied one bedroom and our family, eventually eight children, slept where they could. All the children were born at home with the nurse from nearby Alresford in attendance. To call her someone had to walk or cycle to the town. When one of the children was born the nurse couldn't reach the cottage in her car and had to leave it in the lane, continuing across the fields on foot.

There was an open range in the kitchen over which a bar had to be placed before putting on the kettle or pans. Large amounts of water had to be heated in the copper, especially on washdays.

Nothing was delivered, neither was there a shop in the village. Tradesmen from Alresford left goods, including bread, at the farm at the end of the lane, and the children collected the bread, nibbling the crusts on the way home. Milk was collected from the farm in cans.

The cottage had a very large garden in which the family grew all their own vegetables and kept chickens. Ferrets were also kept and these helped to catch rabbits and hares to supplement the rations. The occasional pigeon appeared on the plate if the owner of the catapult was sufficiently quick.

During the war years the cantankerous shepherd refused to adjust to the need for blackout. One night, during the lambing season, he was out in the fields and, as usual, omitted to shield his lamp. Three bombs fell in the vicinity but fortunately no one was hurt. The shepherd continued to ignore the regulations.

In 1958 shrimps were found in the water from the well and its use was forbidden; at last water was laid on to the cottage, which made life a little easier.

In 1960 we moved to another cottage in the village, which was modernised in 1974. The cottage which had been our home for so many years is now but a memory, as it has disappeared. It exemplified a way of life which had continued for centuries with little change, but has now vanished for ever.'

## ON A SMALLHOLDING

'During the years between the world wars, homes in the countryside did not change a great deal; most were built of brick, or rendered with a smooth or pebble-dash finish with slate or tiled roofs. Old army huts were re-erected and roofed in corrugated iron, lined with matchboarding, well decorated and made comfortable and attractive. During the 1920s most homes were houses, but in the 1930s bungalows became fashionable.

My home as a child was a house on a smallholding of 20 acres on which were kept poultry, pigs and cows. It had six quite large rooms decorated with heavily patterned wallpaper scenes in the downstairs rooms and all-over patterns upstairs. Every room had a small open fireplace with a mantelpiece and downstairs there were hanging oil-burning lamps – upstairs candles; extra heating was provided by a Valor Perfection oil stove with one burner, made of tin, which made pretty flickering patterns on the ceiling.

Floors were wooden, covered with linoleum, carpet squares or rugs. The furniture was very heavy and plain. When the fires went out at night it was quite cold, and water in flower vases could freeze. Beds were warm; lots of blankets, eiderdowns and hot water bottles!

The kitchen was warmed by a cast-iron range with an oven which was polished each day with black lead brushed on. It, too, burned out at night. Heavy flat irons were heated on the top and the kettle always simmered and sang – no airing cupboards then; clothes were aired on a large wooden clothes-horse around the fire.

The scullery had an earthenware sink, wooden draining board and plate rack. Cold water was hand-pumped from an underground tank which held rainwater caught off the roof. In the corner was a large copper, bricked up, with a fire underneath. The water was heated and washing boiled in it. We were lucky to have a bathroom; the luxury of a cast-iron bath with claw feet, hand basin and flush toilet. Cold water was pumped up to a roof tank, hot water pumped from the copper into the bath above. Also in the scullery there was a Valor cooking stove, all metal, with three burners on top of which was placed an oven.

Beyond the kitchen was the larder and dairy where bowls of milk stood for the cream to rise and be skimmed to make butter in a glass churn; the skimmed milk was then fed to the pigs.

Vegetables and fruit were all grown in the garden to supply the

50

family. Some people kept a pig for the household bacon, and with rabbits, pigeons, rook pies and pheasants, families were generally self-supporting.

About 1928 we had a small radio powered by a liquid accumulator, which had to be recharged every week. For transport we maintained a horse and trap, otherwise bicycles or feet were the only means of transport unless a station happened to be nearby, which was our good fortune.'

## CORRUGATED IRON BUNGALOWS

'The few houses existing in Four Marks at the beginning of the century were mostly constructed of knapped flint, but after the First World War servicemen bought smallholdings and many very basic, corrugated iron bungalows sprang up. These usually consisted of four rooms with an outside toilet and no bathroom. Water from the roof was stored in underground tanks and pumped daily to a tank in the roof and so to the taps.

In severe weather windows were frosted on the inside, and taps and pipes were frozen. In dry weather water often had to be drawn from the underground tank by rope and bucket. In hot weather perishable food was stored in a perforated zinc cupboard situated on the north side of the bungalow.'

## LIGHTING THE FIRE

'At Lyndhurst we lived in a very small house, two up and two down with a lean-to scullery, a copper which needed wood and coal to boil up on washdays, and lino on the floor. There was one fire in the kitchen. Some days if we had friends visiting for tea and a game of cards, we would light the front room fire.'

## OVER THE SADDLER'S SHOP

'My father became what his father had been – a saddler, but with the coming of the motor car and tractors in the 1920s, saddlery was a dying trade. He was a skilled craftsman and I liked to watch him, but there were not many things to sell in the shop. In the window would have been saddle soap, shoe polish, dog leads and collars, and curry combs and brushes. I can recall my parents talking when at times the weekly takings were less than £1. What a good thing there were monthly accounts with local farms!

Times were hard, but my father was soft when it came to charging for small jobs. He would say, "That's all right". He got thanked, but a small charge might have boosted takings a little. He once won £10 with a football ticket, which must have been a godsend. Later he was forced to close the shop, but he still did saddlery in his spare time.

We lived at the shop in Fordingbridge High Street. Our home was tiny – cramped even – and people now could never imagine the conditions with which my mother coped. Behind the shop was a dark little room with a table which was raised on hinges when we ate breakfast and lunch (we called it dinner). Cooking was done on a gas stove in a narrow, dark passageway which opened on to a tiny backyard. I think water was fetched from next door.

There was a very steep staircase to the large room upstairs. This staircase was little better than a ladder with wide rungs. There was a window overlooking the street, and the walls were painted green. My parents had an iron double bed with screwable brass knobs. One knob I could unscrew and so it hung over drunkenly. My bed was a single hospital bed, white painted. We had feather mattresses and pillows. I remember my mother "plumping them up". Chamberpots were kept discreetly behind a curtain during the day. The space under the bed provided extra storage room. There was a round mahogany table with a green cover and we had elegant cane-seated bedroom chairs. By the window was an Edwardian easy chair which had turned wooden pillars supporting padded arms, and the front legs were nicely turned too. There was another chair, curved and comfortable with a high rounded back. It was covered in a sort of "American cloth" which was cold to sit on.

In front of the fire was a rag rug with the initials K. H. My uncle, who had been a Royal Marine, made it for his youngest sister (Kate Horsey). I don't remember any other mats over the dark brown linoleum, but I'm sure there were some.

When we needed the privy we had to go through the next premises to the one in their garden.

We lived there until I was ten in 1931 when we moved into a new council house. Heaven. There was no mains drainage in Fordingbridge until late in the 1950s.'

## BUILT OF SHIP'S TIMBERS

'In 1950 I came to live in Hampshire and bought a small cottage in Greatham which at that time cost less than £3,000, and where I still live. The cottage is built of ship's timbers with wattle and daub inner walls, the outer walls being a mixture of rock, brick and ironstone. There was no damp course and no water, electricity or gas laid on. Water was obtained from a well which held surface water and was therefore unfit for drinking. Two hundred swings of the pump sent

*The wedding party gathers for the photographer at Easter 1922. Going straight back to the house for a 'knife and fork' tea was the only celebration most couples enjoyed – and honeymoons were out of the question for working folk.*

enough water for a bath into a tank upstairs on the landing (when we had had a bath plumbed in downstairs!). The water was heated by a coke stove in the kitchen. The toilet was an Elsan (chemical toilet) in an outhouse.

Cooking was done by bottled gas, which was supplied and delivered by a man with a van who also delivered oil for lamps and stoves.

Heating was provided by the coke stove in the kitchen and an open fire in the sitting-room. Any other heat was from paraffin stoves, rather risky as they were apt to flare up and fill the room with soot unless carefully watched.

Paraffin lamps and candles provided light. Washing was done by hand with large items sent to the laundry which called once a week. I used flat irons heated on the stove to iron my hand washing.'

## A TERRACED HOUSE

'In the 1940s we lived in a terraced house in Gunner Street, Portsmouth, which was a heavily bombed area at that time. These houses were built in about 1850 for the dockyard workers. As such these small basic dwellings had had practically no improvements made to them – even by the Second World War. They all faced directly on to the pavement with a shoe scraper let into the wall (which I cannot ever remember being used).

Our house only had a gas supply which was for both lighting and cooking. The gas light required a metal plate between the lamp and the ceiling to deflect the heat. The lamp gave out a gentle hissing noise, a yellowish light which was controlled by chains or a tap, depending how posh your gas lamp was.

The radio, or wireless, provided both entertainment and up to date news. It was powered by a rechargeable accumulator and a little shop in Fratton Road carried out the recharging for a few pence. At the end of the war this radio was replaced by a radio relay receiver. The reception was excellent but it always shut down at precisely 12 pm.

There was no convenience in anything in that house. The toilet was located at the rear of the house and a visit meant going out into the open yard separating the houses. There was no light in the toilet and the damp walls suited slugs and spiders a treat. A visit at night to that place was to be dreaded with little comfort gained from a flickering candle or the light from a torch whose batteries seemed on their last.

The place designated as the kitchen had neither sink nor running water. Any water required had to be brought from the washhouse. Again, a journey into the open yard and into the washhouse, which contained a large stone Butler sink and a single cold water tap.

The washhouse also contained what was fondly described as "the washing machine". This consisted of a galvanised steel container into which both hot water and clothes were put. A flat galvanised steel paddle was made to agitate the clothes by a manually operated handle connected to a rod through the lid. It was really hard work. The water was squeezed out of the clothes by feeding them through the wooden rollers manually rotated.

A gas boiler in the washhouse provided washday and Sunday bathday hot water. Baths were taken in the portable tin bath in front of the living-room fire. Bathday seemed an endless stream of buckets coming and going.

Ironing clothes was by swapping over heated flat irons from the gas ring on the cooker. The cooker was in the kitchen whilst the ironing was carried out in the living-room. A temporary improvement in the ironing task was the gas iron. This was attached to a gas point with a rubber hose and the iron had flames heating the sole plate. I think commonsense stopped its use.'

# THE POLICE HOUSE

'My father was a policeman from the mid 1920s and his first station as a single man was at Havant where he lived in quarters in the old police station in West Street (this was pulled down in the 1960s). On getting married he moved into a police house in Denvilles, Havant where my sister and I were born. This was a new house and of its day very modern. His duties would have comprised traffic duty on the crossroads in Havant (near the church). This would have been performed in shifts of four hours. After being in this area for approximately eight years he was posted to Basingstoke where he had to perform mainly traffic duty. His stay was very brief there as a policeman was required to take over the country beat at Upton Grey.

This house comprised one large room, a scullery, a cellar, one bedroom and a boxroom on the landing with no window. The toilet was up the garden and was a bucket. There was no running water and all water had to be drawn from a well. The lighting was by oil lamps. Cooking was by a kitchen range in the main room or by an oil stove with a twin burner and a small oven on top. The house had a huge garden which produced all the vegetables and fruit we needed and the surplus would be preserved for the winter. Living in the country we had rabbits and pheasants. This was in the 1935–38 era. The other half of the house was occupied by the District Nurse.

Our next move was into Basingstoke where we lived in a terraced house for six months before moving to Whitchurch where we had a modern council house allocated to us. There was a large garden and when the war broke out in 1939 my father also took on an allotment. The house was quite superior to what we had had, although on looking back there was no electricity. It was gas lighting downstairs and we used candles to go to bed with. We had a bathroom but the water was heated in a copper (by a fire underneath it) in the kitchen and then pumped upstairs.

Five years on and we again had a move, this time to another village – St Mary Bourne. The house this time was a purpose built police house but the water was not laid on and had to be pumped by hand to a tank in the roof and there was a cesspit in the garden which periodically had to be emptied.

My father's final move to Tidworth was his last and he had five years to serve before retiring; this was in a police station with three police houses attached. All of this took place before the 1960s.'

# THE POOR HOUSE

'The Poor House lies in the middle of Buriton High Street. It was built in 1790 and must originally have been a place of sadness with couples who could no longer look after themselves cruelly separated, the men in one half, the women in the other.

When I grew up there in the 1940s it was six dwellings. We had two bedrooms, a scullery and a sitting-room. Amenities were primitive; electricity downstairs, one light in the living-room and another in the hall, while upstairs it was candles. There was an outside tap for the six houses, so every drop of water had to be carried in by bucket and disposed of in the same way. On frosty mornings we used the minimum, hoping it would last so that one of our neighbours would go first with a kettle of hot water to thaw the frozen tap. On my wedding day I cycled to the far end of the village for a bath, then cycled back before donning my finery.

Anyone who has experienced outdoor privies must consider indoor sanitation the blessing of the century. The six houses all had their own privy at the top of the gardens. It was no fun to toil up the slope on a dark and wet or wintry night. Cleaning the privies must have been a dreadful task. This was done by the sanitation tanker which called once a week to empty the buckets of sewage. It was known as the "violet cart". It caused much amusement among the villagers, as the men appeared totally unaware of any health hazards and would eat their sandwiches while they worked.

We cooked on a double primus in the scullery, or used a big black range in the kitchen-sitting-room. Chimney fires were very common; a frightening experience as the Registo and surrounding parts would become red hot, instead of black and shining. It was one of my Saturday morning chores to blacklead the range and polish the pokers. Cake making was a hit and miss affair, according to which way the wind was blowing, as this decided whether the oven was sufficiently hot and more importantly whether it would retain its heat.

Ironing was done with flat irons on an old blanket on the big table in the middle of the room. The irons were kept to one side of the range, so they were ready to use. Washing was done in a copper which was in the scullery and heated by wood. It was put to dry on long lines in the back gardens.

Today the Poor House has been converted into four desirable residences, equipped with every labour-saving device. What changes that building has seen in its 200 years.'

# THE CLOCK TOWER

'The clock tower in the centre of Warsash was built in about the 1890s. It was built by Mr G. A. Shenley to house the water tanks to supply water to the Warsash House estate, including various cottages occupied by employees, and also as a yacht store and village clock.

In 1938 my husband purchased the property known as "clock tower and buildings" and we moved into a flat over the coach houses in Shore Road. This flat was entered by a spiral staircase and a long passage on the north side giving access to seven rooms all facing south. Over the next four years or so a great many changes took place. Clock Tower Garage was opened on the corner of Shore Road and Brook Lane, and the coach houses were converted into shops in Shore Road. The ground floor of the clock tower, which was an open archway, was bricked up on the east and west to form a living-room with kitchen and entrance hall to the north. Three flights of stairs were installed where originally there had only been ladders to each floor. The first floor was bathroom, toilet, a large linen cupboard and bedroom number one. The second floor, which originally housed the clock mechanism, was octagonal and became bedroom number two. We had to wind huge weights with the aid of a hand windlass from the ground floor to this height once a week to keep the clock working.

These works were installed by Gillett & Johnson of Croydon. They were dismantled and purchased by Luke Bros shipyard of Hamble and thence to Coventry. They were unique as the mechanism struck ship's bell time. There was a large cast iron bell hung above the first floor window. We got so used to the sound of it we really missed it when it was removed. A small electric clock was installed on the back of the clock face. This floor was occupied by three water tanks which were eventually cut up and lowered for scrap, and windows were put in, in place of louvres. This was our sitting-room, which I do not think we used much but the view was superb. From this floor one climbed a ladder into the dome roof which was like an attic with no windows but air vents. Another ladder took one up to a weighted hatch on to the top of the tower. There was originally a weather vane of a gilded copper sailing ship but this had disappeared many years before we owned the property.

We had one of the first television sets in Warsash with an aerial on top of the tower. The picture was terrible compared to today's reception but we thought it was wonderful.'

# WONDERFUL NEWS

'It was a November morning in 1954. The letter had arrived from the council and we had been offered a house at Leigh Park. Living in a flat, with our two children, this was wonderful news. I could hardly wait for Brian to come home from work; he was on early turn so he would be home about one o'clock.

First, must get in touch with Mum, to look after the children. No phone in those days. Would have to go to Gosport and see her.

Of course, we knew where Leigh Park was. We had been there once, to visit some friends who had a flat by the Cricketers. And Brian's Mum had told us how she had been there on Sunday school outings as a child. Well, it's all arranged, and very exciting. Off we go on Brian's Coventry Eagle motorbike, Mum waving us off. We had the address, and the keys to the house. All we had to do was find it.

We passed through Cosham, along the Havant Road, through Drayton and Farlington. On to the city limits, now we are getting out in the country. At last we were at the Cricketers. "Not far," someone told us, "Stockheath Road is straight on." We chugged on, coming upon what looked and was a building site. No proper roads or footpaths, but plenty of mud. A plank of wood led up to the front door. The terrace of houses were all empty, some still in different stages of being built. Ours was number 48.

It was lovely. A large kitchen and one room at the front downstairs, and three bedrooms and a bathroom upstairs. A large back garden, which looked like a builder's rubbish dump. Bricks and pipes and other unidentifiable objects were everywhere and a stream running across the bottom and, of course, there was mud. But it was all a dream come true. A house of our own, and the children could have

a bedroom each. Now the questions started to come. Could we afford the rent? Where were the shops? Could Brian get to work? Well, he had his motorbike, so that was OK as he had to be at Cosham post office at four o'clock in the morning, so he needed his own transport. Yes, we could just about afford the rent. We had made up our minds, the house was going to be our home. Now, we decided to explore the area. No one else had moved into the other houses that were finished. But two doors away, was a private house with a large garden, belonging to Dr Concannon. Well, that was good news, having a doctor so close. We turned left and found there was a group of shops in Stone Square. Things were going to be all right and Havant was not too far away.

We moved in on 7th December. How quiet it was and how dark. There was no street lighting and it was very cold. Still, we soon had a nice fire burning and the baby settled and David ready for bed. But where was the cat? Oh dear, he had got out, how could we find him? No, he had gone, goodness knows where.

We were settling in slowly. A grocer from Mile End, Portsmouth, had called in his van to ask if we wanted any groceries delivered. "Oh, yes please." He would call one day for our order and deliver it the next so that was a great help. Also, Mr Coleman the baker from Bedhampton called regularly and the milkman too. The coalman was, of course, a blessing.

The first winter had its problems, freezing weather and burst pipes and overflows. Having to walk with the children crying with the cold to find the workmen to come and repair them. Taking the children to clinic in Botley Drive, which seemed miles away, to get the baby's milk and orange juice. Still, we survived. The cat came back after six weeks, looking in a very sad state, but he was pleased to be home. Other families moved in, and we were able to start clearing the garden.

By the summer we were enjoying our new surroundings and neighbours. We had bought our first car for £9 10s, an Austin 7 (if only we had it now). We enjoyed driving to Emsworth and feeding the swans on the Mill Pond, picking bluebells in the woods and picnicking, walking in Leigh Park Gardens amongst the primroses and cowslips and were upset when Leigh Park House was demolished. Going on the Hayling Billy and walking down Staunton Avenue to the Hayling beach.

We had many, many happy days watching Leigh Park develop, Park Parade emerging and the arrival of our own Co-op! Life was lovely.'

# WATER AND WASHDAY

**With no running water, every drop had to be fetched from wells, springs or pumps and was jealously guarded. Washday, which used gallons of water, was an especially hard day. From the lighting of the copper fire in the early morning to the final ironing with irons heated on the fire, it was a day (or days!) of drudgery for all women.**

## ALWAYS A PROBLEM

'Water supplies were always a big problem in Wield till mains water arrived. Although there are some wells, because the village is 600 feet above sea level these are very deep, and presumably difficult and expensive to dig. However, in the late 1920s there was a succession of dry years and things became more and more difficult. During one summer every well in the two villages of Upper and Lower Wield dried up and water had to be collected from the pump at Preston Candover two and a half miles away. For this the people had to pay. Mr Sylvester of Lower Wield decided to deepen his well by 100 feet.

This was done by R. Smith of Basingstoke. They arrived with a small lorry. In order to see clearly down the well a small mirror was used to reflect the sun down the shaft. Fortunately the weather was fine. They could not work if there was any gas in the well so to check that all was clear a candle was lowered down. To deepen the well, hollow pipes were attached to a small, primitive crane on the back of the lorry and dropped down the well on a rope. The pipe was winched up and while any chalk or clay in the end of the pipe was removed another pipe was sent down. The man doing the work was about 70 and nearly all his finger ends were missing where he had caught them in his work.

In about 1936 Mr Sylvester also had built some water collecting pots, called locally Hampshire Pots. These were an improvement on dew-ponds. These are barrel-shaped pits about 20 to 30 feet in depth and about eight feet in diameter, with limestone and brick linings. They were dug both near houses where water could be collected in them from the roof and also out in the fields near a track or place where the water ran down when it rained into the pot. The ones in the fields were to supply water to the sheep and any other animals. We still have one in our field in good condition. However, as the road is now metalled and the water running off it is rather oily it is probably not of a good standard.'

FROM DEW-PONDS TO MAINS WATER

'Burghclere covers an area that includes chalk downland in the south and wooded areas in the north with heathland and marsh in other areas. Due to this diversity man has had to resort to various methods of obtaining water. The earliest evidence of this are the dew-ponds on the downs, one at Ladle Hill Camp and another nearby. These were constructed by excavating the desired area and lining the base and sides with "puddled" clay and straw finished with a layer of chalk. The ponds then filled with rainwater and dew, hence the name. This is an over-simplified explanation of a complicated process that ensured that many of the ponds have not dried up in the intervening centuries. As settlement in Burghclere slowly moved northward wells were dug and natural springs utilised.

There is little doubt that the use of wells led to many of the illnesses which were so prevalent in the past. At the school in 1904 an analysis of the water by Messrs Hickman & Metcalfe was that it was "unsatisfactory". Mr Kelleway (the master) noted that, "The whole of the water drunk by the scholars for over the last twelve months had been boiled by Mrs Kelleway since the water had been pronounced to be polluted by the County Analyst." This must have been a tremendous undertaking for Mrs Kelleway and reminds us once again of the hardships that people faced in the past.

In the garden of the cottage where I was born in 1938 there was a well, but we were more fortunate than some, we had the luxury of a pump in the kitchen with which to bring the water up from the well. This was a blessing as the walk from the well to the house was a distance of some 30 to 40 yards. The toilet facilities were fairly primitive, a small shed with a wooden seat over a bucket. Every now and then the shed would be moved to avoid a built-up of unpleasant residues.

Meanwhile, at the school a lorry would call at regular intervals to empty the buckets from a row of similar toilets. These were memorable occasions, firstly because the visit of the lorry caused a welcome diversion in the school day. and secondly because of the smell which permeated the classrooms even though the sheds were some distance from the school building. The shells of these old toilets are still standing and a double one was left complete as a curiosity.

Piped water first came to Burghclere in the 1930s but only to the

*One of the water men of Titchfield. The wooden-handled bowl used for filling householders' buckets can be seen in the lid of the tank.*

properties that were in close proximity to the main village road, Harts Lane, and must have been a highly prized convenience. The caretaker at the parish room was expected to pay for the water to be piped to the cottage whilst the management committee paid for the hall's supply.

In December 1946 my parents moved from the cottage to one of the post-war council houses at Breachfield and I remember my mother taking my sister and me to see the new house and our delight at running around the house turning the lights on and off and repeatedly flushing the toilet. Of course, we had no electricity at the cottage so we felt doubly blessed by these wonders. People who had moved to the first of the post-war houses had to do without electricity until all the houses in that phase had been finished and so continued to use Aladdin lamps etc, but we moved in to a lovely new house with all "mod cons". The one that must have been a boon to my mother was the washhouse. This was part of the main house but was reached by going out of the back door braving the elements, not so pleasant in winter. The washhouse had a built-in boiler with a space underneath for a fire to heat the water.

Some of the more remote properties didn't have water until the late 1950s. The father of my friend, who lived in Spring Lane, had to take a cart to a nearby spring and fill an enormous wooden vessel with water that had to last the family a week. The residents in Whitway had their water brought to them on a cart from the Highclere estate, although the Carnarvon Arms had its own pumphouse, the remains of which can still be seen under a cloak of ivy and undergrowth.

Now all of Burghclere is piped onto mains water and the old days have been slowly forgotten. However, early maps show where wells were situated, evidence of cottages that long ago fell down and disappeared along with memories of those old, hard times.'

## THE WATER CART

'There was no mains water at Titchfield in the early part of the century and not all properties had a well in the garden, so the water man would pull a large tank on wheels around the village and buckets left outside doors were filled from the tank with a wooden handled bowl. Later a donkey pulled the cart which made his task easier. He was always called "Finisher" because he was said never to finish any job, except his water carrying.

There were dirt roads so Titchfield also had a water cart which was used daily in dry weather to water the streets. It consisted of a large tank, horse-drawn, and the driver had a hand lever to start and stop the water which sprayed the width of the street to lay the dust.'

## TAPS AND YOKES

'In the 1920s there was a windmill in Nether Wallop where the new school is, and a reservoir on the site of the school playground. The mill supplied water to three taps in the village – one by the Ship Inn, one by the shops and the third opposite Pitcot Lane. People in Crabs Hill had to come to this last tap unless they were lucky enough to have a well. A fourth tap was put in at Hilly Close when the houses were built in 1925 and another down the lane by Church Cottages. Mrs Day of Crabs Hill wore a yoke across her shoulders from which she hung the buckets to carry the water home. On a Monday it meant several trips across the road to fill the copper and several baths.'

'My parents and I lived in a small wooden bungalow at Liphook in the 1930s, with a corrugated iron roof. Outside was a bucket lavatory, which had to be emptied on to the garden, as did the sink water which drained from the kitchen sink into an outside bucket. The well, which had been provided for us, did not give enough water and it was never clean, so Mother would put a wooden yoke on her shoulders and walk across to the next field and fill two large buckets from a stopcock – put there to water the chickens. Then she walked back heavily laden. There was no other water supply.'

## WE DIDN'T REALISE

'In the summer of 1953 my husband and I bought our first house, the newly converted kitchen end of an attractive 18th century house in a small village. The vendor, a retired builder, and his wife, who had bought the whole place with outbuildings and 14 acres the previous year for £5,000, undertook to be responsible for keeping us supplied with water, there being no mains then (they came in 1956).

The 500-gallon tanks in the attic were filled from the well in the garage at our end of the house, converted from the laundry room, by a hot air pump (obsolete in the 19th century according to the *Encyclopedia Britannica*, our only handbook). Once the very awkward fire underneath had got going, it took about three hours to fill the tanks before the water started trickling from the overflow and the pump could be stopped. We didn't realise all this on the hot August day we moved in and longed for a wash and tea; alas, the taps were dry and the builder was out for the day. All that we could do was take our biggest saucepans to the pub and say please. We hadn't even a watering can.'


## IT TOOK MOST OF THE DAY

'We had an outhouse which had a built-in copper, sink and a mangle with a cast iron base and two large snow-white wooden rollers. The copper had to be heated as best Mother could, mainly by burning rags obtained from a nearby clothing factory. I can't remember how she managed to fill the copper but I can remember various buckets so presume she had to fill them up any way she could and tip the water into the copper. As the mangle was very heavy to operate, she had to use both arms to wind the handle.

This process took her most of the day. Lunch would be cold meat and mashed potato, the quickest thing she could provide. It was therefore disastrous if the Monday should turn out wet as with little in the way of labour saving devices, every day was booked for a certain job. To dry on such days she would have to light a fire in our sitting-room and the washing would be draped over a large wooden clothes-horse. The clothes were aired in the same way.

The sheets and pillowcases were linen so after drying they had to be pulled into shape before rolling, and put in a large double-handled iron bath ready for ironing. The large tablecloths were all starched and these were subjected to the same pulling and stretching before being rolled and damped down (if they were too dry) before ironing.

Her clothes line was wire so before the clothes were pegged out, this had to be cleaned and it was a very bad day if, for some reason, the line broke!

There were two adults and four children in the house so there was plenty of washing to do. My father wore white shirts, some of which had detached stiff collars which had to be taken to the laundry. If the collars were attached, then mother would open up the collars and lay them on the draining board and taking Fairy soap and a nail brush, would proceed to scrub at the collars before washing the shirts. The only soap powders I remember were Rinso and Oxydol and plenty of soda.

When it came to ironing, she had a heavy flat iron which sat on the top of the black grate in the kitchen – it must have been a boon when she managed to get an electric iron. This was used by way of a two way affair plugged into the light in the middle of the room, consequently as she ironed (no ironing board but a padded sheet on the kitchen table) the light continually moved with the iron!

The whole process was extremely hard work and a job no sane person would look forward to.'

## GREAT CAMARADERIE

'I was born in 1932 in a terraced house in the then small market town of Basingstoke. Washing of clothes was done in a brick copper which had been built in the scullery. This had to be filled with water from the tap and then wood placed in the grate underneath to heat it.

Monday, regardless of the weather, was washday. This entailed my mother rising at 6 am to fill and light the boiler. The whole of the day was taken up with boiling, rinsing and mangling the clothes, so Monday dinner was part of the ritual and we always sat down to cold meat from Sunday's joint and bubble and squeak, with cold fruit pie which had been made the previous day and hot custard. Everybody washed on Mondays and there was a great camaraderie between the women as they pegged out their clothes and the local gossip was exchanged over the fences. The road I grew up in was a hive of activity with everybody knowing everybody else. Across the road was the steam laundry and round the corner was the gasworks. At the end of the garden was the Salvation Army and beyond that the cattle market and railway station.

Sadly nothing remains of any of this except the railway station. All the houses and lots more were demolished to make way for the overspill from London in 1960. My sister and I are grandmothers now with all mod cons in our houses but we look back with nostalgia to a very happy childhood.'

## TAKING IN WASHING

'Most working people at Twyford in the 1920s and 1930s lived in rented houses. There were six cottages in Park Lane where each house had one room upstairs and one down. The landing upstairs was just big enough to hold a bed for two children. Few cottages had bathrooms. On Saturday night the big galvanised iron bath would be put in front of the kitchen fire and hot water from the copper carried in. First the children would be bathed, then Father and last of all Mother, by which time the water would be cool and covered with a grey soapy scum. Lavatories were usually a shed at the end of the garden with a wooden seat over a bucket. When flush toilets were first put into Park Lane two families had to share the same toilet, ten people in all.

Some houses had a washhouse in the garden, fitted with a brick copper for heating water and boiling clothes, but often no tap. A well in the garden and a bucket on the end of a rope was their water supply. Several women took in washing to help with the family budget. One woman did the washing for Shawford House and Brambridge House. This included sheets, tablecloths, maids' caps and aprons. All the whites had to be washed, boiled, rinsed and re-rinsed in water in which a bag of blue colouring had been swished. The cap frills had to be pleated with a goffering iron, heated over the kitchen stove. She then wheeled the clean clothes back to both houses in a pram.'

# FOOD, SHOPPING AND CALLERS TO THE DOOR

**In the days when a pig at the bottom of the garden was a part of life, our food was less varied but fresh and wholesome. Shopping was a pleasure, in shops which had a character all their own, and many day to day foods were delivered straight to our doors by regular tradesmen who became almost part of the family.**

## EVERYONE HAD A PIG

'Everyone at Bighton had a pig in the years before the Second World War, and kept a swill bucket for its food. This was boiled up with potatoes and had barley meal stirred in. Killing the pig was a great event, there was no sentimentality. A licensed slaughterer did the deed. The sides were usually smoked and hung up in an airy place, but there was plenty to share with friends and neighbours.

The larder was as cool as it could be made with marble and slate shelves. About twice a week some of the milk from the farm was put to set in wide shallow pans and after several days the cream was skimmed off; to this day I cannot eat real Scottish porridge without cream! Others bought their milk from a pony and cart, where the milk was ladled out into a jug with pint and half pint measures. Ernie was very obliging and did "messages" for his customers in Alresford, so his trip there made a very long morning.

In summer, there were a lot of flies around and these were controlled by hanging sticky flypapers from the kitchen light – a grisly sight!'

## OUR FAMILY WAS FORTUNATE

'Our family was very fortunate, as my mother was an excellent cook (having herself been "in service" in her teenage days, with several titled families) and even on a modest income, prepared us some delicious, wholesome meals from such things as sixpence worth of bones from the butcher and vegetables from the garden, which became a very tasty, filling soup.

My father was an excellent gardener and he grew all the vegetables imaginable, plus soft fruits such as raspberries, gooseberries, blackcurrants etc. As well as our quite large garden, he had an allotment plot, in which he grew more potatoes, runner and broad beans, marrows etc, and some flowers too – although the flower garden was really my mother's pride and joy and we always had a very colourful garden.

The soft fruits were put to good use and delicious jams and jellies were made and used in puddings, fruit tarts and for our teas. It was always quite a treat, towards the end of our August school holidays, to go with my mother, the neighbouring wives and my little girl friend from next door, to walk about a mile or so to our local fields and woods at Allbrook to pick blackberries, which were made into jam and summer puddings. Some were also put into sterilised jars which were heated in the oven for the appropriate time, so the blackberries and other soft fruits from the garden were preserved, to be used during the winter months when fresh fruit was not available. Bottling was the method used in the 1920s and 1930s before domestic freezers were about. My mother also made an excellent marrow chutney – a delicious recipe which I still use to this day.

We had a very good Co-operative Society branch only a few yards from our home and sometimes I was trusted to take an order to the shop, and the goods would be delivered to our door. If we shopped personally, we could watch sugar, flour, biscuits, etc being weighed up and the butter cut from huge slabs and "knocked into shape" with wooden butter pats. Vinegar was drawn from wooden casks into our own bottles. The Co-op butcher cut whatever joint and size was required and this, too, could be delivered if requested. We had a Co-op milkman, baker and also greengrocer (all of whom had their horse-drawn carts) call at the door – also someone with paraffin and hardware and suchlike, and not to forget the coalman (wearing his cap backwards to protect his head and with a sack draped over his shoulders) with his hundredweight sacks of all sorts of coal, coke and Coalite.'


FOREST FOOD

'I was brought up in Everton, near Lymington in the New Forest, from the 1940s to the 1960s, before cattle grids and fences were built to contain the ponies and cattle. Shopping was quite an expedition once a week from the grocer's Roland Hill in Lymington High Street on the back of Mum's bike. Mum would choose what she required for the week, the sugar was weighed out into cones of paper and butter patted into blocks whilst I was sat on the counter to watch and given a biscuit or sweet. The groceries were then delivered to the house the next day.

As we lived by the sea and also on the edge of the forest, food was quite plentiful so we ate well. Duck, pigeon and rabbit were regularly on the table, so was fish caught by a local fisherman friend. We also kept chickens and grew all our own vegetables. The eggs were preserved in waterglass in a bucket in the larder for baking during the winter months when the hens were off lay – we had to put our hands in this horrible slimy solution to get the eggs out for Mum when we were helping to bake.

The feathers from the chickens were never wasted as we would spend a wet Saturday filling pillows. Even the skins from the rabbits were stretched on a board for weeks to dry and later Mum would make them into fur gloves for my sister and me. I also remember my brother having a rabbit fur pram cover on his pram which must have been the height of luxury.

When Dad harvested the potatoes, with the help of us children, they would be stored in a specially designed potato/apple store in straw. We would gingerly put our hands into the straw to find the potatoes, for fear of mice – I don't know what I disliked more, getting the eggs or the potatoes.

With no freezer (or fridge) Mum would preserve almost anything using all methods; drying, bottling and salting etc. Then came the year of the rose hip syrup, the dandelion wine, sloe gin and ginger beer – do you remember the ginger beer plant? Our two maiden aunts came to stay, as they did most years, and we were sent off to find rose hips by the basket full, jam jars full of sloes and baskets full of dandelion flower heads. I ruined my favourite dress that year and stained my fingers very badly too but it was worth it because the ginger beer and the rose hip syrup were great – we were not allowed to drink the wine or sloe gin!'

TWYFORD SHOPS

'Between the two world wars Twyford was a thriving village supplying most people's everyday necessities. Green King Alfred buses ran frequently to Winchester but the fare was fourpence. When a farm worker's basic weekly wage was 30 shillings many people had either to walk or stay at home.

The largest shop in Twyford was Smith's the baker and grocer. Mr Smith, splendid in a white coat and white apron, presided over this. His white beard and grand manner made the children think he looked like George V. A horse-drawn van was used for deliveries but later they bought a smart motor van. The delivery man tried to learn to drive but he worried so much that his wife found him trying to drive the bedpost in his sleep. He returned to serving in the shop and a younger man took over the van.

Several other shops delivered bread, meat or milk every day. Two dairymen brought churns of milk round in a milk float drawn by a pony. The milk was measured out into customers' jugs by a pint dipper. One milkman put his churns in the dicky seat of his car.

At least three sweet shops kept the children happy even though one of them was kept by "The Witch"! The bonus paid by farmers at the end of harvest brought good trade to the two shoe shops when families were shod for the coming winter.'

## HARDING'S STORES

'Harding's Stores once supplied most of the village from premises in Maury's Lane, the site of the first Methodist chapel in Wellow. Mrs Harding, who once ran the shop with her husband remembers serving her regular customers and was able to give a typical shopping list.

A family of four, working on the land, would probably have a weekly order for eight pounds of sugar, one pound of lard or margarine, two pounds of cheese, half a pound of plain biscuits, half a pound of tea, half a pound of Fry's cocoa, and a bottle of Camp coffee. Flour was not on the weekly list of goods fetched from the shop because it was sold from the van which delivered the bread.

As well as feeding her family, the housewife also had to keep them clean and would need two pounds of soda, a packet of Hudson's washing powder, a Reckitt's blue bag, Watson's soap or a long bar of Primrose soap, a packet of Lux Flakes, and starch.

Other necessities were reels of white cotton thread, leather boot-laces, matches, candles, a Veritas lamp glass, methylated spirits, paraffin oil, camphorated oil (this last for rubbing on chests against the coughs and colds of winter) and blacklead for grates.

Mr and Mrs Harding ran a general store, such as is hardly to be found nowadays, selling many items besides groceries and bread from their bakery. A drapery order would often require tapes, buttons (mainly pearl or linen), braces, calico shirt collars, or cotton striped working shirts. Many families ordered hobnailed working boots, as well as ladies' slippers and shoes. Men's working socks were often hand-knitted by their wives and some women also made their men's working shirts. For these, they would order six yards of Oxford shirting, neckbands and linen buttons.

Mr Harding had four bread vans on the road and hot cross buns were delivered in time for breakfast on Good Friday – the only day in the year on which they were baked. There were other small bakeries in Wellow and deliveries were made to some outlying areas from Sherfield English. There were also two butchers in Wellow, while several came out from Romsey to make deliveries. Milk was sold from local farms and was dipped from the churn in measures of a pint, half a pint and "pennyworths". Some old ladies, living alone, could only afford these "penn'oths" – though without refrigerators the unpasteurised milk would keep for only a short time and was generally bought more frequently than is the case now.

Cellars were rare in Wellow as the water table was too high and in many places would have flooded immediately. Harding's Stores (on higher ground) had a cellar and most people used cool boxes in the garden to keep perishable foods.'

## HIGH CLASS GROCER

'I was born in the village of Hartley Wintney, in the cottage my parents lived in until their death. My father was the manager of a High Class Grocer's called Mercer Harvis Ltd. It was a large shop, Tudor-style timbers outside and inside a high ceiling, polished wooden shelving and counters, hidden from the shopfront windows by dark green half curtains on brass poles.

There were three counter staff as well as my father, two bakers in a separate bakehouse out the back, one errand boy who rode a strong bike with a huge basket on the front and "Missy" – the lady in the office. As a little child I was in awe of her. She sat bird-like on a high stool in front of a huge sloping desk, full of large ledgers with rainbow edges. Her office was within the shop but hidden behind huge black and gold display tins of different teas, and the windows on two sides of the desk were coloured glass "church windows", so being small I could not see "Missy" until I stood inside the door. She would look at me over the top of her owl-like gold glasses. My mother paid the grocery bill on a Monday afternoon and this was always done in the office. I still have her account book today: ¼ lb suet 4½d, 2 lb sugar 8d, tin salmon 1s 8½d, bacon 5d, 1 lb sausages 1s 1d etc.

My favourite person within the shop was Mr Gibbs the baker. He always called me "Little Mac" (father was nicknamed Mac) and would bake me a special tiny cottage loaf (burnt especially). He would wrap it up and hide it under the covers of my doll's pram when I called at the bakehouse door. It was "our secret". He was a lovely man, forever covered in flour and always wore a tall white chef's hat and white apron over cotton striped trousers. I always came away with flour on my nose and cheeks.

*In the early 1900s Susannah Bennett had a bread round in the New Forest. She took orders, collected the bread and delivered it. She always hoped for an order of twelve loaves so that she was eligible for a free loaf – the baker's dozen.*

I loved the various smells in the shop. Fresh ground coffee sold in stiff blue bags, sliced bacon and ham cut as you waited. Butter patted into shape and wrapped as you wished, fresh buns and "candle grease" buns and various fancy cakes all laid out in a large glass cabinet with a mirror at the back. Rows of biscuit tins with glass tops – every make possible, to be weighed out and sold in blue or white bags (no prepacked items in those days). I can still see my father deftly folding over bags and bags of sugar, dried fruit, coffee and tea – all done while the customer waited. It was a grand shop, much respected by the village folk and beyond. The staff were always courteous and people still talk of my father and the shop today.'

TREATS

'There were two village shops at Rotherwick which seemed to stock all necessities. One had a low window with a deep shelf which held boxes of sweets of all descriptions – dolly mixtures, liquorice, pear drops, every imaginable delight for a child.

My father attended the cattle markets at Winchester, Southampton and occasionally Salisbury. Sometimes he brought home special treats. The ones I remember best were the small pinky-fleshed Canary Island bananas, the tangerines at Christmas, and the small cottage loaves from Salisbury, costing one penny each.'

## CALLERS TO THE DOOR

'During the early 1920s Mapledurwell had a bread delivery from a small bakery in Old Basing twice a week by horse and cart. Some people made their own. Also a Mr Terry from Odiham used to deliver meat and groceries once a week on Saturdays. The order was placed a week in advance, but it was usually about five or six o'clock before he arrived back at Mapledurwell, so in the summer, after the goods had been in the cart all day, the fats were nearly melted and the meat half-cooked. The fats were put into a pail and suspended down the well, and the meat washed in vinegar and water, and partly cooked ready for Sunday lunch.

Later there was a carrier cart service run by the Gregory family from Hook (near Odiham) on Wednesdays and Saturdays. It started from Hook, through Greywell, Up Nateley, Mapledurwell and Old Basing into Basingstoke. It called at all the houses in the villages, collected the orders, did the shopping in Basingstoke, then delivered the goods on the homeward journey. The charge for this service was less than sixpence. The cart looked like the old Western covered waggons, but not so tall, and it could accommodate two passengers. There were no bus services from the villages then, but you had to take your chance of a space on the cart, as it may have picked up its quota of passengers before it arrived. You had plenty of exercise in those days, you either walked or cycled.'

'During the 1930s, tradesmen called at our house in Bitterne. The baker in his white apron carried a large wicker basket to the back door and Mother would select loaves from this. The horse-drawn baker's van was beautifully signwritten. I remember in winter the muffin man carrying a wooden tray on his head, ringing a bell and calling out his wares. The milkman arrived very early in the morning delivering milk in pint and half pint bottles.

The coalman, wearing a folded coal sack on his head and a leather apron, delivered coal, and always swept up any he happened to spill. His flat bed cart was pulled by a large white shire horse and swinging at the back of the cart was a nosebag of oats, and a leather bucket for water. The dustman collected the bin from behind the garage and returned it to its place, but not before he had sprinkled pink powder in and around it!'

'We had three grocers in Lyndhurst, one for each class of people – the gentry, middle class and working class. The fish man and the oil man came weekly, the latter with kitchen utensils as well as oil (for lamps and heaters). The butcher came three times a week. Locals seldom went outside the village. The tallyman called and clothes and household goods were purchased paying so much a week; remember mothers had been left widowed with large families from the First World War and this was the only way they could clothe the children.'

# FROM THE CRADLE TO THE GRAVE

**We were more likely to be born, to suffer our illnesses and to die in our own homes in the past. Doctors had to be paid for and most families relied on home cures handed down through the generations. Infectious diseases, however, were rife, particularly scarlet fever and diphtheria, and many a child spent weeks in the isolation hospital cut off from family and friends. Communities got together to provide services, such as home nursing, and the local chemist was often called on to diagnose as well as dispense medicines.**

### HAVING A BABY MEANT HOME DELIVERY

'Having a baby in the late 1950s or early 1960s meant a home delivery unless it was your first or fourth child, when the delivery would be in one of the few hospital beds which were available. Mothers could, however, still choose to have the baby at home but the midwife would probably prefer that numbers eight, nine or ten should be in hospital. Where there was a history of a difficult previous birth the advice was for hospital delivery.

Hampshire led the attachment of nurse/midwives to general practices so the mother would know the midwife who was to deliver her quite well. They would meet at ante-natal clinics and mothercraft sessions as well as home visits. The midwife had 24 hours off duty per week and a Saturday/Sunday once a month, so it was unlikely that she would miss many of her "Mums". Whenever the midwife went out she left a slate at her front door with a list of all the calls she would be making and their approximate time. A relative or husband could then find the midwife. However, most calls came in the night which was less disruptive to the daytime work which still had to be carried out. Midwives often had less than three hours sleep at night and this could happen on consecutive nights. In the early 1960s a midwife's pay went up to £1,000 per annum.

It wasn't unusual to find homes which still had electricity downstairs only, water drawn from a well and fireplaces in all the rooms. A single bed for delivery was preferred but was not always available. Husbands were encouraged to be present at birth. They were another pair of hands to help stoke the fire, trim the oil lamps, carry the gas and air machine and delivery bag as well as support their wife. It was not unknown for the other children to be present at the birth and they would certainly be brought in soon after delivery to be reassured that Mum was well and to approve of the new baby.

There was no high technology in those days. The midwife listened to the foetal heart with a stethoscope that resembled an ear trumpet. She carried pethidine to relieve pain in the later stages of labour and a disgusting mixture to be taken by mouth if it was really needed earlier on. All mothers had an injection after birth to control bleeding and could have gas and air if they requested. Doctors were rarely present at delivery but would come out if problems arose. As a result of the care taken when booking and the history that was recorded, those who might present problems were siphoned off for the hospital and so there were few problems. As a result the infant mortality rate was very low and the maternal rate was negligible. After the birth the placenta or afterbirth was either burned on the house boiler or taken

home, well wrapped up, by the midwife to bury in her garden and help produce the next good crop in the garden.

After delivery a mother would have a roller towel firmly stitched or pinned round her abdomen for 48 hours, which was understood to give support and firmness to a deflated waistline! The midwife visited twice a day for three days and then daily. A bath was permitted on the seventh day and the mother bathed her baby on the tenth day. She started to get up for short periods of time from the eighth day and by the time the midwife finished visiting on the 14th day she would be ready to start taking over the household and would probably be breastfeeding her baby.

Terry towelling nappies were usually used in triangles and firmly tucked round the baby to give maximum protection where it mattered. Babies were dressed in a nappy, vest, nightgown and bootees and wrapped firmly in a flannelette sheet before being placed on their side in their cot, crib or a drawer.

Most mothers enjoyed the cosseting they received, were rested by the time they had spent in bed and had plenty of time to get to know their baby, and the feeding arrangements be they breast or bottle were well organised. The other children adapted quickly to their new arrival and were pleased to do quite a bit of fetching and carrying. This was a time for the whole family to rejoice.'

## HOME CURES

'To cure earache, Grandmother used to place herbs between brown paper, heat with the flat iron, and then keep it in place over the ear with a large handkerchief.'

'A sure cure for whooping cough was said to be to put one new laid egg into a jar with a gill of vinegar. Cover with parchment to make airtight and leave for 24 hours. The shell will now have dissolved. Take the inner skin off the egg and beat the egg for ten minutes in the vinegar with six ounces of brown sugar. The dose was one to two teaspoonfuls according to the age of the child. This recipe was given to my mother by her painter and decorator in 1920!'

'A cure for ringworm was to squeeze the liquid from the tiny leaves of lichen (probably houseleek) growing on a dairy roof, mix it with a little cream and anoint the sores – this was a gipsy remedy used at Wellow.

For the common cold, eat a boiled onion, stuffed with pepper, last thing at night. The patient can be relied on to deny any remaining symptoms of a cold the next day!'

# IN THE FEVER HOSPITAL

'Diphtheria! So that was what I had when I came from school feeling unwell. It was 2nd November 1922, and I was nine years old.

Next morning Mother, with her neighbour, examined my throat and decided. The next I knew was late in the evening when a nurse, with a red blanket, came into the bedroom. She said she was Sister Kaye, and wrapped me up like a mummy. She carried me downstairs to a waiting yellow fever van.

Next I found myself in B Ward of the infectious diseases hospital, Portsmouth. I was soon surrounded by blue gowned, white aproned nurses. I was to be given an injection, and was praised for being so good. Days passed.

One morning a nurse said, "Your little brother is coming in today." I knew I didn't have a little brother and said so. But the nurse and I had a difference of opinion, and it was left at that. The truth was that the "brother" was the 18 month old son of the neighbour who had looked at my throat. I had sisters only, and not one of them contracted the disease.

Time passed. The patients decided their own progress by the food, soup to start, followed by fish, white, boiled, not delicious, then mince and we knew going home followed.

By now Christmas was getting near. The wards were being decorated, but to me home was the place to spend Christmas. Just a few days before Christmas I was discharged.

Life at home was normal after that until June or July 1923. I was back in hospital, this time with scarlet fever. But I knew about hospitals, so accepted all they did for me. One night my legs were giving me much pain, and when a nurse took my temperature, it was 104° or 105°. I was wrapped in a blanket and reported to the day staff. I was the centre of attention for a little while.

This time I received a little parcel each week containing all kinds of goodies. After six or seven weeks I was allowed home, by which time the school had started the summer holiday.

I learned many things by watching the ward maids at work, and one of the most useful things was how to scrub a wooden floor!'


## MORE RELAXED THAN NOW

'A country doctor's life between the wars was much more relaxed than nowadays. The story is told of a local doctor at Braishfield who one day took his wife along on his rounds. Outside one farm she sat forgotten for four hours while her husband ate supper with his patient's family!

Home remedies included goose grease, deer fat and, of course, syrup of figs.'

## GETTING HIS PRIORITIES RIGHT

'The doctor at Droxford, before having a car, did his rounds with three horses – one for him, one for his groom and one spare which the groom led. The doctor was also the chief fireman, so he had to get his priorities right, either to help with the fire or attend his patient, and he often arrived with dirty hands and clothes.'

## WALK TO THE DOCTOR

'In 1927 we moved to a bungalow outside Ropley. If you needed the doctor you had to walk two miles to the nearest village. On one occasion my baby sister scratched my mother's eye and it was so bad she had to walk to the doctor on the Monday morning and he said she had to go to hospital. She then walked home to tell my father, walked two miles to catch the bus to Winchester (an hour's journey) and had to stay in hospital for one week.'

## A VILLAGE EFFORT

'A village effort was started in 1930, the object to provide a nurse to visit local Hordle families in need of nursing assistance and midwifery. Her wage and expenses were paid by collecting the sum of twopence per week from villagers who became members of the nursing association and by donations from more wealthy inhabitants (these donations ranged from ten shillings to five guineas, considerable sums in those days).

Monthly meetings were held by a committee of villagers. It is interesting to read that in 1932 the nurse was paid £120 per year and lived rent and rate free in a bungalow built by the association for the sum of about £360. The parish was divided into several districts, each of which was served by voluntary collectors who not only kept the twopences coming in but who saw at once who needed nursing assistance. By 1932 the nurse had been provided with a secondhand Trojan car, which cost £15. By 1936, she was paying about 270 visits each month around the village.

The association ceased to be responsible for the nurse when the National Health Service was started in 1948 and eventually the bungalow was sold and the proceeds invested. The interest kept the association in being as a way of helping the aged and infirm of the village, mostly at Christmas time and it is still in being to provide a fund for general charitable purposes among the people of Hordle parish.

In these days it is difficult to realise that a weekly contribution of just less than a modern penny could make such a service available.'

## GETTING TO HOSPITAL

'In about 1860 a carter broke both legs in a farm accident at Thruxton Down Farm. The doctor came out from Thruxton village in a pony and trap, and decided that the patient needed to go to Salisbury hospital. The vicar at Quarley conveyed the patient in his donkey cart to Grateley station, and the patient then went on the train to Salisbury. The donkey, being made to gallop on the way to Grateley, started braying at this ill-treatment and this, it is said, started the use of the "two tone" emergency horn – a first for Andover!

By 1890 a six foot long Moses basket with a hood at one end, a three foot wheel at either side and the middle, and a small wheel at front and rear, pushed by one man at the back and pulled by another at the front, was used to carry patients to the local Andover hospital in Junction Road, and the "pest house" in a field on the north side of Vigo Road.

In 1928 the first motor vehicle ambulance took up its duties in Andover, and patients paid for the use of this service. In the 1930s a Mr Fennel went round on a Monday delivering invoices for the use of the ambulance in the previous week. When the National Health Service began, the Ambulance Service was "started" by Hampshire County Council with two vehicles, three drivers and one part-time attendant – no radio, and initially no phone link. If the ambulance was out the police put a Red Cross sign in the police station for the ambulance to call in and phone Hampshire County Council. Radio soon followed and progress was made. The area covered by Andover was from the Berkshire border, round the Wiltshire border to Romsey, and the A34 on the eastern side.'

## THE CHEMIST

'Before the advent of the National Health Service and free treatment for all, local chemists filled a very important function in the community. Many people could not afford to see a doctor except in dire circumstances. For them the chemist had to take the place of the doctor for all ills. In fact, most people would go to a chemist anyway before bothering a doctor. So chemists were, in the main, pretty good diagnosticians, and some were better than others.

One such was Mr H. R. Eyre in Junction Road, Totton. He was a very clever man who would have liked to be a doctor but could not afford the training. Instead he had taken up pharmacy. He was also a dispensing optician of outstanding ability.

His service to the district was broadly based. Besides the pharmacy and optical work, he pierced ears; he also syringed them and was generally willing to have a go at any challenge that presented itself short of surgery. But his talents stretched beyond the human sphere into veterinary practice as well. And when all else had failed he was suitably equipped to "put down" any domestic pet brought to his door.

Despite wartime shortages, his shop was stocked from floor to ceiling with every conceivable type of merchandise relating to his various professions. Business was conducted in a small gap in the towering display on the counter where earnest discussions would be conducted, *sotto voce*, between himself and the customer. A decision would be reached and away he would go to dispense the remedy. As long as one could hear a rustle of movement from the back of the shop all was well. Silence indicated a long wait. But people would wait, albeit with increasing frustration as the shop filled with customers until eventually a queue formed on the pavement outside. Of course the original customer thought their prescription must be of immense complication to take so long to produce.

In fact Mr Eyre had probably slipped out the back way to the post office up the road and fallen into conversation with someone en route. Or maybe he was testing a patient's eyes. He would eventually return, by which time the customers would be in an ugly mood. Profuse apologies would be offered and business would proceed at a more tolerable rate. However, the process would be repeated time and time again throughout the day as other distractions claimed his attention. But he would never employ help in the shop. His was a personal service of which he was justly proud. As a result no one ever got out of that shop in less than an hour. The remarkable thing was that although everyone grumbled relentlessly about the delays no one would dream of going elsewhere, and there were, in fact, several other chemists within a few hundred yards. His gifts were legion and commanded the utmost loyalty and respect of his customers. Sadly he died an early death and was a great loss to the community.'

THE LAST JOURNEY

'During the first half of the century most deaths took place at home. A clergyman would often be present at the time of death, or called to attend soon after, in order to administer the last rites. Each village

80

*A hand wheel bier and horse-drawn mourners' carriages outside the asylum in Alton in the early part of the century.*

or street had a woman who would come to the house to lay out the deceased (often the same woman who attended at the time of a birth). She would arrive with her bag of equipment to wash, dress and generally prepare the deceased for their burial.

The church bell would usually toll, sounding out the death knell. This was often repeated at the time of the funeral, calling the mourners to church. (This practice was temporarily suspended during the Second World War, as the church bell would have been rung to raise the alarm in case of invasion).

The undertaker attended the house to measure for the coffin, which was then hand-made, probably of oak or elm. Country estates often kept a stock of timber, felled from their own grounds, for such purposes. The undertaker returned to the house with the coffin, usually under cover of darkness. The deceased remained at home, in the parlour or the bedroom, until the time of the funeral. Family and friends, however young, came to file past the open coffin, paying their last respects. People took a death in the family in their stride. It was not at all unusual for infants, children and mothers in childbirth to die. Diseases such as diphtheria could rob a family of several children within a few weeks.

When the time of the funeral came, the coffin was transported on a hand wheel bier, or in a carriage-built hearse drawn by black-plumed horses. The mourners followed the coffin from the house on foot or in mourning carriages, of which there could be many, due to most people not owning their own vehicles. A long funeral procession made a grand sight, members of the public stopped and bowed their heads as the cortège passed by. Motorised hearses, forerunners of those used today, came into use in urban areas during the late 1920s. However, the horse-drawn hearse was still in frequent use long after this. During the war years, horses were again used to help conserve petrol supplies.

There were many small firms of builder-undertakers, who hired hearses and mourning coaches from carriage masters, and most would have owned a wheel bier. Many funerals took place in the afternoons, this allowed the building workers to go home at lunch time to clean up ready to act as pall bearers. In some villages local men carried the coffin wearing white milking smocks, which covered their everyday clothes, enabling them all to look the same.

Burial took place in churchyards in rural areas and cemeteries in city areas. Graves were often dug up to six deep, enabling them to be reopened for further burials. Cremation became available at Southampton in 1932 and Bournemouth (then in Hampshire) in 1938. The uptake was slow at first, but increased steadily.

Black was traditionally worn at the time of a death. Black armbands were worn or a black fabric diamond may have been sewn onto the sleeve. These continued to be worn for a suitable period of mourning.

Flowers have long been associated with funerals; in Victorian times they were carried to mask unpleasant smells. The traditional round wreath or cross, often of lilies, placed on the coffin became a customary symbol of respect. Most war dead were buried, wrapped in an army blanket, where they fell. However, many were later exhumed, placed in coffins, and reburied in War Grave Commission cemeteries, either at home or abroad. Some families had their loved ones repatriated to their own locality, thus many churchyards and cemeteries contain a few war graves.

During the earlier part of the century, there were those who were denied a Christian burial. Murderers may well have been hanged publicly, but they were buried quietly in unconsecrated ground within the prison confines. Likewise, up until 1961, it was a criminal offence to be found guilty of committing suicide. Such persons were sometimes transported along back roads to their place of burial in unconsecrated ground.'

# CHILDHOOD & SCHOOLDAYS

# BACK IN TIME

**Visiting grandparents could take us back to a more distant past, which even then seemed less hurried and more secure.**

## THE ROCK ON WHICH OUR FAMILY WAS BUILT

'Granny was a tall, upright lady almost always dressed in black with a lace neckpiece which nearly came up to her chin, and her hair was drawn back to form a bun. When she went out she always wore a tall hat with a velvet bow; this she kept on with a hat pin, and as a small boy I was always frightened she would stick it through her head.

Queen Victoria had been on the throne 30 years when Granny was born into a small family butchery business right on the county border at Emsworth, and that is where she grew up.

When she married Grandad they came to Winchester to live as he was a soldier serving in the Rifle Brigade. Grandad was discharged from the army after the Boer War as medically unfit – due to rheumatism – and Granny was told she would have to support him for the rest of his life, and at that time she also had a family of three small children. To help keep them, they bought a small off-licence in Western Road in Winchester. This she ran until 1916 as by that time Grandad had recovered enough from the rheumatics to set up a smallholding and market garden in the nearby village of Littleton.

A new house was built on the land in 1916 where she started a new life. Although she had left school when she was only twelve years old, she kept the business books and accounts in a very fair hand. Her family butchery background came in very useful; Grandad killed a pig once a fortnight and he also kept chickens, turkeys and ducks, all of which were prepared and dressed by Granny for him to sell from his pony and cart on his round in Winchester. She also made wonderful sausages from an old family recipe.

Granny lived by the clock, up at 7 am, breakfast at 8 am, dinner at 12.30 pm, tea at 4.30 pm, supper at 9 pm, bed at 10 pm, and woe betide Grandad if he was late for his meal. They believed in hard work and plenty of food, a large proportion of which they produced themselves. There was always bacon for breakfast, a large meal with pudding for dinner, tea was bread and butter and jam and usually a fruit cake, supper was sometimes soup and perhaps something which had been left from dinner.

*It was never too early to give a hand with the washing! This young assistant lived at Overton in the 1920s.*

After the midday meal when things had been cleared away and washed up, Granny would disappear upstairs to wash and change into her afternoon frock. We were very often invited to tea and I remember standing on a chair at the kitchen sink to wash my hands. We also had to brush our hair and "quiff" as Grandad called it.

If we were ill in bed with the usual children's illnesses, Granny would always come and read to us in the afternoon. With us boys she might have been strict but she was always kind.

Whatever the weather she could always be found at evensong in our little village church on a Sunday evening. The church was quite a walk from her house and I can remember the rector saying as she walked into the church on a very wet and windy night, "Brave woman."

She served on the Parochial Church Council and was a member of the Mothers Union, and a founder member of the village WI, which was formed in 1924. During the Second World War she ran and collected the National Savings in the village, she organised the knitting of garments for the troops (my brother and I had to learn to knit scarves), and a family of blind evacuees also lived with her for a time.

I can never remember her sitting doing nothing, she was always reading or knitting, and in her later years when she could no longer get to church she liked to listen to the services and hymn singing on the radio. Granny lived to the great age of 92, and now I am older I realise my Victorian Granny was the rock on which our family was built; she was always there.'

## EVERY SUMMER

'Every summer we would visit our grandparents in the village of Curdridge. They lived in a picturesque thatched cottage near the church. We arrived by steam train at Botley station and walked through the lanes to Curdridge, passing the strawberry fields where Granfer would be sitting on straw bales packing freshly picked strawberries ready for market, and keeping an eye on his pigs. Gran would be busy either washing or ironing as she used to do the laundry for the large houses in the village. Gran always wore long skirts and boots. Her long hair was done up into a bun and tucked under a knitted woollen hat. The toilet was an earth closet in the copse and the only light was an oil lamp or a candle. Water was from the well. To us, as children, it was sheer magic to go to bed by the light of a candle, sink into a cosy feather mattress, and listen to the church clock striking.'

## MY GRANDFATHER'S HOUSE

'Brookside, the house on the left as you entered Anna Valley from the Salisbury-Andover road, had been built by Grandfather Tasker, along with the ironworks at the other end of the village, after he was hounded out of Abbotts Ann because of his staunch stand against witchcraft. The low two-storey house stood back from the road. On two sides it had a cobbled veranda with a delicately curved copper roof, now green with verdigris, supported by ornate iron pillars. On either side of the front door stood "Gog and Magog", awesome Grecian figures. Inside the hall one was faced with an illuminated motto on an arch proclaiming that "Christ is the Head of this House", leaving no doubt as to where the family loyalty lay.

At the foot of the stairs stood a three foot high decorated wooden Ali Baba jar. Lifting the lid released an overwhelming scent of rose petals thrown in over many decades.

Miss Tasker, Aunt Elizabeth to us, had been our mother's brides-maid in 1911. She kept house for her aged father, played the harmonium on Sundays in the village hall, supplied eggs and vegetables as gifts from the garden to cottages in "The Square" where most of the workers lived, and led numerous women's meetings in surrounding villages, travelling by bicycle or bus.

Uncle Tasker looked like an old patriarch with his long white beard. He spent most of his time, often asleep, in his study surrounded by ancient books and even older Levantine pots. Entry for us was by invitation only. After breakfast he would read out of an enormous family Bible.

Every August in the early 1920s we would be dumped on Aunt Elizabeth. Always our first action on arriving was to dash down the garden past beds packed with delphiniums, lupins and phlox and edged with low box hedges which we brushed with our hands to get the smell; past cages of currant bushes, through the heavy wooden door in the thatched flint wall, along twisty paths through hazel bushes to the boathouse. Here waited the solid old boat on which, out on the river Anna, we would spend most of our time.

Before a meal a gong would be banged up at the house. We were expected to present ourselves, ten minutes later when another gong sounded, hands washed and hair brushed, ready for Uncle Tasker to say grace. Totally free between meals, at the table we had to be on our best behaviour. Afternoon tea in the drawing-room was our greatest test, having to balance a tea cup in one hand and avoid dropping crumbs on the carpet.

There being no electricity, at bedtime we each selected an already lit oil lamp off the huge chest in the hall to light us up the shadowy stairs. A copper can full of hot water stood ready by the washstand to be poured into the large porcelain bowl. Water had to be pumped by the old windmill on the hillside across the road. The gentle tick-tock of the grandfather clock on the landing lulled us to sleep.

The first job in the morning was to clean the lamp glasses with newspaper in a cupboard adjoining the spacious kitchen with its vast cooking range behind which cockroaches lurked. A night-time sport was drumming them out to be caught in waiting bowls of boiling water. Down a step was the always cold dairy. Here on slabs of slate stood large shallow bowls of milk waiting for the cream to settle to be used fresh, made into butter or eaten sour with blackcurrants – delicious.

Before dawn on Mondays the fire under the copper in the washhouse would be lit and the copper filled by buckets ready for the army of women from the village who, all day, would scrub, rinse, wring and mangle. By contrast on Saturdays, the local gentry, suitably dressed in white, would come to play tennis or croquet. On both occasions we were kept out of the way.

An evening treat for us was to be taken into the darkening Works, after the men had gone home and the furnaces damped down, when the only sound was the chirruping of the crickets.'

## THEY WERE WEALTHY

'I spent my childhood summers in the 1920s with my grandparents who lived in the small New Forest village of Fritham. Nearly all the villagers had a few cows, some pigs, and chickens, and some had a heavy working horse. My grandfather was the local preacher and a colporteur (a book pedlar), and in his pony and trap he visited the nearby villages selling his Bibles and religious tracts. The little chapel was packed every Sunday for the morning and evening services, and my normally gentle grandfather put the fear of God into all of us as we sat waiting for the thunderbolt to strike. I clung to my grandmother, and was always very relieved to get out of the chapel in one piece!

The villagers were mostly almost self-supporting with milk, butter, eggs and vegetables. Excess milk was put in great churns and left in the road to be collected early morning by a large cart drawn by two horses.

Granny's cool dairy had large flat dishes filled with milk. The cream was skimmed off for buttermaking in her churn, and the skimmed milk went to the pigs. Wednesday was Ringwood market day, and Grandad would set off on the 13 mile journey with butter, eggs and Bibles. It was an all day excursion, and as I drive there and back now for a quick shopping expedition, I often think how times have changed.

I remember the hay being cut with scythes, the men walking down the field in line. As one field was finished, the men all moved to another, and so all helped each other. Bracken was collected from the forest, stacked and used for animal bedding.

As a child I roamed the forest alone without fear. There were always forest workers about mending fences, digging ditches, clearing fallen trees, and all had a cheery word for me. Now, the ditches are overgrown and trees lie where they fall – food for the insects they say, but I think it is lack of labour, and the forest has an unkempt look about it to my eyes. The ponies, too, have changed. They were once small, brown and hardy, but they are now bred for riding, and come in all colours. Nor are they so hardy.

Entertainment was all home-made of course, with church teas and games on the green, concerts in the little tin hut by the chapel, Band of Hope and the Ladies' Sewing Circle. The children walked the three miles to school in the next village of Bramshaw, and my father tells me that Granny gave him a hot potato in his pocket for his lunch. It never survived the journey to school, he admitted! "Did you have school dinners?" I asked. He laughed at the idea, but said they were allowed to help themselves to water from the well in the courtyard throughout the day. To the end of his long life, however, his writing, arithmetic, grammar and spelling were perfect.

There was no water or electricity in Granny's house, and every morning two buckets of water would be lifted from the well at the end of the garden, and carried back to the kitchen on a shoulder halter. And the dark, spider-ridden privy under the walnut tree was a nightmare for me, especially on a dark windy night, when the candle flickered and shadows threatened. Granny would stand at the kitchen door, calling out encouragement as I made the trip in record time!

Gipsies would come out of the forest and walk through the village sometimes and I loved to stand at the five barred gate and see the piebald horses, and the collection of dogs under the carts which rang with pots and pans hanging everywhere. Granny always held my hand very tightly as the gipsies went by. I had blond ringlets, and she wasn't taking any chances!

Such happy memories of long days running wild in the forest, picking flowers, catching tadpoles, watching the animals, "helping" with the milking and buttermaking, and climbing trees with the local children. On the go all day, and it didn't cost a penny. Talking of which, my grandmother gave me a penny pocket money and I spent it a farthing at a time over the week, down at the one small village shop/bakery/post office. How old Mrs Winter must have blessed me as I pondered over my purchase, but I'm sure I had more pleasure out of that weekly penny than the children do today with their money.

These lovely summer holiday days would end with the three of us sitting round the table as the oil lamp hissed quietly. Granny would be mending, while Grandad wrote his next week's sermon, and I sleepily read a book before taking a candle up to bed, and jumping into the most delicious all-enveloping feather bed. Religious tracts lined the walls of the bedroom, and in the corner stood a marble washstand with a rose decorated basin and ewer; my cold water morning "wash" was more of a "lick and a promise" I suspect. The weekly bath in front of the ever burning kitchen fire with the big black kettle hanging on a hook, took care of the corners I had missed!

Compared with my bright sunny home in Croydon, I remember Granny Bellamy's farmhouse as dark, with lino or bare boards. The only mats were hand-made from rags, and as my grandmother always wore black, the rugs were predominantly dark. But there was always laughter, bright fires, kittens and so much love and affection; parishioners calling, a rabbit or brace of pheasants left on the doorstep. My grandparents had very few worldly goods, and what they had they shared, but looking back I now know they were very wealthy.'

# DAYS OF FUN AND FREEDOM

**Whether we grew up in a town or a country village we shared a freedom in the past that sadly today's children will never know. Though times could be hard we found pleasure in small things, made friends of children and adults alike, and rarely found life boring!**

### AN ODIHAM LAD

'I was born at No 45 High Street in the front room above my father's butcher's shop. I used to play with a little wooden horse on a platform with four wheels. It went everywhere with me, round the garden, up and down the street. The men in my father's shop used to tease me dreadfully about it and threaten they would take it to the slaughter-house behind the shop to have it killed!

On Sunday afternoons we sometimes had tea at Lodge Farm, with my uncle's family. Here the river Whitewater runs about five feet from the back door and the orchard, over the river, is reached by a small wooden bridge. One afternoon all the family crossed safely but I managed to fall in the water soaking my new white sailor suit. I still remember being dragged home by an extremely annoyed father.

At the age of five I went to Buryfields school in the village, walking there with Miss Shearing, one of the teachers. We sat in tiers in class, like at a football match today, and we were all taught together. Normally I went home for lunch because it was so close, but sometimes I stayed on Mondays. They made pea soup for lunch on Mondays and I liked this so if Mum gave me a penny I could stay instead of returning home.

At eight or nine I went to the London Road school, where Mr Tinley was headmaster. About this time I joined the Wolf Cubs who met every Wednesday evening at my old school, Buryfields. I was also a member of the church choir, in time becoming head choir boy. If we attended all the practices, plus matins and evensong for a month we received two shillings and sixpence . . . such wealth. I can remember spending some of this buying sweets for my mother. We could be quite naughty in church, eating sweets during the sermon, and messing around with chewing gum and silver paper. The organ blower at church was a real character and for some reason he liked to wear a cassock. He kept this in a cupboard behind the organ. One day before choir practice, dressed in my white robe, I decided to play a trick on Freddie. I hid in the cupboard where it was quite dark, and when Freddie reached in to get his cassock this white shape rose up and let out a blood-curdling scream. Freddie ran for his life, down the aisle and out of the church, swearing he'd seen a ghost.

At the age of eleven I went to Odiham grammar school where I stayed until after my 16th birthday. By now I was a member of the Boy Scouts and we had a drum bugle band and a trek cart . . . I felt most important. I also played football for the school in the first eleven side. We had our field in Hatchwoods Meadow (where Archery Fields is now). I always played in goal and because we had a good team I didn't have a great deal to do. On one memorable occasion, I was chatting to the new wife of one of our masters, who himself was the referee, feeling very pleased that she had noticed me, and unfortunately completely missed an attack coming. In the ensuing scuffle around the goal I suffered the ultimate indignity of having my shorts pulled off by one of the opposing side! More concentration on the game was obviously required.'

# A SHORT CHILDHOOD

'I lived in Bramdean, halfway between Petersfield and Winchester. We had one shop, a pub, village hall, church and school. I was one of six children. Dad was a gardener and we lived in my uncle's house, no rent, we could cope, just.

Attended school in the village until eight, then senior school at Hinton a mile away until 14. Girls all wore pinnies and boots. Three teachers, two classrooms. We were taught parrot fashion, tables, spelling, poetry. We did arithmetic, writing, PE, singing, religion. Twice yearly the girls had a month of domestic science locally. Hand inspection daily, head inspection monthly, if dirty the nit nurse sent children home.

Teachers were fair but strict, and boys and girls were caned if we misbehaved. We had a pit lavvy and squares of newspaper. We paid a penny a day for Horlicks, if money was short an Oxo and bread sufficed. Playtime was happy at school, skipping, balls, rounders, tag, wooden hoops, shinty, hopscotch.

Home at four to rabbit stew, hunks of bread. Jam or lard and sugar. Dad kept bees, honeycomb was lovely. Wash up, out to play hide and seek, paperchases, until dark, no toys – we had none.

Sunday, best clothes, usually jumble, different from school days. A penny paid for attendance at Sunday school. It was a bequeathed charity. Church next, most of us between nine and twelve were choir girls. Back home, Sunday roast, rice pudding, ginger cake for tea.

Chores, every child did them, mine was washing up, scrubbing the porch clean, cutlery, fetch the milk 7.30 am.

Wintertime, Mum would tell stories, toast hunks of bread over an open fire. Sometimes we would listen to the wireless. This had an accumulator. We had electricity in 1930.

Great treat was the Christmas party at the big house, all children had presents. Home we did not have enough money. A stocking, sweets, orange and apple, it sufficed. Snow was welcomed, trays, cardboard, pieces of wood, no sledges, we loved it.

Spring, flowers to pick, nests to find, hours of rambling, no toys, no holidays or bus rides. Trips to seaside yearly. Summer months haymaking, pooking, riding haycarts, making ricks, tickling trout in river, good fun.

Summer holidays, picnics, penny for lemonade powder made two bottles, bread and jam, out all day, made houses, ate hawthorn leaves, bread and cheese we called it. Sorrel, underground nuts, blackberries, nuts, this was the menu. Dyed faces with blackberries, with feathers we were Indians. Boys smoked old man's beard but it only smouldered, little devils.

Harvest, following the binder with sticks to catch rabbits on the last trip. Corn was sheathed, picked, later threshed, another day out, killing rats and mice, home to a tin bath in front of the fire, tired but happy.

Left school at 14, domestic service, six shillings and eightpence a week, buy my own uniform, work from 6.30 am to 10.30 pm, half day off a week. My childhood was over.'

## AUNTY PAYNE

'One day when I was five my parents left me at Aunty's to play with my cousins whilst they went to see "Aunty Payne". When they came back the grown-ups went into the other room. We could not hear a thing as they were whispering. Soon after I was six, my Dad collected me from school with my night things and a bag of sweets to share with my cousins. He told me to be a good girl and he would come and see me tomorrow. I remember Aunty slicing up a lovely chocolate roll. It is funny how food away always tastes better than at home! The next day my Dad came to take me to school. He was grinning all over his face and hugged his sister. She was crying with happiness as now the family name would be carried on as I had a baby brother and he was going to be called George after Grandad. When we got home it was so strange because "Aunty Payne" was there. My mother was not in her own bed but in the big bed in the spare room and she was holding a little bundle with a very red face. "Aunty Payne" attended all the confinements in the family. Mothers in those days stayed in bed about a fortnight. "Aunty Payne" was very modern and liked to smoke and have a glass of stout to keep her hard at work.

My dad was also a heavy smoker. Players Navy Cut cigarettes in those days were elevenpence halfpenny for 20. The counter at the back of our grocery shop was all burn marks where he used to lay his cigarette down whilst he was serving the customers. No such thing as hygiene then! The bakers used to smoke but they rolled their own and used to knead the dough in the big bins with a cigarette in the corner of their mouths. They turned their heads occasionally and dropped the ash on the floor. Sometimes they were too late and it went into the dough. Nevertheless, our bread was the finest for miles around!

My friend and I used to walk for miles with my brother in the pram. We were quite safe in those days to go to the woods and pick bunches of lovely white violets. They smelt so beautiful. We did not bother with the blue dog violets as they had no scent. The primroses looked so delicate after the winter snows. Sometimes we found oxlips and cowslips and occasionally pink orchid. The white anemones were so graceful but it was a shame to pick them as they did not last long in water. The bluebells were the next to flower and sometimes there were a few white bells. There was a lovely crab apple tree in the woods and my mother always used to make a few jars of crab apple jelly. This was lovely and clear with a distinct flavour of its own.'

## A CHILD OF THE 1930s

'When I look back to my childhood in the 1930s, I realise now what a wonderfully innocent time I had. To me everyone was either good or bad. My family, school teacher, the government, the Royal family, were all without blemish in my eyes and only the occasional burglar or murderer read about in the paper was bad. I knew nothing about sex until I went to boarding school in 1938 and then the information was pretty meagre.

I was six when my youngest brother was born and I and my elder brother were sent away for three weeks to relations and the first we knew about the new baby was when we returned. I remember being most annoyed that my friends knew I had another brother before I did! My mother, of course, was still in bed with a "monthly nurse" to look after her.

I was the eldest of three, having two brothers, two and a half and six and a half years younger than myself. My father, a farmer's son, had served throughout the Great War in Egypt and then France, gaining his commission in the Wiltshire Regiment. In 1920 he came to Bedhampton to run Manor Farm and met and married my mother, a farmer's daughter, in 1922. By the time I can remember anything, we were comfortably off. We ran two cars, our farmhouse had been built in 1900 and had electricity, telephone and running water and we even had a large radiator in the hall running off the hot water system. My mother had quite a lot of help in the house. When we were younger we had a daily maid, a mother's help and a woman to do the washing etc. We also had a gardener and a back door man to clean shoes, cars, and do the grates etc. We loved our "mother's helps". The first left when I was about six to look after her father and Miss Copus left about 1936 to get married. After one more "mother's help" who was not a success, Mother had two maids, one living in. These were young girls who wore uniform. Pale green dresses in the morning with large white starched aprons and white caps, and after lunch they changed into dark brown dresses with small lace-edged coffee coloured aprons and a small band of the same colour material round their heads.

There was a very definite class structure in those days. Most of my parents' friends had maids in uniform. They seemed to have names like Alice, Gertrude, Beatrice and Lilian. Some of the really large houses in the village had menservants and nannies in uniform with flowing veils. We would meet them pushing their perambulators when we were being taken for our daily walk with my little brother in his pram. We were never asked to their parties, in the same way we didn't ask the children who lived in the cottages near our farm, to our house.

We were taught good manners from an early age and expected to be polite to everyone whatever their walk in life. My father was a stickler for time. Meals had to be on the dot. We children didn't stay up to supper at 8 pm until we were in our teens. I cannot ever remember being late for a meal. For breakfast we always had porridge or cereal, eggs in some form, sausage, bacon or fish every day, toast and marmalade. Lunch was meat, usually hot with two vegetables, except Mondays when we had the Sunday roast cold with potatoes in their jacket and a milk pudding (rice, tapioca, macaroni, semolina) and another such as treacle tart or bread and butter pudding. Tea was bread and butter with jam or fish paste and at least two types of cake. This was our last meal, but my parents would have a supper dish such as macaroni cheese, omelette or Welsh rarebit etc.

Chicken was a great treat and only provided on special occasions, mutton served with suet pudding, beef and pork being the usual fare. Although we were farmers and my father a keen shot, my mother didn't care to serve game or rabbit. We were not allowed to be fussy. You ate what was put in front of you. The only concession was to me as raw milk upset me, so I was given water to drink. To this day, this is my main drink and I never have any hot drinks, but I can eat anything!

I went to a very small school run by a teacher called Miss Dunning, a wonderful woman who seemed as old as the hills to me, but was probably in her thirties. I can remember learning my letters by running my fingers over a card about five inches square with the letters in sandpaper. The background of the card was pale pink for consonants and pale green for vowels. We then progressed to cut out letters in red and blue and made words with these. I think I learned to read very quickly and I loved sums. I used to sit up in bed with a page of them that my mother had written out for me. There were only about eight of us and when I went on to a larger private school in Havant in 1935 I was well ahead of my contemporaries.

In 1938 I went away to boarding school which I didn't really enjoy, but at the outbreak of war, my father wanted the family to be together so I came back to the school in Havant and stayed there for the rest of my schooldays. My brothers however went off to boarding school towards the end of 1940.

Church was attended regularly, alternate Sundays at 11 am for matins. I think my parents went to communion on the intervening Sundays, but I had no idea what this service was like until I was confirmed. I used to enjoy helping my mother do the church flowers when it was her turn. I also helped her run the cake stall at the church fête. Sometimes she was in charge of the teas instead of the cake stall. Over the years I presented several bouquets to various fête openers and I can also remember presenting a bouquet to the wife of our Member of Parliament at the time of the General Election in 1936.

My father, as well as farming, had started a large milk round and he introduced milk in schools in the area. He also had a lime business, burning chalk from a nearby chalk pit, and a retail coal business. He was a magistrate, churchwarden and on numerous committees, which helped Havant hospital and other local charities. My mother and I were therefore expected to help with these various money-raising activities. All of which I thoroughly enjoyed although so young.

Of course there was no television and my parents and the mother's help would play games with us after tea. Card games such as snap, Old Maid, Beat Jack out of Doors, and later on Lexicon, Sorry, Newmarket and then later still whist, solo and bridge. Hide and seek was a great game in the summer and we picnicked often. Sometimes only in the farthest corner of the garden, but that didn't matter.

In the second half of the 1930s my brother and I were allowed to play anywhere on the farm. This included the marshes at Bedhampton where we had marvellous games. These marshes are now covered with roads, incinerators and rubbish dumps. As long as we were back for lunch at 12.30 pm we could go for the whole morning. What a change now. You wouldn't let a ten and eight year old go off on their own for several hours today!

George V's Silver Jubilee was celebrated in May 1935 and all the children in the Bedhampton and Havant area were invited to a film show in the Empire cinema in Havant. Stuart and I were allowed to go. The first time we'd ever been to a cinema! I can remember sitting spellbound at this amazing sight of people moving and talking on screen. I can't recall what the film was about though. In the afternoon we had sports on the playing field at Bedhampton. We were all given a Jubilee mug and a book about the Royal family which I still have.

Two years later in May 1937 we were celebrating the Coronation.

Mother once again was organising the teas and in between running in the races I helped her.

As a middle class child in the 1930s, I was lucky. The depression didn't touch us and we were innocent, happy children. Becoming a teenager and the start of the war came in the same year and life became very different.'

## A CHILD OF THE 1940s

'Being born at the end of the war, 1944, Portsmouth's problems were not something that I was aware of until later on in life, although there were plenty of visual signs as I was growing up. My father was in the police, recruited as a war reserve in March 1939, and served with the traffic department full time throughout the war. My mother spent many a lonely and scaring night alone, sometimes too scared to go to the shelter. This situation was eased when they moved to Drayton, slightly away from the main targets, and with good friends. This was where I first lived until 1957.

I vividly remember playing in the large garden and how, in summer, the blankets were washed and laid on the grass to dry in the sun. The garden was a great gathering place for visitors, who used to call for tea, always bringing their welcome with them, perhaps some tea, sugar or bread to help. I did not realise the importance of this at the time, but it was obviously because of shortages.

My grandmother lived in the North End area. She was a great walker, who loved her cup of tea. My mother and I used to meet her halfway, either at the Co-op in Fratton Road, or Lyons Tea Rooms in Commercial Road. This probably did not happen that often, as it was quite a treat. We would have a cup of tea, a cake and a chat. Sometimes we would cut our cakes in half, so that we could see what each other's tasted like! I also remember going to the Savoy Ballroom at South Parade, again for the teatime treat.

I was not that aware of rationing, but remember clearly going to the shops at North End and being given sixpence to buy myself some sweets in the Chocolate King shop. It was some years before I realised that this marked the end of sweet rationing, as I often wondered what all the excitement was about. For some time after the war there were shortages, as I am told that bananas were not readily available, and when they were, I surprised everyone by not actually liking them!

In the first winter at Elm Grove, I was ill. Nothing serious with today's modern medicines, but worrying in those days. The doctor charged a fee for home visits, which must have been a strain. This was just before the National Health Service was started. In the early

*Children of the 1940s had to grow up fast in a dangerous world. Harry Arnold and his sister Kit are standing beside the blackout panel at their house in Havant in 1942.*

1950s I had several illnesses, which warranted the use of the newly available penicillin. This was given in those days by injection, by a community nurse, who used to call once or twice daily. They were very smart, always with a crisp white apron and a navy blue bag! If you were ill, there was the luxury of a coal fire in the bedroom; if you were well, you jumped into bed warmed only by a hot water bottle!

In 1953, the Queen's coronation was celebrated by street parties all over the city. I was invited to one in Grosvenor Street, as Elm Grove was not able to be closed to traffic, being a main road. I recall sitting at long tables, with lots of grown-ups gathered behind us. We queued up at the end, to be given an apple and an orange as a going home present.

When I was quite small, obviously, I was taken to the beach by my parents, but by the late 1950s I used to meet friends there, and we would take our lunch or tea and meet at a pre-arranged area, near South Parade Pier. It was not thought dangerous as we all learned to swim at primary school. Other dangers did not seem uppermost in people's minds then.'


## ON THE COUNCIL ESTATE

'I spent the 1950s on a council estate (Harefield) on the eastern side of Southampton. The house itself was one of a terrace that ascended the hill rather like a flight of stairs. We had a kitchen and "the other room" downstairs and upstairs two bedrooms and a bathroom. Outside the kitchen door to the street (there was also a back door to what I recall as a quite spacious garden, as well as the usual front door) was a glory hole where the coal was kept and where activities such as shoe cleaning took place. We had a coal fire in "the other room" and although we had quite adequate indoor plumbing, a winter treat for my sister and me was to have our (weekly) bath in the tin bath in front of the fire. I was too young to concern myself with such trivialities as how the hot water got in to the tub – but we did certainly have a washing boiler in the kitchen so perhaps this was used.

At the top of the road was "the woods" and at the bottom "the shop" with on the opposite corner "the prickly field" – a square patch of land covered with gorse which was wonderful for hide-and-seek and dens but infested with nasties such as "bloodsuckers". What I significantly do not remember is any kind of confinement. We went – singly, in pairs or in groups – on errands to the shop and we played mostly out of doors – tracking, exploring or imagining in the woods or the prickly field.

This was a time when today's life of automation, pre-packaging and communication was emerging. Possibly the less affluent environment of the council estate may have been somewhat behind other areas, I do not know, but certainly we had no car, fridge, telephone or washing machine and though we knew people who did, these were not the norm. The local shop was a hybrid – it had the exterior of a modern mini-market but I can remember loose biscuits and block sugar and salt. The milkman called, of course, as did the baker, the coalman, the laundryman and sometimes – drawing us children like the Pied Piper – the rag and bone man, dispensing goldfish in exchange for old clothes and other junk. The rag and bone man certainly came in a cart drawn by an old nag, but one of the others – it must surely have been the coalman – had a splendid carthorse which we would rush out to see and sometimes stroke and whose "offerings" were gladly collected after its passing by any rose-growers.

There were "hang-overs" from the war – pig-bins dotted about the estate for our food scraps; National Health orange juice; and in the city centre bomb sites with which I was familiar but which I never connected with bombs until years afterwards. As is so often the case with childhood memories, it seems to me that life was simpler and less stressed than now – we had enough but not a great deal and we didn't waste our energy in envy and impossible dreams.'

## GROWING UP

'My friend Ellen went to Woolworths and bought herself a pair of "diamond and sapphire" earrings for sixpence. I couldn't be "copy cat", she wouldn't like that, so I bought a pair of "real cultured pearl" earrings, also sixpence. We used to go for walks with our beads and earrings and imagine we were rich princesses or film stars. I put mine in my hanky before I went indoors but unfortunately we were late getting home one day and my Dad was waiting for me with a little wooden stick that he would tap my legs with and send me up to bed. This particular night as I ran upstairs the earrings fell out of the hanky. You would have thought that I had stolen the Crown Jewels and of course I cried quite loudly and that brought my mother to see what all the fuss was about. She said she would keep them for me until I was older as they really weren't suitable for little girls.

I often think of that incident as I'm still very fond of pearl earrings and wear them quite a lot, and make-up too!'

'My mother never wore any make-up and had her hair done up in a bun at the back of her head. We had a customer in our shop at Church Crookham who obviously dyed her hair jet black, as sometimes you were able to see the white roots showing, and she also used powder on her face, which of course made her look very pale in contrast with this black hair. I was always told I would end up like this if I "put that muck on my face" and by the time I was 25 my face would be wrinkled and raddled!'

# TREATS AND GAMES

**Holidays were few and far between but trips out were eagerly awaited and we made the most of long summers spent in the open air. Our games followed the seasons and needed imagination more than equipment.**

## SUMMER DAYS

'I was born in 1916 at Griggs Green, near Liphook. I had one sister Isabel, two years younger than me. We were fortunate children with the love of both our parents and wanted for nothing.

Summer holidays from school were very happy ones. Our house was situated at the foot of Weaver's Down and we were able to walk directly from our little woodland on to the common. We had great freedom to wander about the local countryside but most of our time was spent on Weaver's Down with our local friends and often our cousin Audrey, who had beautiful red hair and freckles, on holiday from London.

We spent hours making moss houses with the many different kinds of mosses which we found on the common, using a different moss for each room. We decorated them with wild flowers and any kind of pretty stones or pieces of glass we could find. Fir cones were used to look like fireplaces and sand was collected and used to make garden paths around our moss houses.

There were also days spent bird watching; we would take notepads to keep a record of all the birds we saw, carefully listing types and numbers. Some days we would record in the same way the many varieties of butterflies and moths which we saw. The warm summer evenings were good for listening to the wood pigeons and the humming noise of nightjars. Bats flew low over our heads with

101

great speed making a piercing squealing noise. Once we had one in our bedroom and Father had great difficulty in getting it to fly out of the window. I don't know who was most frightened, my sister, me or the bat.

Summer holidays also gave us the opportunity to enjoy the company of our herd of goats and we would awake to hear them calling for us to let them out onto the common. We had about eight nanny goats and one billy who was a devil; Father coped mostly with him. The nannies were very friendly and quite clever, they are not silly creatures and given the opportunity can be quite bright. The young kids were a complete joy to us children and we would play games with them. We taught them simple tricks like jumping on our backs if we bent over and they would come for walks just like a dog, stopping every so often to eat a choice bit of grass and racing us to spots which they knew well. My father built a stable for the goats just like a miniature cow byre with food troughs, hay racks, an efficient drainage system and an enclosed run for the kids. Our neighbours had a pack of red setters and our goats became very friendly with them.

It was a wonderful childhood to look back on.'

'When I was born in 1921, Chandler's Ford was a small village. The tiny cottage my parents lived in had only two bedrooms, so when I was a year old we moved into one of the first council houses to be built at Fryern Hill. Life was transformed for my mother, to have a bathroom, even though water had to be heated by a coal-burning copper.

Spring was a magic time for us, as there was a beautiful bluebell wood across the fields near us, where our father always seemed to know where to find birds' nests. Then we would pick bluebells, and if we found the odd white one, we thought that very lucky.

At Easter most men did not work on Good Friday and, weather permitting, they planted their first potatoes. My Dad had an allotment and I can remember us taking him tea in a blue enamel can, with hot cross buns for all of us. Easter Sunday was the time for perhaps a new dress or hat, or even black patent leather shoes to wear to Sunday school.

With summer came Sunday school outings, either to Hayling Island or Lee-on-Solent. The Southern Railway steam trains went all the way there in those days. Then our teachers would distribute our lunch bags, and we all happily anticipated what we were having. My father worked on the railway, so we were able to travel on either free passes or privilege tickets. It meant that we visited the London Zoo or one of the seaside resorts each year.

One summer activity was to go to Shawford Downs with the wooden sledges that my brothers and their pals made. We used to walk the three miles, packed up with sandwiches and lemonade. The day was spent tobogganing down the grassy slopes and toiling back up again. Then the long walk home again, but no one seemed to mind. We also used to have Sunday walks by the river Itchen at Brambridge, picking bunches of watercress for our tea.

A most important occupation for all children was to go out "wooding". My sister used to push me in my chair, a wooden one with carpeting seat and back. Then the dry snap wood was piled onto the push-chair and I would have to walk home. Everyone tried to stock up with coal at the cheaper summer prices, but, even so, the wood helped to keep us warm in the winter.

My father sometimes had to lodge away on weekdays, to save travelling back and forth to a job. Then we would go to bed early to save light and heat, and Mother would read to us from one of her Sunday school prizes. Our favourites were either *Little Lord Fauntleroy* or *John Halifax, Gentleman*. It has meant that all four of us have a love of books, and also taught us the value of simple pleasures.'

## COMING TO HAMPSHIRE

'In 1938 I went on a seamanship course in Portsmouth harbour. At that time there were two wooden ships moored there and used by organisations such as boys' clubs. I went to the course as a Sea Ranger. The staff lived on the ship *Foudroyant*, which is now being restored at a North East shipyard, and the course members lived on the ship *Implacable*. Unfortunately, this vessel became beyond repair and was sunk in the Channel a few years after the end of the Second World War.

It was a hard week's training – I remember that on the first day I was on the rota for the duty boat. This meant rowing over to a jetty at Gosport to fetch the milk as the first job and then ferrying the staff between the *Foudroyant* and *Implacable* whenever necessary. We were certainly exhausted by bedtime. We worked in port and starboard watches and had to sling our hammocks for sleeping at night. We also had to roll them up each day with the correct number of knots and stow them. They were inspected, so it was worth making a good neat job in the first place rather than have to do it again. I think we had a ship's cook as I don't remember having anything to do with the galley, but we had to clean down the mess tables, swab the decks clean and polish the brass. Our course included lectures on sailing and some practical experience. We had gig races and I

*Fun on Southsea beach in the late 1930s. For many Hampshire children, a trip to the seaside was still a rare treat.*

remember having a turn at the steering wheel on the launch when we took a trip to Portsmouth Hard, in order to visit the *Victory*. It seemed reasonably easy to line up in the right direction but needless to say I wasn't allowed to dock the vessel! During this training we wore *Implacable* hat bands round our Sea Ranger hats and I still have mine.'

## A GREAT DAY OUT

'South Farnborough was a great place to spend a childhood in the 1930s. We had the RAF and aerodrome on one side and the army and Aldershot on the other. We could play on the aerodrome except at flying times, when red flags would be put out. Sometimes we were taken for a walk past the hangars and we would look through the cracks in the doors at the planes, which looked so huge to us children. Every year Aldershot had its tattoo lasting a week, and each evening our mother would take us to watch the traffic along the Farnborough Road, as cars, carriages and coaches streamed by. It was very exciting to watch the soldiers going from the barracks all dressed in various costumes for the parts they were going to play in the tattoo. A special time was when royalty came and we would

104

wait for hours to see them all dressed in their finery. On one of the matinée days all the local schoolchildren would walk from their schools, some three or four miles, to the arena. Our headmaster walked in the front carrying the school flag, followed by all the school. It was quite a sight and a wonderful day out.'

'Every Christmas the Women's Institute at Sherborne St John gave us a treat. We had a huge Christmas tree from the Vyne estate, covered with presents, and mountains of thick bread with quince jam, and bread pudding to follow! The WI was also responsible for my seeing the sea. In 1921, we paid one shilling a week, and on the great day we waited in The Square, where Mr Benham's charabanc picked us up. We all tried to get on the back seat, as you got some protection from the wind and dust from the folded down hood, otherwise it was just open air and our mouths got full of grit from the unmade roads. We went to Bournemouth, starting at 8 am and arriving there at noon. I saw the ponies in the New Forest, and was amazed when we got to the sea to see this water that moved! I was allowed to paddle with my frock tucked into my bloomers. We all sat in a circle and had lunch of cucumber sandwiches and home-made lemonade. We returned at 6 pm, and as everyone wore large hats, with pins through their buns to hold them on, no one got sunburnt.'

## HOLIDAYS WERE NOT EASILY HAD

'Born in 1947, I was brought up in the centre of Portsmouth. I lived in a terraced house with my parents and grandmother. I spent some time playing in the street. It was easier in those days. We had no car, as was the case with most of the neighbours, so tag, kingie, hopscotch, roller skating and ball games were safely undertaken. The Shearer Arms provided a superb wall to pay two-ball and dropsy against.

Holidays were not as easily had in the post-war years. Money was conserved and any holidays I had were mainly stays with relatives in Bournemouth, Didcot and York. We did, however, have days out. We tended to head for the country (Lovedean, Horndean, and Rowlands Castle) in the spring and autumn when the spring flowers and autumn fruits were the main attraction. The summer months were mainly centred around the sea front. We would walk to St Mary's church to catch the No 4 or 7 bus to the sea front, or if we could, a green Southdown bus. These had the advantage of stopping right by the prom and meant a shorter distance for carting stuff to the beach. I remember that the sight of the *Queen Mary* or *Queen Elizabeth* was always greeted with joy. Then I would get in the water and ten minutes or so later I would get the moment when the wash came ashore and I would jump up and down in bigger waves.

Sometimes our trip to the sea front was in the evening when we could view the lights and fireworks. I loved seeing the seals with their bouncing ball, or the squirrels climbing the trees by the Rock Garden fountain. Only standing space could be had there when everyone gathered to watch all the changing lights. Occasionally we walked to New Road and caught the No 11 bus to the Hard where we would walk to Old Portsmouth or take the ferry to Gosport, stopping to watch the Mudlarks collecting pennies in the mud by the station approach road.'

## OUR GAMES

'In those days youngsters made up their own games and amusements. Children in the Stramshaw area of Portsmouth, or rather, those that had a bicycle fitted with a sort of step attached to the rear wheel and paraffin lamp to front and rear, used to race each other, two youngsters to a cycle, the person at the rear hanging on for grim death, around four streets forming a square, with no fear of meeting any other traffic such as cars, and very competitive these races were. No prizes for the winners, just thankfulness that the two on a cycle came back safe and sound.

Another daring but exhilarating game we used to play was running across the logs in the water. This took place at a place called Rudmore Wharf which is now the Continental ferry port. The planks were in deep water, mostly moored together but the occasional ones being loose. The object was to run over these logs which submerged if you stood on them too long, and reach the farthest log away from you, some hundred yards away without falling in and getting wet. Yes, very dangerous.

Another of our games was to gather about 15 to 20 of us together and go to Alexandra Park to play football. The goals were trees, which are still there. "Felix" the park-keeper did his best to forestall us but most times we managed to dodge him.

Our treat for the year in those days, when most of us went to Sunday school, was to venture via the Horndean tram which ran from Cosham, along the foot of Portsdown Hill, past the George Inn, and then picnic at Petersfield, and it seems that in those days the day was never spoilt by rain. I remember buying a bar of chocolate for my mother but on the way home, due to hunger, I ate one square of chocolate. When I presented the chocolate to my mother and said I was sorry that I had eaten one square, she burst into tears. At the time I wondered why but now I've aged I can understand.

Another venture was to get on the tram at a certain point and go right round the city for one and a half pennies, mostly on a Saturday. Concealed in our pockets were our pea shooters, out of view of the tram conductor. Each time the tram stopped on its journey, out would come the pea shooters aimed either at passengers getting on, or passers-by. We were a wild lot, but with no really malicious intent.

On most Sundays I and my brother, smartly dressed, as were our parents, would walk along Stamshaw foreshore at the rear of Alexandra Park. Us two boys, well behaved mind you, and parents behind us would walk as far as Hilsea Lido, passing Stamshaw swimming pool and on to the main A3 London Road at Portsbride with its square police box and constable. We then entered a small track (which is now Northern Parade). This track, with fallen trees either side, led to what is now the front gate of Alexandra Park. This track got very wet and muddy at times. So who cleaned all our shoes when we got home?'

'The children at Bashley played a game called Old Mother Hastings Broke Her Basin – one child lay on the ground while the others jumped over her legs.'

'Children's games were simple and required little or no improvised equipment. Bungle Barrel was a rough team game which only required a wall for support. Marbles, five-stones and bows and arrows were popular. Skipping ropes, whips and tops were often played with on Odiham High Street as traffic was less frequent and slower moving than today. Pigs' bladders, begged from the butcher, became footballs and the games often took place in The Bury. The local blacksmith would provide an iron hoop and handle for sixpence. Many children bowled these along for hours. Cad in the Hole was a popular game with boys as it was played with sticks, and was also often played in The Bury.'

### AIR WAVES

'In 1924, one day at breakfast my Dad said, "It's come!" What, I wondered? After work he cycled off to Basingstoke, returning with a square box strapped on the carrier. He then proceeded to put it on the table, attached a length of wire, which he put through the window into the rainwater butt, attached a pair of headphones, clamped them on his ears, and then on Mum's. He said I could have a listen too. The headphones were put on my ears and I heard a man singing *Yes, We Have No Bananas*. I said, "Dad, who is it?" He replied, "A man in London!" I was very puzzled, so he proceeded to explain all about air waves. So I went outside and listened intently, but couldn't hear a thing, only cows mooing in the distance.'

# SCHOOLDAYS BEFORE THE SECOND WORLD WAR

**Long walks to school, learning to write on slates, drying off clothes on the classroom stove and huddling round it in cold weather, no school meals and little equipment. Schools changed very little from one generation to the next and learning was often basic, but many of us have cause to thank those dedicated teachers of the past.**

### WHEN MY FATHER WENT TO WAR

'When my father went to war in August 1914 we left Aldershot and eventually settled in Gladstone Cottage, Droxford, where my father was born and raised, and I became a pupil at his old school.

We had three teachers, the headmistress being Miss Brown who had taught my father. The seven to 14 year olds all occupied one large room, the juniors sitting at one end and the seniors at the other, presided over by Miss Brown from a massive desk on a dais.

At 8.55 the school bell was rung by one of the senior boys and at 9 a hand bell summoned us into orderly lines outside the boys' and girls' porches. The day always started with a hymn and the Lord's Prayer, with a special service on Fridays. After roll call we settled to lessons.

I was always good at needlework and was honoured by being allowed to embroider the headmistress's undies. I scalloped the neckline and did broderie anglaise work on the front of her camisoles. In the winter we senior girls knitted long black stockings for her and when the feet got worn we unpicked them to the ankles and re-footed them to last another year.

There were no organised games or sport but we did have to do drill outside in the playground, weather permitting. Most of us had sufficient exercise walking the two or three miles to school and back. Those unable to go home for dinner brought sandwiches and drank water from a tap in the backyard. In very cold weather Miss Brown made cocoa for us from a kettle on a big stove that heated the room and allowed us to toast our bread if the fire was red enough.

On very hot days the big children carried desks outside under the large lime trees and the classes took turns to have a lesson in the open air. Occasionally we went for nature walks and when blackberries were ripe we were all taken over the downs to Mary Hill to pick them and they were sent away somewhere to be made into jam.

On 24th May every year we celebrated Empire Day. Various retired Admirals, Generals and Majors came to "inspect" us as we lined up on the school green, and heard us sing patriotic songs, including the *Marseillaise*! The rest of the day was a holiday.

When school broke up for Christmas every child filed by the door of Clark's, the village grocer and draper's, to receive an orange and a Christmas card.

The school building still serves the village as village hall. The school green, now tarmacked and used as a car park, is known as The Square.'

MARCHWOOD SCHOOL

'The village school at Marchwood in the 1920s consisted of three main classrooms – one for the infants and standard one, another for standards two, three and four and the third for five, six and seven. Boys and girls were segregated at playtime, apart from the infant boys who stayed in the girls' playground for protection from the older, rougher boys.

It was a Church of England school and received no assistance from the State. Each morning the first 45 minutes were devoted to scripture. We learned all the commandments, catechism and Bible stories, having begun the lesson with a doxology. The main subjects were the 3Rs, history, geography, music and singing, crafts and needlework. We studied quite an amount of Shakespeare, learning passages off by heart, also poetry.

Discipline was strict. Both girls and boys were caned and 100 lines after school had finished were commonplace. Children, however, seemed to accept whatever punishment was measured out to them and parents rarely interfered.

One of the special days was Empire Day – 24th May. It was a school holiday. First we went to church in the morning for a service of thanksgiving for "our Empire". Then we all walked to Lloyds recreation ground where we had buns and lemonade. In the afternoon we had races and games, after which we had tea in the church hall.

In May each year a maypole was erected in the playground and each playtime chosen children would dance round it, the lovely coloured tapes making intricate patterns on the pole.

Some years the school held an autumn bazaar where our work would be on show, also cookery competitions etc. On one occasion a lady from Ipley Manor came to open our show. There was always a lady of importance in the village to do this and a child from the school presented her with a bouquet.

There were no school dinners so we took sandwiches and when it was cold we were allowed to make cocoa, the water having been heated on a Tortoise coke-burning stove.

There was an eleven-plus examination called the scholarship for those who wanted to continue their education and attend Brockenhurst school. This was out of the question for most children as parents could not afford to pay for the necessary books and uniform. By and large the people of Marchwood were far from affluent. The school ran a clothing and boot club, people paying what they could afford each week. They struggled to beat the deprivation of those days. During the years of mass unemployment soup kitchens were set up for the children of the unemployed. No Welfare State, but it was a close community, with people caring and helping others.'

## EARLY DAYS IN SHIRLEY

'The sight of the rather decrepit single storey building, now converted into lockup garages, standing immediately opposite the end of Colebrook Avenue at its junction with St James Road in Shirley, makes it difficult to believe that it was once a small thriving school. Originally named Denehurst, it became St Catherine's in about 1924 when the Revd and Mrs Lathom took over. My association with it began as a pupil in 1925 at the age of seven, at which time Mrs Lathom was teaching the younger boys; the Revd Lathom and his two assistant masters, Mr Mills and Mr Williams, being responsible for the classes of older boys. A change in ownership took place in 1926. In 1927 the new owner, Mr Clement Bloy, amalgamated St Catherine's with Banister Court school, which had just closed. The buildings in St James Road were vacated and Whithedwood House, in Whithedwood Avenue, became the premises for the new Banister school.

In 1925 I lived at 147 St James Road. My journey to school must have been one of the shortest on record, a matter of 20 or 30 paces to the gates. Between home and the school was a single house, the end house of the terrace, the front room of which had been converted into a shop. The shop has long reverted to an ordinary dwelling, and St James' churchyard, originally bristling with row upon row of tombstones, is now a park.

In the 1920s much of the area between Twyford Avenue and Wilton Road was undeveloped; part of it was marsh where the desire to catch newts overcame the fear of our parents' wrath when we returned covered in mud. Near Twyford Avenue, roughly where Branksome Avenue now begins, was a large gravel pit filled with water. It was an irresistible, and perhaps dangerous, place for boys. Here we built a raft from oil drums and pieces of wood and had "pug" fights with the abundance of clay to be found there. In St James Road, where the Methodist church now stands, was more open space, and it was from the horse chestnut trees that grew there that we replenished our stock during the conker season.

Opposite the recreation ground in St James Road were some large red-bricked houses of which the one at Bellemoor Road corner is the only survivor. A classmate and particular friend of mine lived in the adjoining house. His family were farmers and his relatives had butcher's shops in the town. The extensive garden had many fruit trees and Ellen, the housekeeper, kept a watchful eye on Jim and his friends when the apples were ripening. Of other friends who lived within a short distance of the school several were sons of local shopkeepers; the father of one was the manager of the

Rialto cinema in Shirley Road; yet another's father was the landlord of the Bellemoor Inn. Playing bowls in the garden of the inn was an occasional pastime, but more often we preferred to career around the common on bicycles, over the "bumps" or along what seemed, to youngsters, adventurous paths through the bushes. Fishing in the ornamental or cemetery lakes was another enjoyment, as was sailing boats on the yachting pond.

Only a few cars and lorries were to be seen in my early days at school and the fact that boys were able to whip tops along the road is indicative of how infrequently they came along. A well remembered car, a solid-tyred Trojan, belonged to the vicar of St James' church, but horse-drawn vehicles predominated.'

## BUTTON BOOTS AND DOLLS

'I was born and brought up in Eastleigh in the 1920s. I started school at Winchester Road infants in January 1925 and remember wearing high button boots to my knees, the buttons of which had to be done up with a button hook, an arduous task for my mother. I walked to and from school four times a day, almost four miles in all, although my mother took me the first time in very deep snow. The toilets at school were in a block across the playground, a freezing adventure during that first winter. Heating in the classrooms was a large round stove with a huge chimney, very warm if you were lucky enough to sit close to it, but not so good in the four corners of the room.

We played vigorous games in the playground to keep warm in winter, with a child at each end of a long rope and any number in the middle skipping. Another game was hopscotch, drawn out on the playground with chalk. Marbles also was a favourite, both at school and home, and, of course, bowling a large iron hoop along the pavement controlled by a stick. Whip and top was played in all seasons, which I could manage even when quite small.

My first doll had a wax head which melted when I left it in front of the fire. I also remember having a large celluloid doll, again not very suitable as it dented if not handled with great care.

I think the most exciting moment of my childhood was when I was given a baby doll with a porcelain head and opening and closing eyes. It was dressed in a long christening gown lavishly trimmed with lace and a veil to go over its face. It was the custom for very young babies when carried in their mother's arms wrapped in a shawl, to have a large lace type veil over their head and face.'

# BOOKS AND KNITTING

'I attended the primary school at Sherborne St John in the 1920s, and we had slates, with pencils, and blackboard and chalk to do our writing on. Oh, the dust from the chalk! We had one reading book a term, and as I soon learned to read, I had finished mine by the end of the first week. I used to ask, "Can I have another book, please?" Whereon I was told to read it again, so in the end I could almost recite the book word perfect. We had to learn to sew using a sampler book and we made men's shirts, and for knitting we made socks, and woollen vests for ourselves. Mine never seemed to grow quickly enough, so I would knit a line and then keep stretching it underneath the desk.'

# SCHOOLING IN TWO GENERATIONS

'I was born in the 1920s in Hambledon. My father was a tailor, more properly a breeches maker, his mother was the village midwife and my mother was a children's nurse to two vicars, one at Hambledon and one at Petersfield. Their families had been in the village for generations, since 1830 in my father's case and since 1680 in my mother's. My father's family trade was tailoring and on my mother's male side they were blacksmiths.

Both of my parents and all their brothers and sisters (twelve of them) went to the same village school. Mr Evans was the headmaster from the 1890s up to just after the 1914–18 war and was a strict disciplinarian according to legend. Of course, most children left at twelve but the majority could read, write and do some arithmetic. My father, born in 1886 and working in the tailor's shop at age twelve, wrote the most beautiful copperplate.

I went to the same village school; the first teacher I can remember at the age of five was a Miss Newberry. The infants classroom had a big iron stove in the middle of the room, around which our coats were hung on a wet day. Our lunches for playtime were all put together on a shelf and you had to be able to recognise your own packet. The lavatories were across two playgrounds and to today's eyes very unhygienic, and of course we only had cold water and a roller towel in the cloakroom.

As I grew up and moved through the classes, my teachers changed to Miss Samways, then Miss Pearson and finally for the village school, the headmaster, Mr Browning. Memory plays tricks but I do remember a Doctor Joliffe lecturing on the dangers of alcohol and showing a frog pickled in the stuff to ram the message home, after which we had to write an essay. There was also an itinerant musician called Piccolo Peter (or was it Joe?) who played the piccolo in the High Street with all the kids following him and being late home for dinner.

Other things happened which were not so pleasant. There was an outbreak of diphtheria, during which some children died, and we all had a throat swab taken every day. Also, visits from the school dentist were absolutely terrifying, he had a foot-driven drill which must have put children off visiting a dentist for life.

I and two friends passed the scholarship just before the war started and so left the village school to go to Purbrook Park county high school as it was then called, and that was a very different experience indeed.'

## PICKLED ONIONS

'When school dinners began in 1929, surplus vegetables were donated by private estates in the Boldre area and some were grown by the boys on their gardening lesson plots. Shallots were pickled by the girls (in the evenings), and sold to finance sports equipment, hence the poem – 

> Onions, pickled onions, who'll buy our pickled onions?
> Onions, pickled onions, oh do a sample try,
> Perhaps you'll think we're silly because we live at Pilley,
> But as the days grow colder, you'll thank the kids at Boldre,
> For onions, pickled onions, who'll buy our pickled onions?

At the time, for punishment, instead of writing lines, children had to skin onions!'

## A TWO-SCHOOL VILLAGE

'In my schooldays (1915–1926) the village of Overton had a population of just under 1,000 yet it had two schools situated in the centre of the village – one opposite the post office and a smaller one (for infants) in Red Lion Lane. This mixed infants school catered for 50 to 60 children from four to six years of age. The staff consisted of a governess and two teachers. It was a red letter day when, early in April, the "top class" was marched down Red Lion Lane, through the High Street, and handed over to the master and governess of the "big school" for more serious instruction.

This was a divided school and at no time did the boys and girls intermingle. Playtime was taken at different times – the boys going first. The number of children attending this school fluctuated between 80 to 90 boys and 100 to 110 girls. There was no transport for children to the schools. Those living at Ashe Folly, Burley Lane, Frost Hill, Northington, Brick Hill, Apple Dell etc often had a bleak walk to and from school, yet they were seldom late and their attendance was often better than those children living near the school.'

## IT WAS BASIC

'In the middle 1930s, life at The Worldhams' village school was, to say the least, basic. We had outside toilets of the non-flush variety, and water for drinking and hand washing had to be fetched from the spring at the bottom of the hill each evening by the caretaker's husband.

The school, which was situated on the side of a steep hill, comprised two rooms, one approximately twice the size of the other, and two porches, the girls' porch being sandwiched between the school and the school house, where the head teacher lived. This fearsome lady was referred to as the "governess". There were two teachers, one in the "big room" teaching children from standards two to seven. Children started at the age of five, as soon as they had had their fifth birthday, in the "little room", using slates and pencils, later progressing to chalks and boards and eventually paper and pencils.

The heating was provided by a tall, round, iron stove which stood out in the room encircled by a black metal guard by which stood a large bucket of coal, which was fed into it at intervals during the day. The playground was a rough, stony area around the building, but during the summer months we had the use of a nearby field, which was luxury indeed. Our head teacher was very strict, with a strong right arm which she exercised regularly using the cane.

This was a hop growing area and our summer holidays were arranged so that we could go hop picking for the four weeks of September. We looked forward to this and the promise of a new pair of shoes or a new jumper added to the enthusiasm. We walked to the hop garden, arriving to start at 7 am. Halfway through the morning we had a break and then worked on till lunchtime at noon when we stopped for an hour and ate our sandwiches. We had to hold these with paper because of the nasty, black stain which coated our hands and tasted so bitter. At 1 pm we started again and continued until 5 pm when we trudged wearily home after the hops had been measured in large five bushel baskets. These were emptied into surplices and taken by horse and cart to the hop kiln for drying. Little wonder after the first week the novelty had worn off, and the promise of new things had little effect.

Sometimes the holiday was extended for a further week which

*Empire Day at Middle Road infants school, Sholing in the 1930s, with children dressed to represent a country of the British Empire. Always popular, Empire Day meant an afternoon off school!*

was received with mixed feelings. For the hop picking season, the village people were joined by pickers from Southampton, Portsmouth and London, and travellers with their horse-drawn caravans. The townspeople treated this as a holiday, living in a series of small wooden huts, built by the farmers usually close to the hop gardens. There was a communal cookhouse and cold water tap for their use.

During the war there were a few changes. The gas masks we were issued with were carried backwards and forwards to school and were hung on the backs of our desks during lessons. Sometimes we had a practice session, much to everyone's amusement. The windows were covered with a lace-like material, glued to the window-panes to prevent flying glass in the event of an air raid. During this period the school was filled to capacity with children who had been evacuated with their families from Southampton, Portsmouth and London to occupy the empty houses in the area.

Whilst on our nature walks we collected rose hips, rich in vitamin C, to make into syrup for use in the absence of oranges. We also collected foxglove leaves which would be dried for digitalis tablets.

The highlights of our village year were the village fête, a summer outing to the seaside and a Christmas party held in the village hall with a Christmas tree and presents.

We found pleasure in simple things – picking wild flowers or looking for birds' nests. We knew the haunts of certain flowers; the field that was full of horse daisies all summer, the little coppice where we picked purple orchids in the spring, the swamp where the kingcups grew. We climbed the hangars to pick primroses, bluebells, white and purple violets, where also grew the hazel and wild cherry trees. In the autumn we collected the nuts to store for Christmas and hopefully could reach some of the ripe cherries. Although they were rather sour, we would eat them.

We liked to lean over the door of the forge, watching the blacksmith put the shoes on the farm horses, and in the winter sliding on the frozen pond. Life was so much simpler then.'

# SCHOOLS DURING THE WAR AND AFTER

**War brought new problems to schools, coping with air raids and overcrowding by evacuees, but at last it was over and we were into a new world – though little enough changed!**

117

# BASINGSTOKE THROUGH THE WAR

'I started school in Basingstoke in September 1939 at the age of five, initially for half a day only as the school population was increased with evacuees.

My first memories are of air raid and gas mask drills. During an air raid warning we had to sit under the desks, crowded together away from the windows and with our gas masks at the ready. All the windows were criss-cross taped to prevent glass shattering, and some windows were half bricked up.

The building was an old Board school with outside loos and two asphalt playgrounds, one for girls and the other for boys. We all lined up in classes before marching into school with our teacher. Our class teacher taught us everything. I remember all the times tables round the walls which we learnt by rote (but I never forgot them), my reading books were the *Milly-Molly-Mandy* series, and we learned to add and subtract with counters which were kept in small Oxo tins. When we had mastered the basics we had mental arithmetic tests every day, and spelling tests were a regular feature.

Lessons were formal with everyone seated at double desks with tip-up seats attached. Once we progressed to "proper writing" we were given pen holders and nibs and used the powdered ink in the inkwells. These were collected weekly in trays and we took turns in washing them out, a messy task as a favourite occupation was filling up the inkwell with blotting paper.

At playtime we skipped, played ball against the school walls, had spinning tops and whips, played leapfrog and hopscotch.

Our school was always overcrowded. One class was taught in an old drill hall – the pupils were marched in crocodile each day from the main building. Physical exercises were done standing in the aisles between the desks.

Everyone had a daily gill of milk in the old fashioned bottle with the cardboard top where you pushed the straw through the hole in the middle.

In 1945 I sat the first eleven-plus examination. I remember being allowed to go to the corner shop with my ration book and buy a whole bar of chocolate to eat in the play period between the two parts of the exam. I bought a bar of Fry's Sandwich Chocolate – and did not share it with my friends!

I passed the exam to go to the high school for girls. Oh, the pride to wear school uniform and the excitement of wearing it on the first day! A new headmistress was appointed as I started and, for that time, she was very progressive. She changed the uniform from the traditional box-pleat gymslip to a grey skirt and jumper with an aertex shirt, navy gabardine coats, plain lace-up brown or black shoes, and a grey beret with school badge. In the summer we wore maroon blazers with a school badge and were allowed to go hatless!

During the first year the school was decorated internally. We returned after the holidays to find the traditional dark green and brown had been replaced by pastel colours, different in each room. I suspect our headmistress must have fought very hard for such innovations. We were lectured on how lucky we were and how we were expected to take pride in, and care for, our surroundings. When I left that school five years later the decorations were still a joy – I don't think graffiti had been thought of, and in any case we would not have dared!

The original school building comprised only four classrooms, two laboratories, a domestic science room, library and hall. Also an office for the headmistress and a staff room so small that it was impossible for all the staff to sit down together. The part time school secretary's office doubled as the stationery cupboard. In addition there were four "temporary" wooden classrooms and cloakroom, and two additional brick classrooms. These, although newer than the wooden rooms, did not have radiators but were heated by a coal stove at the front. Because of lack of space one class had to "live" in a corridor with books kept in lockers. Also on occasions small groups were taught in the caretaker's front room.

We had a playing field which was suitable for rounders, two netball pitches and five tennis courts. Hockey was taught in the local park which was only a short walk from the school. Swimming lessons were at a local open air baths and classes were bussed there each week in summer. The baths were unheated and the water became dark green before it was changed.

We had annual prize-giving days which were held at the boys' grammar school which was a modern building with a large hall and stage. Our annual school play was staged there also.

It was a traditional education with everyone taking their school certificate and, if they continued, higher school certificate. My main memory of examinations is of two of us doing a Latin retake in December. The only room available did not have heating so we sat in our outdoor coats and with our feet off the floor on boxes. Our invigilator was a retired clergyman who sat in outdoor clothes, including hat and scarf! I am pleased to say we both passed!

During my schooldays, 1939 to 1951, I was never taught by a married teacher – and apart from retiring, teachers seemed to remain in their post and were in many cases teaching a second generation.'

# TEACHING IN PORTCHESTER

'My first post was at Portchester secondary school in September 1953. The school was very modern for the time, having been completed in 1939. The classrooms were light and airy, with specialist rooms for crafts and science and a large hall/gym and dining-room.

A nucleus of the staff had long been with Mr Ted Harman, the headmaster. He had lost a leg in the First World War and when angry would be heard stumping down the corridor to chastise an offender; all the children immediately sat a little straighter and looked a little anxious in case they had incurred his wrath. The deputy head was "Dad" Stone, a wonderful character. Truanting was not unknown even in those days, particularly on sunny Friday afternoons. Then he would cycle down to the castle to look for offenders. Once some boys had climbed onto one of the boats. Its irate owner untied the mooring rope so they were marooned until the tide turned.

There were about 400 children, some of them coming by bus from Southwick and Boarhunt. They were real country children and knew the best places for mushrooms, blackberries and chestnuts.

The children had a good basic education with the more able taking O levels or a commercial course. They were also prepared to run a home with domestic science and needlework for the girls, and gardening, woodwork and later metalwork for the boys.

Three annual events stand out. There was sports day, so efficiently organised by Arthur Barker and enthusiastically supported by the parents. At Christmas a pantomime was produced which was enjoyed by children and staff. Finally in February was eleven-plus day, for selection to grammar schools. The children from the local primary schools attended and sat three papers; maths, English and verbal reasoning. Few found this an ordeal; they seemed to relish a visit to the "big" school. At the end of supervising the exams the teachers had the task of marking and checking the papers and this meant a long day. One morning a girl had a trying cough, my fellow supervisor produced a bottle of linctus and a hairy spoon and dosed the child. I hope this did not account for her failure. She was bright and ended with a good degree.

Equipment was limited, even the school cash box was hidden in a dustbin of lentils in the store room. Registers were kept most strictly in red and black ink, until I spilt a full bottle of red ink down myself.

Today the nucleus of the old school is surrounded by many additional buildings and has superb modern facilities. I think, however, it lost its family feeling, for we knew the names of every child and their background.'

## SOUTHSEA SCHOOLDAYS

'The saying that your schooldays are the happiest of your life does not seem to be true at the time, but in hindsight there is a lot of truth in the remark. It was a very happy school, St Jude's, Marmion Road, Southsea. Although the building was very old, heated mainly by open coal fires in the classrooms, the staff did their very best to ensure everyone played their part.

I particularly remember the summer term, when Mr Lucas, the headmaster, ensured that if the work was done by lunchtime on hot days an afternoon by the pool was on the menu. The academic side of school life was very important and a high percentage of pupils went on to pass the eleven-plus exam, but this was balanced by a need for recreation.

It seems as if we spent a lot of time swimming, and often a large crocodile of children walked across the common to Children's Corner and its pool. Mr Haywood was in charge of the pool, and encouraged us to learn to swim. We were charged twopence for the afternoon and sixpence if we wanted to take our tea and stay on later. Every year there was the swimming gala at the pool, with a large crowd of parents to cheer us all on! Sports day was also a big event, which was held in the Castle Field, now the D-Day Museum site. In those days, there was still a military presence, making it quite an honour to hold such an event there. Towards the end of the summer term, the school outing was always something to get excited about.

Hambledon was the destination on more than one occasion, with a large picnic on the edge of the cricket ground, opposite the Bat and Ball. There were always games organised, with the inevitable game of cricket, led by Mr Lucas and Mr Harrington.

The school was a church school with strong links with the nearby St Jude's church. Every Monday, a procession of pupils would make its way along Marmion Road, for a service taken by the vicar, Mr Abbott. There was sometimes a special service on Sundays, when the school choir performed.

The classrooms were very large, with the inner wall in some rooms being a wooden divider, which could be pushed back for special lessons. The classes were made up of about 43 pupils, arranged in rows of desks and chairs. Discipline was strict, but very fair, with everyone encouraged to develop good manners. This was in evidence when regular visits were made by local dignitaries who were school governors. One in particular was Mrs Sharpe, who was an Alderman of the City and showed great interest in the school's activities.

Mr Shrubb, the caretaker, was loved by all and made sure that the fires were well stoked. On cold days we were able to choose whether we wanted hot or cold milk, with the little bottles placed inside the fireguard for those who preferred hot milk mid morning! I remember this as a particular feature of being in Mrs Warren's class.

School dinners were available, but were cooked at a central kitchen and brought to the church hall nearby. A lot of children lived reasonably near, so the majority went home to lunch.

Resources were limited, by today's standards, with no large playing field, just a tarmac playground. There was a small park nearby, which was used for games, and in a furniture repository across the road, two rooms were used as overflow classrooms. It might not have been comparable with today's primary schools, but it gave us all a good start and a sense of security in those post-war years of the early 1950s.'

# THE WORLD OF WORK

# ON THE LAND

**Farming has long been the backbone of Hampshire's country life, but how things have changed in the last 50 years, since horses provided the power on the farm and hop and fruit picking was an annual excitement.**

## SO MUCH HAS CHANGED

'Farming, within my memory, has probably changed more than anything else since the 1920s or 1930s. There were few tractors, and what there were, were heavy and used mainly as stationary engines for running elevators and grinding corn.

The work was very labour intensive and time consuming. Whereas now, one combine harvester can deal with a crop of corn in one action in a few hours, those days the corn had to be cut and bound into sheaves which were then stooked or shocked into groups of three, left to dry for a few days, loaded into horse-drawn waggons, taken to the farmyard, and built into ricks. These would then have to be thatched and left until the spring when the corn would be threshed, put into sacks and stored in the barns until sold. The sacks weighed two or two and a half hundredweight depending whether wheat, barley or oats; very heavy.

Wheat straw was used for thatching as it is longer. The other straw was used for litter for the different animals, some types more suitable than others. The corn would have been sown in the autumn (winter wheat, barley etc) and in March. March dust was always thought of as being worth a "pound a peck".

Sheep farming was very different too. In the Odiham area, they were mostly Hampshire Downs sheep and lambing was carried out in specially built pens or folds made from hurdles with thatched shelter. The shepherd would sleep in a hut on wheels which had a coke fire, in order to look the ewes over through the night. Lambing usually was timed to begin at Christmas so that lamb would be on the table by Easter. Now all sheep under a year are lambs and one never hears of mutton.

A dairy farm was very intensive too. The cows were brought in twice a day for milking and this involved a very early start. In all but the very worst weather they lived out of doors. Dairy hygiene was fairly primitive, and only in the 1930s did it become more strict.

Pigs were often kept in sties but there was a developing trend for keeping them in "arks" or free range, in a similar method to that used for poultry. Poultry were kept in deep litter, free range and in cages. Animal feed was often prepared at the farm and meal was ground from home-grown corn. Slabs of cattle-cake were crushed. Roots, turnips, swedes and kale were grown for cattle feed, and sheep were fed directly onto the crops, the folds being moved daily.

Sprays against weeds and artificial manures were in their infancy and crops were often lost to beetles, flies and pigeons. The litter from all the animals was built up in the yards and when well rotted would be spread on the land. All this meant that there were many more men employed full time; a 600 acre farm would probably employ 20 to 25 men as well as casual labour for hoeing, harvest, dock pulling among growing corn to name but a few. There would also be ten to 15 carthorses, shires, Suffolk punches etc.

The 1920s were difficult times for farming, land was cheap and prices low. There was a slump in every way. The war wrought many changes, food was desperately needed and incentives were offered. New breeds of corn were found and combine harvesters developed, replacing threshing machines.'

## LIFE ON THE FARM

'The first house I remember living in was in 1916, a four roomed, thatched cottage on a farm, three miles north-east of Basingstoke.

My father worked on the farm as a carter. He had to get up early. The horses had to be fed, watered, groomed and the stable cleaned out, and start working in the field by six o'clock in the morning. He didn't come home until five o'clock in the afternoon. Then the horses had to be groomed and fed again. Then when the horses slept in the stables, Dad had to go again to give them hay in their racks for the night. This was called "racking up". All this work for about ten shillings a week.

Every year, Michaelmas fairs were held, where surplus livestock was sold. If a man was not satisfied with his job, he would take the animals to the fair and get talking to the farmers to find out if they were wanting another workman. He would apply for the job, and if the farmer agreed to employ him, he would pay the man one shilling hiring fee. Once this shilling was accepted, he could not change his mind about taking the job.

The women seldom went out to work. Some went to work in the harvest fields, stacking the sheaves of corn in six or eight sheaves, standing with the grain upward off the ground to dry. This was called "shocking". The pay was one shilling an acre; if the size of

*Taking a break from the haymaking at Westfield House, Rowlands Castle in the 1940s – with the jug to be handed round!*

the field was ten acres it would take two or three days to earn ten shillings.'

## A FAMILY CONCERN

'On the day when I was born at Wellow, my mother told me that she lay in bed, listening and worrying about my older sisters and brother. She could hear them trudging up and down "the bricks", carrying logs of wood for the fires. That was 30th November 1920. "The bricks" were a line of large paving stones which led from the yard to the back door. The wood was stacked between the chicken house, a lean-to at the back of the cart houses, and a grain store on staddle stones which was divided into four storage compartments. The logs of wood were placed on a sawing horse and cut into pieces with a cross-cut saw – this was probably about five foot long with a handle at each end, and we spent many hours pulling in turn to saw through the wood.

The chickens were not restricted in any way – free to scratch and wander throughout the farmyard, the orchards, nearby fields and sometimes into the house. We endeavoured to keep them out of the kitchen garden. Collecting the eggs meant a tour of all this area and, if we heard a hen cackling, it was wise to check where it was so that we could find the nest. It was not unusual, in the spring, to see a hen return to the yard proudly leading a family of baby chicks. I do not remember ever hearing of chickens being killed by a fox – maybe they were not as plentiful, or maybe the Hunt was more successful in keeping the numbers down.

The wood was cut for the open fire in the kitchen. A smaller fireplace in the next room, the front room, was only used on Sundays in winter time and there was a tiny fireplace in my parents' bedroom. I never remember seeing a fire there – I never remember seeing anyone ill in bed – but maybe there was a fire when I was born. The kitchen fire was open with a large fireplace. Bricks were built up on either side, the fire was made on top of the oven and ashes were put underneath it if anything was to be cooked in the oven. A bar about three inches wide stretched over the fire and various saucepans were balanced (or not) on it. It was not unknown for a saucepan of potatoes to overbalance into the fire and then clouds of ash filled the kitchen. A kettle and a large saucepan hung from hooks above the fire. Everything was very black and sooty. During the winter we were always pleased if there were a few loose bricks, so that we could wrap them in paper and take them to bed to keep our feet warm. There was great rejoicing when my mother's twin sister gave us a stone hot water bottle, but there were rather a lot of beds to share it between. There was a copper in the kitchen which was stoked with small twigs and faggots every Tuesday. We had a pump in the kitchen and a huge wooden sink quite a yard square, so that we did not have to let a bucket down the well.

Chimney sweeping meant that my father or brother took a hoe or some similar implement to rake down the soot in the lower part. The chimneys were very large and every so often they would catch fire and that would clean them. Chimney sweeping was a very dirty job – everything had to be removed or covered and pictures and china had to be washed before being replaced.

There was a set job for each day of the week. On Monday my mother made butter. As soon as the cows were milked, the milk was separated – the cream was stored in huge earthenware containers in the dairy, a large room off the kitchen, facing north, with large paving stones on the floor. The skim milk was poured into two half barrels which always stood just outside the back door and contained any kitchen waste, and this was used as a base for the pigs' food, mixed with bran and barley meal. What farmer's wife would tolerate that at her back door today? Every Monday the cream was tipped into the churn and my mother turned the handle until it turned to butter – sometimes it took hours. Then she weighed it into half pound blocks and shaped it. My bedroom was over the dairy and I can still remember the "pit-pat" as she wielded it into shape. A few people came to collect their supply but I remember, as soon as I was old enough, having to deliver it, in a box tied to the carrier of my bicycle. It was no joke in summer time, when it became softer and softer, cycling from Cross Oaks to various customers, including two aunts in remoter parts of the scattered village. My sister used to take eggs and butter to Miss Smith, headmistress of Barton Peveril school, which we attended.

Tuesday was washing day and everything was rubbed and scrub-bed before being put into the copper – not straight into a washing machine as today. There were two large baths on the kitchen table and farm clothes tended to get very dirty. The mangle stood in the corner of the dairy – large wooden rollers, with a screw at the top to push the two rollers closer together, and another handle to be turned for what seemed hours. The clothes were folded and fed through the rollers, with a bath underneath to catch the water which was squeezed out. Then they were hung on lines among the apple trees in the orchard or, on wet days, draped around the kitchen after we had retired to the second room. At times the mangle could be used on dry sheets as an easier form of ironing.

After the washing was completed, the kitchen floor was thoroughly scrubbed – not easy on the knees, as the floor was made up of bricks, unevenly laid.

Most of the family retired about 10 pm, but it was quite common for my mother to sit up until 1 or 2 am mending our clothes. There was little money for new, and everything was handed down, so, as the fifth daughter my clothes had been well worn before they fitted me.

Wednesday was ironing day and the flat irons were lined up on the bar over the kitchen fire and had to be well wiped before they could be used. No ironing boards – just an old blanket covered by an equally old sheet spread over the kitchen table.

Thursday, it was back to buttermaking again – the length of the task depending on how long the butter took to "turn". The cry, "It's coming", was greeted with cheers of relief by all. Groceries were delivered by a Mr Hankin from Southampton, later Summerbee and Hankin, and he took our surplus butter and eggs.

On Friday the house had to be cleaned right through – five bedrooms, two flights of stairs, two "passages" and two "lounges" a word not heard then. No carpets or vacuum cleaners – stained boards round the edges, a piece of linoleum and, if you were lucky, a small mat, often a home-made rag mat, to step on when you had the courage to get out of bed. There was no heating and we were glad to have feather beds and patchwork quilts. All the mats had to be carried downstairs and shaken, sometimes put on the clothes line and beaten.

There was not a lot of furniture or ornaments to be dusted – a few religious pictures probably handed on by my mother's parents. Each room had its washbasin and jug, although we often washed downstairs where it was warmer. We had a round bath about nine inches deep which we used in the summer, having to heat the water over the fire or in the copper and carry it upstairs (and down again after use), but in winter we tried to manage a bath in front of the fire. It was hard work to keep clean. Needless to say, there was a chamberpot in each room and these had to be emptied when the beds were made – as proof of the cold, it was not unknown for the contents to be frozen in winter.

On one occasion my father and brother, having carried fruit to be stored in the attic, climbed along above the ceiling where they dropped down into two rooms – no windows, no stairs – but they found clay pipes there. We can only imagine that this was where the workmen slept.

Saturday was baking day and the fire had to be well stoked before my mother could start making cake for her large family, although cake was not as plentiful then. Whenever fruit was in season, she

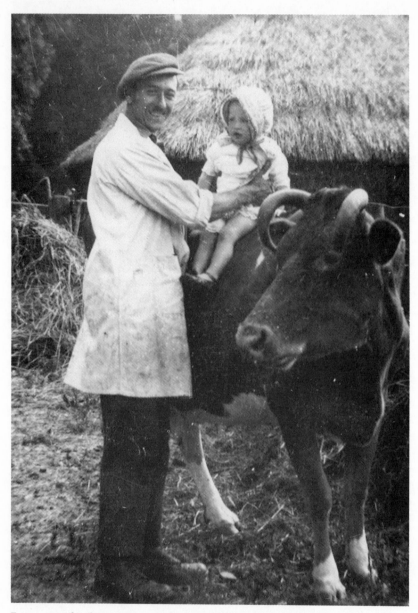

*Farms were family concerns – and it was never too early to get used to the livestock! Behind the farmer and his daughter, at Hursley in 1928, is a neatly thatched rick, a common sight on farms before mechanisation.*

130

would be making jam and there were usually several shelves of jam in the dairy. We always had a pig for the house. Salt was rubbed into the sides and then it was taken to the bakery at Buck Hill (on the Romsey-Salisbury main road), where it was smoked. In one bedroom there was a bacon cupboard – it looked like a wardrobe, but it was backed onto the chimney.

Sunday – the "day of rest". Every day, before she could think of her household tasks, my mother with Father and later my brother and second sister had to milk the cows, feed the pigs and chickens and then, after breakfast, the men went to the fields and Mother would turn to her normal routine. So, on Sunday, it was just the same until after breakfast. In the early days my father went to church but there was a rather bitter quarrel between members of the Church Council, which is best left as history, and after that he used to change and retire to the front room and read until he was called to carve the Sunday joint. Yes – read, mainly Byron or Shakespeare, rather strange for a man who left school to help his mother provide for the family as soon as he reached the required standard of education at the age of eleven. Mr Noake, the then headmaster, commented, "What a waste!" He could recite the *Ancient Mariner* from school-days and often helped us with our history homework. My mother sometimes sat in the orchard with a book on fine summer Sundays – for about two hours, and then back to work, tea and then milking again. My sister helped on the farm with haymaking etc and when there was a rick to be thatched, we carried buckets of water from the stream to damp down the straw – down with empty buckets, climb back up with full.

We had one oil lamp for the living-room and a small oil lamp in the kitchen. Lanterns were used to check on the animals and "rack up" at night and there was a row of candlesticks in the kitchen for us to use when we went to bed.

During the summer the cows were allowed to graze along the sides of the road and I used to take my homework and sit on a gate while I looked after them. Sometimes there would be a call to cycle to Romsey to the Test Valley Ironworks to collect a plough share and bring it home. How I hated that!

I suppose that the most primitive thing about our life was the "toilet", if I can elevate it to that name. We walked up a long path, with box hedges on either side and turned left into a little shed with two holes over a ditch. Presumably the liquids were purified or at least no danger to health by the time they reached the river. The solids – I shudder. An elderly workman and later my brother had to shovel it out on to the vegetable garden, where it was dug in to produce, no doubt, good vegetables. What joy there was when we had a new shed built, in front of the old one, and where there was a bucket. The same happened to the contents, as it still did in Wellow for many years, until well after the war, but at least a hole could be dug and the contents covered over.

My father had little choice but to buy Cross Oaks in 1920 when the Embley estate was sold – his father-in-law said that it would be a millstone round his neck for the rest of his life. He must have wondered if that was true in the early 1930s when he, my mother, brother and sister (whose wages were the princely sum of half a crown per week) worked a full year and were worse off at the end. The best move was in the mid-1930s when they contracted with Brown and Harrison's dairies in Southampton to sell the milk. They had to get up in the middle of the night (or so it seemed) to have it ready for the lorry. My father used to call me when he brought the first load to the "cooler" at 6.30. They were still milking when I left at 7.15 to cycle to Romsey and on to Barton Peveril by train. I was always in trouble for arriving at school with dirty shoes from where I had made my way across the cow yard to kiss my mother goodbye before starting on my way. Buttermaking had never been very profitable and many farmers relied on the regular milk cheque to keep them going and pay the bills.

We had all our own agricultural machinery, all horse-drawn, grass cutter, binder, plough, harrow, rakes, a large waggon and smaller carts. The only machine which came in was the threshing "tackle" which used to come chugging along the road from the direction of the church and fill up with water at the stream. A few neighbours used to help as two men were needed on the rick being threshed, two to feed the machine, and two to build the straw rick. Someone had to attend to the sacks of corn, take them to the store and fix empty ones. The cats were always waiting to see if any rats came from the rick. Some of the corn was taken to the mill at Sherfield English to be ground – barley for meal to feed the pigs.

My brother's one ambition was to have a tractor and he saved every penny. He caught rabbits with a ferret or with a "long net", shot pigeons, caught moles and sold the skins and we all picked daffodils and blackberries which were taken to Southampton for sale – just to get some money for Christmas presents.

The men ate bacon, egg and fried bread for breakfast, or boiled eggs, probably with porridge, and ending with bread and jam – but there was always butter, which was rare in those days, when people mostly ate either butter *or* jam on their bread. There was a cereal called "Force" with a picture of a male doll on the packet and it was possible to get this doll, called "Sunny Jim", and there was another cereal, Grape Nuts. We always had roast on Sunday and usually cold on Monday, then rissoles or cottage pie, steak and kidney pudding, fish – fresh herrings or (my pet hate) boiled cod with a white sauce with boiled eggs in it. On Saturday, it was often pea soup – thick with split peas, lentils, etc. We had rabbit quite often and pigeon pie. The "shoot" was let and, on occasions, my father was given a pheasant, which was a rare treat.

A man came with a horse and cart to deliver fish – huge cod – and was obviously nicknamed "Fishy". I cannot remember the butcher ever coming in a horse and cart, he had an old van and always used to bring a few bags of sweets with him which he hoped my mother would be tempted to buy.

We had fruit in season and apples and pears were stored on straw in the attic, with onions, which lasted until spring. The Barney pears, very hard, were stewed slowly in the oven with brown sugar and were delicious. Rhubarb, blackcurrants and gooseberries were also turned into jam, especially rhubarb and ginger, also marrow and ginger, and plum jam with the stones left in. A few strawberries were bought for jam. Egg custard made from the "beastings" – the first milk from a cow after calving, was a favourite and we sometimes had rice boiled in a cloth, with golden syrup. There were plenty of steamed puddings with various fruits which oozed juice as they were turned out onto a dish and, of course, spotted dick (suet pastry boiled in a cloth with dried fruits – the "spots") and jam roly-poly, also cooked in a cloth. The less enjoyable apples were made into cider. We did not have much fruit, apart from what we grew, but we always had oranges, figs, dates and nuts at Christmas. One of the men who shared the "shoot" always sent us a large box of chocolates at Christmas – oh, the temptation to open it before Christmas Day! We always had my mother's two sisters, with the husband of one of them, at least for Christmas Day. My uncle, Percy Moore, who was organist at Wellow church for many years, used to entertain us with songs like *Little Brown Jug*, *Uncle Tom Cobley*, *The Death of Cock Robin*, etc. During the war he had entertained his friends and he used to sing at the concerts at the old village hall – a wonderful organist, singer and choirmaster.

My father would never sell calves at a day old, as many did, but when the dealer came to buy the young bull calves the cows all recognised his transport and became very upset, whether it was their own calf or just one belonging to another cow.

Except when my father went to Salisbury market and brought back smoked haddock, sprats or even winkles, tea was mostly bread and butter with jam, golden syrup or even, on occasion, sugar spread on the slices. Most of the cake was home-made, or scones over a girdle, with occasionally a lardy cake from the baker. He used to bring the bread by horse and cart from Buck Hill and, as we were the last on the round, we often had to wait up for him until after 10 pm. If my father had a bad cold, he would have onions boiled in milk or water before going to bed. We always had cocoa to drink for supper – what a joy to have visitors so that we could have coffee!'

WORKING WITH HORSES

'When I started work in 1924 for Lothian Bonham Carter at Buriton I was just 14 years old and went straight into work with horses. He owned 24 good strong working horses and two light horses, one for the bailiff to ride all over the estate to look at his workforce, crops and the flock of sheep and fat bullocks, and the other light horse was for the trap for going to the bank and the market.

The stables were just inside the big farm gate on the left hand side, twelve stables, and two loose boxes for the light horses. Four horses were kept the other side, four at Heather and Baker's yard and four at Faggs Farm at the top of Haws Hill.

A carter had four horses to work and care for. His days were long, starting at five o'clock in the morning, feeding, taking them to the water trough for a drink, cleaning up their beds of straw, home at six for breakfast, and back again at six thirty to await orders for the day's work, and harness up for the certain jobs. All had to be out of the stables by 7 am and on the way to the fields; one hour was allowed for dinner. The horse's feed was in a nosebag. After the day's work, back to the stables at 4 pm for a drink, a feed of corn and cleaning off the mud and grooming their coats, and getting straw for their beds, and five o'clock home for tea and rest. Back to the stable at 7 pm, another feed, hay for the night, bed down with straw, another groom, putting their corn up in nosebags for the next day. Eight o'clock finish for the day and home. That was every day of the year, except for the summer months, then they were turned out to grass for the night at five o'clock, but next morning back to work at a quarter to five to get them in from the meadow, clean them, feed them, home again at six for breakfast, then back again by six thirty to get them ready for work again.

They all had their own names, and in the dark of an August morning you could not see them, but if you stood by the gate and called their names they would come galloping in, ready for a feed of corn and a grooming. A true friend, worth looking after, never letting you down, and always trying his hardest; just a working horse.

The blacksmith came from Petersfield, a Mr Chitty, a short tubby man but as strong as a horse. All 24 horses were shod in rotation, he knew just when they wanted shoeing and the measurements of each one were kept in his head. In the winter shoeing was done by candlelight when they came in from the fields at 4 pm.

Our horses were very sensible. They knew when you spoke to them and over the years, working with them each day, you spoke to them like a human being, and took pride in them. Somehow they knew when they were going home at the end of the day's work, and one rascal would not go by his stable after 4 pm and would defy anyone to make him.

Ploughing each day was a pleasure with two good horses, a steady plod all day, and in step with each other. The work for horses was 360 days a year, ploughing, cultivating the soil, drilling the corn, grass cutting, turning the grass into hay, pulling the waggon loaded with hay to the ricks, and cutting the corn with a binder, a machine that cut the corn and tied it into neat bundles called sheaves. The binder took three horses to pull, from nine in the morning to eight o'clock at night.

Horses were wanted again to gather the corn in, into ricks, then in the autumn and winter for cultivating the fields, pulling the carts up on the hill with food and hay for the cattle each week, food for the sheep, straw and hay, for litters to lie on, getting waggon loads of flints from Holt for roads, hauling timber and trees to the saw bench. The horses were wanted each day for hundreds of jobs, and they could do it because they were well fed, and looked after with pride. In the spring, when they were turned out to grass in the meadows, it was good to see them galloping and rolling about in their freedom. But the Princes, Daisies, Drummers, Punches are no more. One of man's best friends.'

## MOVING ON

'I was born at Wyck in 1935 and in 1945 my father changed jobs and we moved to East Worldham. Moving day was nearly always 29th September (Michaelmas) if you worked on a farm.'

## CHICKEN AND FRUIT

'Father worked on a free range chicken cum fruit farm at Liphook. Trees were planted in rows and the ground between was ploughed with a one-horse manual plough. Although the chickens were shut in chicken houses (after being rescued from the apple tree branches), foxes would often try to pull them by their legs through the slatted floor. To prevent this, hurricane lamps were lit and left hanging from the apple trees. Christmas would find Mother in a shed, plucking. She wore a sacking apron to protect her clothes and had a large bath

*Bedding strawberries at Burridge in 1922. The heavy clay soil required a great deal of work before becoming suitable for cultivation. Soft fruits were an important local industry.*

in front of her to collect the feathers. She had to be careful not to tear the breast skin as it spoilt the appearance of the final trussed and cleaned bird.'

## THE FRUIT FARM

'I was born in Burridge and my earliest recollections were of a very striving family. We had about ten acres of land and grew mostly strawberries. The whole community was quite new. The land had been sold in 1910 by the Hood estate to cover death duties so all Burridge road was in little sections. They reckoned that if you had two to four acres of land to grow strawberries you could make a living. They were all very hard-working folk. They all had the same standard house, sort of square, three-bedroomed places. My father built a shed and then lived in it till the house was built.

My father's first job on returning from the war in 1918 was laying drains. It was very heavy clay land. People often wondered why he started growing strawberries on such heavy land but he wanted to be near the river which he loved so much. He did not mind the toiling.

The local men all had horses and had to grub the land and clear away the oak trees. Burridge, Warsash and Swanwick and about ten years later, Botley, all grew strawberries. Warsash and Swanwick had the very early ones. The stones there warmed the land so that was why they were early.

They kept a lot of horses at that time in London and so it was traditional that you went with your horse and cart to the station and collected truck loads of "London dung". That happened in the autumn. There was no artificial manure in those days but they had this tremendous tonnage of good strong horse manure.

The baskets they used for the strawberries and currants were wicker, holding about three or four pounds, and the prisoners at Winchester Prison were allowed to choose whether they made mail bags or strawberry baskets. Later on a basket factory began at Swanwick and the baskets were made from poplar wood.

At Hoads Hill, Wickham we had a stall by the side of the road where we sold strawberries, blackcurrants, beans, potatoes, raspberries and loganberries. This was one of the first of these little stalls in the 1930s, which the council did not seem to object to. It went very well.'

## STRAWBERRY MECCA

'Curdridge was a strawberry mecca. Many of the fields were divided into strips where the various owners grew and picked strawberries. My grandparents did just that and in the picking season my mother used to go down to help. She used to tell of picking strawberries which were then packed into "chip" baskets, labelled, and taken to Botley station by pony and trap for the train journey to the wholesaler in Reading. As children we loved these visits. Unfortunately, with the outbreak of war in 1939 the strawberry fields were taken over to grow corn, and in many cases the strawberry harvest never returned.'

## MODERNISING

'During the Second World War Mr Shortis of Lower Wield Farm and Mr Dumbell of Wield House Farm decided it was time to modernise their harvesting equipment. They and Mr Paris of Moth Farm, Brown Candover both had a Kennedy & Kemp grain drier installed and ordered Massey Harris combine harvesters which had to be imported from the United States. Unfortunately the ship bringing them across the Atlantic was sunk but luckily Mr Shortis, who had sold off his old equipment, had kept one binder and so was able to get in his harvest.

Eventually the new combines arrived, with their canvas driving belts which continually needed adjusting during the day as the temperature and humidity changed. This early machine needed two men at least, one to drive it and the other to stand behind him on a platform and hang sacks beneath the four vents on hooks while corn poured through the hoppers to fill them. The top of the sack would be tied up, then the sack was dropped gently down a slide at the rear of the machine and left on the ground to be collected later. The combine had iron wheels, which after the war had new axles put onto it and some German aircraft wheels fitted which had been bought up by an enterprising agricultural engineering firm. These wheels had rubber tyres.

Before the use of combine harvesters the corn was left in stooks in the field until it was dry enough to be put into ricks. When it was required it was threshed out. Probably one of the main causes of the reduction in the owl population was due to modern grain storage reducing greatly the numbers of mice and rats. The ricks used to be simply heaving with them.'

## FATHER WAS A SHEPHERD

'We came to Compton on 9th October 1929. There were twelve in the family; I had two brothers and seven sisters – the youngest sisters were born at Compton – that meant five of us going to school together. We knew hard times, and as children we nearly starved, living on just swedes, turnips, carrots, cabbage stalks and a rabbit now and again. We all had to learn to sew, mend and knit from an early age, also make cloth rugs from clippings.

Father was a shepherd and in charge of 1,000 sheep with two dogs. He would shepherd the sheep over Compton Down to cross the main road at Wayside Cross (no longer visible) to graze the flock on Shawford Down. Late afternoon back across again, standing in the middle of the road to stop the traffic, holding up his stick or shepherd's crook. Usually all went well, but sometimes motorists would get impatient and start tooting their horns. Sheep frighten easily, but all in all it was a sight worth seeing. The barn, at Compton Street, now a private dwelling, was used for shearing sheep; it was our duty to take down father's dinner. It was intriguing to watch the speed of the shearers, extra hands taken on temporarily for the job.'

'For Alresford Sheep Fair we children used to get up at 5 am to drive the sheep to the fairground. It was quite a job to get them past the butcher's shop because they could smell the blood from the slaughterhouse behind it. Drovers came great distances to the fair and once they had delivered their animals at the fairground they would seek out some grassy land and sleep in any corner they could find.'

## HOP GROWING AND PICKING

'Hops were introduced to this country from Flanders in 1525. The plants were grown chiefly in Kent, but also in the counties of Hereford, Sussex, Worcester and Hampshire. Latterly their cultivation was mainly in Kent and Hereford.

Hops are still grown at Bentley. Apart from this, there were growers at Crookham, Farnham and Alton. At Hillside there was a garden known as Hordles, and earlier there were hops growing on the west side of King Street at Odiham where Mayhill school grounds now are. Palace Gate Farm dealt with the hops from Hordles.

At Winchfield there were three gardens which belonged to Mr Dennis of Bridge Farm (now Bailey's Farm) at Potbridge and this is where the drying kiln was situated. (In Kent the kilns were referred to as oast houses.) The building was of brick and housed ovens on the ground floor with a large room above with a specially covered floor upon which the hops were spread for drying. When the process

was completed, and it meant a day and night job for the dryer, the hops were loaded into "pockets". These were long (about twelve foot), high quality sacks, bearing the name and address of the grower and so strong that approximately 200 bushels of dried hops could be rammed into each bag. The bag was secured by a circular iron clamp over a rim above a hole in the drying room floor, dropped through and held securely by hinged half-circular iron sheets. A presser was wound down into the pocket to compress the hops. This was worked by handle and rack.

The hops were afterwards sent to the chief market, which was at the Hop Exchange in Southwark, south east London. (It is interesting to note that before the introduction of all-figures in the telephone code, there was an exchange called HOP.)

The Hop Exchange later became the Hops Marketing Board but still functioned from the Borough in Southwark. This board dealt with all claims from hop growers, who often experienced storm damage from hail. The principal use for hops was for brewing, but they were also found in medicines.

Hop picking time in the early 1900s was a period of great activity and excitement – for the younger generation anyway. Early in the year Mr Dennis of Bridge Farm would call and collate the names of all families who were prepared to go hopping in the autumn. A few selected women would be chosen to tie the hops to their poles. This was done in May when the young shoots (several to a root) would be assisted to climb. The poles were of ash, beech or hardwood – about seven feet long – and rather stouter than runner bean rods. They were inserted by the roots of the hops which were about two feet apart in double rows. A wider space was left between the rows to allow access. When the time came for picking, the villagers were informed and upon their arrival at the garden they found that wide avenues had been made by the pole-pullers. Large wicker bins had also been placed at fixed intervals along the avenue – one for each family – and beside the bins were the pulled hops ready for picking. The bins were flattened oval in shape – they held seven bushels – and brown markings around the inside indicated how many bushels had been picked.

Work started early – 7.30 am. Sandwiches and drinks had to be prepared before leaving home and it was usual for each family to have a truck (probably a Tate & Lyle sugar box mounted on a pair of old perambulator wheels) or a mail cart or perambulator if there were small children going to the hop garden. Favourite drinks were cold tea, lemonade or home-made Salisbury beer. This was a highly concentrated essence to which sugar and boiling water were added to make what was a luxury non-intoxicating drink.

140

Each family took one or more umbrellas. These were handy in case of rain, but if fine, one of the family (usually grandmother) would sit on a stool and pick hops into the umbrella. The younger hoppers stood by the bin and after placing the pole with bine (stem) attached over it would drop the hops in. Leaves were frowned upon and the tallyman would quickly point them out and make a suitable deduction in his account book. The tallyman kept a strict record of each picker's work, and could be called upon as soon as a bin became full.

Just before the close of day (about 4 pm) the pole pullers would go around calling loudly "No more poles", and shortly afterwards the tallyman would again attend and note all final pickings. The hoppers could be seen delving into their bins just before his arrival hoping to raise the level of the hops. They were apt to settle down quickly. It was an unforgiveable offence for anyone to carelessly knock the bin and children were forbidden to go near until after the departure of the tallyman. The bins were emptied on the spot into large canvas holders called "surplices", picked up shortly afterwards by horse and cart and removed to the kiln.

Apart from wasps and flies, which always seemed more plentiful at hopping time, there was excitement everywhere when Tommy Judd, of Hartley Wintney, came along with his handcart selling bulls-eyes, peppermints and toffee. In addition, local bakers brought round bread, doughnuts, cakes, etc. Mr Hill of North Warnborough (known as Fishy) also with handcart, purveyed bloaters, herrings, etc. At a higher level, Messrs John Eighteen of Reading called regularly with wet fish of all sorts. They had a horse and cart.

Upon arrival home there was always the problem of removing the brown stain on fingers. Modern bleaches were not available, but a good hard rub with a block of pumice moistened with soft water from the nearby pond usually did the trick, but hardly sufficient to remove the scent of hops which gave an edge to the appetite.

The hopping usually lasted about three weeks at Winchfield, there being two gardens at Chevertons and one opposite the brickyard on the Winchfield Road, known as Tossells. Sometimes boys were allowed to go to the drying kiln and take potatoes to bake. They could also witness the filling of the dried hops into the pockets, a large triangular canvas shovel being used.

To complete the cycle, Mr Dennis would call with the money a few weeks after hopping and pay the pickers in cash. In 1909 the payment was a penny halfpenny per bushel.'

'Until 1953 when disease attacked the vines, Buriton and Weston, which lie south of Petersfield, had extensive hop fields. Hop growing was really a twelve month job. To start, there was the stringing. This was done by men. In Buriton they used ladders, not stilts as at Weston. Then the women came and did the training, putting the strongest vines to grow up the strings. This was done twice, then the men took over to train them as they reached the top. Later the lower leaves were stripped by women, and men earthed up the roots. The vines were regularly sprayed for pests and diseases and weeded between the rows.

Nearer the harvest in September we wrote to the foreman for a basket. He would give everyone a number and a date to start. Very early on that morning we arrived on the field and were put into groups of 20 with a wire-puller who cut down the vines and was in charge of the gang. The outsiders from Portsmouth who used the huts at Cowhouse Farm (these were only removed in 1993) or camped in what is now Heatherfield, had their own leader and gang. It was all fairly arranged so if you had an outside position coming up, you had a more central position on the return.

Everyone had a certain distance to pick. We emptied our baskets into sacks and a tallyman came round about three times a day and measured and entered the results in his book. With large hops called Fuggles, a family could pick 80 or so bushels a day. We were paid between a penny farthing and threepence halfpenny a bushel, with more money for small hops, called Goldings.

Picking lasted three or four weeks and school holidays were arranged to coincide with the harvest and the children often had an extra week from school. Later they had a special pass giving them leave from school during hop picking. We always hoped this would finish for Taro Fair day which is still held in Petersfield on 6th October.

The hops were dried in the kilns in Bones Lane and I can still remember the smell of drying hops which filled the whole village. Today those hop kilns have been converted into very nice houses. Hops still grow wild in some of the hedges, so they have survived a long time.'

'Our house at East Worldham was very close to the Three Horse Shoes public house and after hop picking each year in the 1940s, they would have what was known as "Horse Shoe Fair Day". The travellers would come from miles around to trade in their horses, carts and anything else they wanted to sell. The horses were paraded up and down the road and there was always a lot of haggling over what price a horse was worth; quite often by the end of the day a few fights had taken place.'

# IN SERVICE

**The 'big house', and many smaller farms and middle class homes, employed a number of servants and this was a major source of employment until the 1950s, especially for girls straight from school. There were the outdoor staff on the bigger estates as well, such as gardeners and gamekeepers. With the right employer, it could be a good life.**

LUCKY ME

'Christmas Eve 1917, I was with other girls helping to decorate the village church at Sparsholt when my Dad came in and said, "You must come home, Mother says, and go to help in the big house". Dad was gardener there and we lived in one of the cottages belonging to the three maiden ladies who lived in the big house. So of course I was expected to do as I was told. I was just 14 years old.

My very first job was to put a whole loaf of stale bread through a wire sieve and I thought perhaps I would be trained as a cook. I only ever wanted to be a nursemaid. Well, after six weeks I had to go and live in. I shared a room with the housemaid. There was an old housekeeper who had been the nanny to the three ladies, and there was the cook, a parlourmaid, the housemaid and myself who was the between maid and had to help everyone. I wore a pink cotton dress with cap and apron in the morning till two o'clock, then I had to change into a black dress. The dresses came to the tops of my shoes. The first time I put on the black dress I cried and the cook said, "What are you blubbering about?" and I said, "I feel as if my mother has died in this black frock."

The maids were locked upstairs at night and in the morning someone had to go for the key which one of the ladies kept and we came down and had a cup of tea. My job was first to clean the housekeeper's fire, that was 6.30 am, then I had to lay kitchen breakfast. We had really good food always. Each maid had her own box of tools to clean grates and we each had a jar of tea leaves to sprinkle on the carpets before brushing them with a stiff brush into a dustpan, and we had to brush the carpets the way the pile went. There were no nice soap powders then, so we had to use soda which made my hands crack often and become so sore. We, the parlourmaid and I, had to lay table for the ladies and I had to sound the gong at

143

seven for them to get dressed for dinner in the evening. I liked doing that then, at 7.30, to say dinner was on the table.

There was only one bathroom and only one lady used it. Everyone else had a hip bath in their room and cans of water had to be taken upstairs by me. I was a nervous girl and the shadows thrown by the lamps made me feel all creepy. There was what was called the morning room and pictures all round the walls of their ancestors. All the frames were gilt and the eyes sort of followed me round the room.

The saucepans were very heavy black ones and we only had a wire brush to get them clean which was hard work for a 14 year old. We only had some stuff called Monkey Brand to clean the two toilets. I had to bail out the water, then rub and rub until the pan was clean. I had to scrub the red brick scullery floor and wash the passages and the big kitchen floor. With the help of the housemaid I had to clean beautiful silver. We had to use our thumb and finger to put the stuff, on then rub it off with two or three other cloths.

After breakfast we had to march into the dining-room for prayers. First the old housekeeper, then the cook, then the parlourmaid, then the housemaid, then me. We sat facing the ladies while one read the gospel and said other things. Then we had to turn round and kneel down while one of them read prayers, and as the First World War was still on there were such a lot of prayers. Sometimes the young housemaid and I got the giggles as the old housekeeper said Amen too soon. No men friends were to come into the grounds. One lady said she could smell a man one evening. It was one of the girls there with a young man who was smoking.

I was allowed out once a week from two till seven thirty and every other Sunday till ten, and every other Sunday for church. I was told that if I didn't break anything they would put sixpence into the war effort each month. I was there nine months and I broke so many of the kitchen things there was no money of mine for the war effort. The first morning I was there, the small shade of a lamp I was carrying fell off and broke and I was so frightened to tell but I asked the housemaid, "Who shall I tell?" and she said Miss M, who was the youngest and was about 50. Anyhow, I said, "I'm very sorry, miss, but I've broken a lampshade," and she said, "Do you know how expensive they are?" I said, "No, miss," and she said, "They are sixpence halfpenny each". And yet they were very wealthy people.

There were big tables to scrub, grates to be cleaned out and blackleaded, steel fenders to be cleaned, hearths to be whitened and rugs to be taken out and put on the line and beaten. There was furniture to be polished with wax sort of stuff and always someone to see it was all done properly. The old housekeeper liked me, I think, and always called me "little one", not by my name. She and I used to make the ladies' beds together.

Another job I hated was doing the slops. I had to take a can of soda water and three cloths and a slop pail into the bedrooms and empty the chamberpots and the washbasin and wash tooth glasses and soapdishes and then wipe the washstand down. Often the youngest lady would be in bed as she had heart trouble. I was so nervous doing things in front of her I used to sort of hold my breath.

Mother and Father said I was a very lucky girl to be in such a good place of service with good, real old-fashioned gentry and that I'd get a proper training, but how I longed to be a nursemaid. Then one afternoon, when it was my time off, Mother, who only lived across the road, said, "The new vicar and his wife want a girl to train to help with their baby. Why don't you go and see them." So off I went. I remember I had on a purple skirt and white blouse which had a sailor collar, and I had a white straw hat and my hair in a bun. The lady was young and pretty and chatted to me and said I could come there to the vicarage in one month. The ladies were a little bit angry, really, as I was getting on well, they said. They paid me at the rate of £10 a year but of course bought my dresses, aprons and caps and if I had a cold they gave me cinnamon, which I hated.

Anyhow, I was helping the housekeeper make the beds one morning and I happened to be alone for a while so I picked up the pillow and I stood in front of the long mirror and I held the pillow like it was a baby and the housekeeper came into the room and said, "Little one, little one, what are you doing, dancing with a pillow?" I didn't like to say, "No, I'm pretending I'm holding the baby where I'm going to learn to be a nanny."

I went there on 9th August 1918, which it was the baby's first birthday. The housekeeper there showed me up to the nursery and said, "They are out for their walk and you are to thread ribbons through these little dresses," which I did. Then I saw them coming up the drive, the lady pushing a very big pram and the baby who had fair hair curling and I felt all happy.

At first I only cleaned the nursery and the pram and sort of helped downstairs, then I had to read baby books and watch and learn how to go on and when we were out with the baby I was told I must talk to her and point out interesting things to her. I went on holidays which I would never had had if I'd not been a nursemaid. Then the new baby arrived and I was more and more trusted and then came the day when I was to be called Nanny. Happy me!'

## A NUMBER OF STAFF

'I was employed at Bordean House as third housemaid of three, from 1927 to 1929. A very large staff was employed there – butler and footman, two lady's maids, sewing maid, three kitchen staff, two chauffeurs, and six gardeners including Mr White as head gardener.

Work was very hard in those days, with long hours. We started work at 6.15 am and at 9.30 pm we all had to be in our bedrooms when the butler rang the "bed bell". My salary was £1 a month and my food. Our time off duty was one half day a week, usually starting at 3 pm. On one Sunday morning we had to attend Langrish church, the next Sunday we were off duty from 2.30 pm to 9 pm. When I left in 1929 it was to gain further experience.'

'My two sisters and I were trained as domestic servants at a house in Easton, which kept a staff of ten – Ethel as between maid rising to housemaid, Josephine as scullery maid rising to kitchenmaid and cook, and me as under parlourmaid to the head parlourmaid. The head servants were strict disciplinarians, but we enjoyed good food, free uniforms and outings half a day a week plus a half day on alternate Sundays. We had two weeks unpaid holiday a year, and my wages were £30 a year, paid quarterly.

After four years I moved on to a much larger establishment, with a staff of 30, a much more relaxed and happy place. By then wages had risen to £50 a year. I married in 1935 to a gamekeeper whose wages were £2 a week plus a tied cottage. I missed the comfort of service, but felt good to be free of answering bells.'

146

## THE KITCHENMAID

'At the age of 14, in 1927, following in the footsteps of my older sisters, I went into service as a live-in kitchenmaid in a large house belonging to two elderly sisters, where I earned five shillings a month. The ladies of the house kept the wages and then handed all the money over at once at Christmas. For mornings a blue dress with a white apron had to be worn; for afternoons a black dress and white apron. The staff had to provide their own uniforms.

For the kitchenmaid the day began at six o'clock by lighting the gas lamps. Then the kitchen fire, which had to be cleaned with steel wire first, had to be lit and the cook's breakfast prepared. Next came the preparations for the other breakfasts, cleaning the kitchen, preparing the vegetables, washing dishes – always having to work hard. One half day a week and every other Sunday afternoon was free, but everything had to be cleared up before I was allowed out and staff had to be back by 10 pm. Five members of staff lived in, two upstairs maids, the cook, the pantry maid and the kitchenmaid; someone came in "to do the rough" and to carry in the coal. It was the task of one of the upstairs maids to clean the bedroom hearths, light the fires and carry up the cans of hot water every morning as well as for the hip baths which were placed in the bedrooms. There was little time and even less money to spend on entertainment, but walking along the nearby seafront or shop window gazing was possible, although most free time was spent visiting home.'

## THE GAMEKEEPER AND THE SHOOT

'Before the First World War the Bonham Carter estate at Buriton had six or seven keepers and about 4,000 birds were killed each year. There were also shoots at Ditcham, where the Cades lived, and Chalton on the estate of Major Jarvis, the MP. There was virtually no poaching. It was rabbit poaching because Butser, Wardown and Holt were all rabbit warrens.

There were hundreds of rabbits there. These were shot on Fridays, pheasants on Saturdays. Before they shot they had men stopping the burrows with creosote and tar. It was all downland with gorse patches where the rabbits lay out. One day they killed 800 rabbits on Wardown. They sold them to butchers from Portsmouth at a shilling each. Villagers could buy them for eightpence.

We fed the pheasants oatmeal, barley meal and corn with hard boiled eggs mixed in and minced, boiled, rabbit meat.

There were about eight pheasant shoots a year. We had partridge shoots before the pheasant shoots started. My mother prepared the lunches for the shoots. My father used to go to Petersfield market and buy two pigs. He killed one and used it for the next two shoots and saved the other for the following two.

There were about 18 beaters and ten keepers from neighbouring estates, plus our six keepers who dealt with wounded birds. The 30 or so boys who acted as stops were paid eightpence a day and their food, which was two sausages, bread and mince pies, the sweet sort. A barrel of beer was provided for the beaters.

Colonel Algernon Bonham Carter was very strict about carrying guns correctly and if a man was a bad shot or shot dangerously he was never asked again.

The Colonel did believe in everyone enjoying themselves. He had a cock day for the beaters when he acted as a beater. Also a rabbit day, mostly on Boxing Day, when he would provide the lunch and port. We usually shot between 300 and 400. Finally at the end of the season we had a hare shoot.'

# OTHER WAYS WE MADE A LIVING

**There were of course dozens of other ways we made a living in the past, and these are just a few of those that bring back memories – from the chimney sweep to power boat building, the village shop to aircraft making.**

### VILLAGE TRADES AND CRAFTS

'Many businesses flourished in Highclere in the 1930s, until the changes in agriculture began to take effect. There were blacksmiths and a wheelwright, farm workers, coal merchants and carriers, a haulage contractor, a brickworks, builders, carpenters and under-takers, water diviners and well diggers, a stonemason, a factory producing aircraft parts, musicians, a doctor and a midwife, a garage and a general store, a cobbler, and a post office with a local postman.'

'When girls left school at Abbotts Ann there was little to do but go into service. If they did not have a live-in position they had to walk, often for miles, to be there on duty at 6.30 am. Married women did casual farm work and gathered flints from the fields for road surfacing. It was not until after the Second World War that the roads in the village were tarred.

Some men were estate workers – woodmen, gardeners, game-keepers etc. Others were farm workers, but a large number were employed at the Anna Valley Ironworks. There were also jobs in Andover shops and as carriers. In the early 1930s a builder set up business in the village and began to employ some men. There were two blacksmiths, an undertaker and a cordwainer in the village (the children could earn a penny for taking shoes to the cordwainer!)'

VILLAGE ENTERPRISES

'Many villages owe their fame to one resident or one activity but Hamble has become prominent for at least three ventures and very many famous names. Many of these are commemorated by the names of village roads.

The College of Air Training was the first of its kind in the country. Where pilots were trained and where Bert Hinkler, Amy Johnson and many world-famous names landed, housing developments have sprung up, many echoing the past. Barton Drive, named after the first director, College Close, Astral Gardens, Pegasus Close and others.

C.B. Fry, famous cricketer, athlete and scholar, together with his formidable wife, ran the *Mercury* training ship for boys for nearly 40 years. Newcomers might wonder at "Mercury View" in Satchell Lane, but when these houses were built the residents could see the training ship at her moorings. *Mercury* is commemorated more recently by a housing estate whose roads all have some bearing on the ship or the Fry family. Older residents have many memories of the boys marching through the village on public occasions and the sound of their bugle calls.

Aircraft have been manufactured in Hamble since earliest days. In 1911 the Luke brothers, better known as boat builders, started in a very modest way with a two-seater plane capable of 65 miles an hour. This was a short-lived affair but Fairey Aviation occupied Hamble Point for decades.

The first Englishman to fly, Sir Alliott Verdon Roe, came to Hamble in 1914 and built a factory where many well known aircraft were produced. He not only lived in the village but is buried close to the church. Verdon Avenue is named after him.

Aircraft have been manufactured here, too, since 1936 at British Marine Aircraft, later to be known as Folland Aircraft, then as British Aerospace.

149

British Petroleum celebrated the seventieth year since the construction of the terminal on the Hamble bank of Southampton Water in 1994.

But the general public chiefly associate the name of Hamble with sailing – and sailing of every description from the largest and most dignified yacht to the smallest dinghy. Hamble River Sailing Club was founded in 1919 while the Royal Southern Yacht Club and Royal Air Force Yacht Club transferred from Southampton in 1936 and Calshot in 1951 respectively.

It is strange that aircraft and oil have superseded farming and boatbuilding, both of which flourished within living memory, but such is modern life. Rope Walk, Admiral's Court and Mariners Close bring a whiff of the sea but the only reminder of farming is the very modern name "The Bartletts", in tribute to the large farming family.

The village blacksmith, shoemaker, baker and coal merchant have all vanished from the scene during the past 70 years.'

## THE POWER BOATS

'The Power Boats factory at Hythe during the war was under Scott Pain and had almost everything to build the boats from the raw wood and steel. We had machine shops which made the prop shafts, and we made the propellers; we grooved them to shape and dipped and plated them in a coppersmith's shop. I cannot be really sure but we had the best part of 2,000 people working there, with girls in all departments, about 300 or more and they did a good job.

The working hours were Monday to Friday nine hours a day and on Saturday 8 am till 4 pm. Tucked in the middle of that we would do one all-night stand nearly every week. Not everybody was on nights, only a set number. They were long nights!

My first introduction to the British Power Boats was working a planing machine. This had four thirty-inch blades in the block. Some planer! It was used chiefly for the four inch by three eighths of an inch planking for the boats. After a few months we moved to the "jig shop" or prefab shop. All work in the shop was passed by inspectors. It had to fit in the boat first time. Most of the boats were motor torpedo gunboats or 71′ 6″ × 68′ rescue launches. I had a jig made which was the same camber of the deck, to prefab the wheelhouse and bridge of the 71′ 6″. I have made 30 or 40 for the boats. We made the frames of the boats. They had to be bevelled at different stations to fit into the sweep of the hulls. From the jig shop they went to the frame shop where they were assembled.'

# MY CHIMNEY SWEEP GRANDFATHER

'I remember, and this will date me, when we lived with my chimney sweep grandfather in a terraced house in the Eastney area of Portsmouth.

The front room, only ventured into on special occasions, had a small table just inside the door on which was a large book. Into this went the names and addresses of customers. The regulars knew the procedure – put your hand through the letter box, locate the string, pull it through and there was the key to the front door, open the door and write your request in the book.

From the front door was a long dark passage with two rooms and the stairs on the right before you reached the kitchen. This led to the scullery, and for those of a tender age the scullery was the utility room of yesteryear. The scullery, as well as containing the copper, also housed the gas cooker. The copper was a large metal drum with a gas burner attached under its base. Every day of her married life my grandmother had to fill the copper with water to be heated for the bath. In those days we had zinc baths which were portable. Ours lived in the backyard and was hung on the wall. There was just room for the bath and the copper to be in the scullery at the same time. The hot water had to be transferred to the bath in a galvanised bucket. I don't recall there ever being an accident but I suppose my grandmother had plenty of practice filling and emptying the buckets every day.

As well as the daily bath the sooty clothes had to be washed. But there were no quick drying, easycare fabrics in those days. Thick cotton shirts and underwear were all heavy with soot. After the washing the clothes were wrung by hand to extract enough water so they could be taken into the backyard to be squeezed by the big wooden rollers of the mangle. In the dead of winter this was a thankless task. The clothes were pegged out to dry and were brought in at night as stiff as boards to be hung in front of the dying embers of the fire to finish drying.

My grandfather came from a long line of chimney sweeps dating back to the 17th century. In those far off days it was a very lucrative business as all buildings had fireplaces.

When my dad was a small boy he and his brother were expected to help in the store. This enormous store, or so it seemed to a small boy, was piled high with soot. Dad and his brother had to sift out the pieces of brick and cement and shovel the soot into sacks. Every spring a local farmer would collect the soot to spread out on his fields.

Dad recalls vividly the tragic night that a fire destroyed the stable and the horses perished. The stable had housed about six horses which belonged to the local baker, greengrocer and my grandfather. For these tradesmen it was their living destroyed because there were no insurance policies to cover such losses. During the following weeks there would often be the rattle of the letterbox and on the mat would be an envelope containing money. Maybe just a few pennies from a nearby household or maybe £5 from a grateful hotelier with whom my grandfather had a contract.

Grandfather didn't quit and for the rest of his working life he pulled and pushed his cart round Portsmouth laden, by the end of the day, with soot.

I can still smell and taste the soot as I recall these memories. My grandparents, especially my grandmother, had a life of drudgery which would defeat many of us today, but, at least they could leave the key safely in the front door.'

## THE VILLAGE SHOP

'My family and I came to Lindford stores in September of 1955, as owners of a really typical village shop. It was a large Victorian building that gave us three large bedrooms, sitting-room and dining-room, and a kitchen added as an afterthought from the previous cooking arrangements of "a pot hanging over an open fireplace" in the dining-room. Facilities in the kitchen were few, an ancient Aga cooker and a low-set earthenware sink with just a cold tap – these to back up the workers in the shop.

Entering the shop through the single door, to my "modern" eye, one encountered the dark drabness of the original village general store, but what an abundance of varied stock we held. We boasted a post office counter where locals came for their pensions, allowances and suchlike as were available in those years. From the post office counter ran a white marble topped counter from where we served from the many drawers, cupboards, and jars that ranged on shelves all around the shop. The drawers, three deep, stood along one side, mounted by shallow shelves with display stock, such as candles, matches, oil lamps, wicks. Blue paper bags of sugar which we weighed up ourselves, stood beside packets of biscuits and tea, whilst hidden away in the depths of the drawers were mouse traps, reels of cotton, needles, pins, so many accessories that I do not think we ever knew just what we really sold. On the very top of these shelves were large tin containers, dark green, lettered in gold, with the types of tea, eg Ceylon, China, though all were empty now and were relics of yesteryear. Bacon, butter and other fats were sold from a glass cabinet; how health authorities would cringe at the sight

152

of this unit! A wide selection of jars of sweets, sold by the quarter, and weighed in our early days into twists of paper to make a conical bag, formed a busy section of a bustling little shop. We sold a vast amount of paraffin for many people in the village used it in stoves for heating their houses and for cooking as well, but we did have a very large fridge which held our stock of bacon and fats for stocking the glass cabinet in the shop.

Our customers were all local villagers and did most of their shopping in our shop and one other similar in Lindford; the older customers would collect their pensions then shop for all their needs, there was no need to look further than the stores apart from clothes and hardware. Anyone with more than they could carry would have their shopping boxed up and delivered by my husband in his van. Many people came with their cars and we had a wonderfully friendly existence with our customers. Coughs, colds, corns, sprains and the like could all be relieved with some preparation we had on the shelf. In a very short time we learned of most of the backgrounds and needs of our local people and consequently the shelves took on more stock to cater for their wants.

The previous owners had also been bakers and to accommodate their trade they had a large bakehouse in the garden where during their long working life the bakers had coal delivered to keep the ovens going. Flour was delivered into the loft of the bakehouse and the large airy room was a place of extreme activity, not only baking bread for the shop but for a wide delivery area, and also many luscious cakes. We were not bakers and the disused bakery was eventually pulled down. Trading in those early days was good, without the cut-throat competition we had during later years.'

## THE BUTCHER'S SHOP

'One of the most important and enduring influences in my life was the butcher's shop. As well as the shop in Odiham my father owned four others, in Fleet, Hook, Crondall and Hartley Wintney. All the slaughtering for the five shops was done at Odiham and at any one time we would have six to seven full time staff at Odiham, including errand boys. Sheep were kept in our orchard prior to slaughter and as a child I was allowed to help move them. The drover, a man called "Dukie" Cowdrey, was a real character who persistently said things backwards, much to my amusement. He had won the military medal in the First World War.

I can remember quarters of beef hanging on the veranda outside the shop, summer and winter. Especially dramatic were the Christmas displays, turkeys and geese hanging on the wall above the veranda and trestles covered with straw outside the shop, full of all kinds of game. Inside the shop meat was sold at one side whilst the other side was an off-licence. People would always buy meat by weight, not price, as often happens today. A horse and cart was kept to make deliveries.

Work in the shop started at 6 am and on most weekdays finished about 6 pm but on Fridays and Saturdays we wouldn't finish until 9 pm.

Refrigeration was in its infancy. To keep meat cool we had a sealed room. Here the walls were packed with sawdust for insulation and we had three galvanised tanks which we prepared in the following way. The tanks were first drained of the previous brine, then for each tank a two hundredweight slab of ice was chopped and to this was added a 56 pound bag of freezing salt. The tanks were then placed in the cold room. This process was repeated every Tuesday, Thursday and Saturday. The ice came from the Aldershot Ice Co or the Reading Ice and Cold Storage Co. The shop had its own water supply which was used until about 1932. There was a well in the large cellar under the shop. The temperature in the cellar stayed at about 45°F summer and winter. The water from the well was pumped by a gas engine to storage tanks in the roof, from where it was used for domestic purposes as well as for the shop and slaughterhouse.

Work was hard, with long hours, but it did have its lighter moments. Not long after leaving school and starting work I was asked to kill and prepare the guinea fowl. An errand boy was deputised to help me but unfortunately he was careless when opening the cage door and all the birds flew off. We gave chase as far as the cemetery, and having the foresight to take our guns, the day was saved!'

EASTER AT THE BAKERY

'At Easter time we all had to mind our Ps and Qs as the bakers were very overworked and tired and short-tempered. They baked bread on the Thursday before Good Friday, double the normal as they didn't bake on Good Friday, but they had to work all night on the Thursday to produce the hot cross buns for early Friday delivery. These trays of buns were placed along the passage which ran through the house. A few buns can smell lovely and spicy but with the fragrance from trays of hot cross buns wafting into our bedrooms all night, together with all the noise, we never had much sleep. I had to get up and bag up the orders and deliver them very early on my bicycle. Friday night the bakers had to come back and make the dough (double again) for the Saturday bread as there was no delivery on Easter Monday. By the time it got to Easter morning

154

and we had an Easter egg or two and went to church and sang the Easter hymns, life seemed more normal after the hard work of the weekend.'

## AT THE POST OFFICE

'In 1915 I was employed as an office girl at the Head Telegraph Office in Southampton, overlooking the Old Docks. We saw soldiers marching to troop ships to embark for France, and later endless hospital trains returning with the wounded. I shall always remember these two contrasting sides to the Great War.

Then I became more ambitious and obtained permission to teach myself telegraphy; which meant after an eight-hour day staying behind an hour to learn the Morse code and to make myself proficient on the key. At that time most telegrams were sent and received in Morse and, when received, written in longhand ready for delivery. When the man I replaced returned from the war in 1920 I worked for a year in the telephone room but was then offered a staff vacancy in Bishop's Waltham which was then a salaried sub-office.

Arriving in Bishop's Waltham my lodging was with a Mrs Cobbett in Bank Street; her late husband was a descendant of William Cobbett, the author of *Rural Rides*. There were also three Miss Cobbetts who ran a school in Free Street; the school fee was sixpence per week for each pupil!

Bishop's Waltham post office exterior was just as it is today but then it contained not only the postal counter but also a 31-manual telephone exchange, a Morse key, and the only public call box, with the Labour Exchange upstairs. As counter clerk for eight hours each day I dealt with all postal, banking and pension matters and also ran the call box and telephone exchange, though not the Labour Exchange!

The books were balanced after 7 pm each evening although this was not so easy on Saturdays when the Salvation Army played in the Square. I never recall having time for coffee although we did have half an hour for lunch. The office was open from 8 am until 7 pm on weekdays and 9 to 10.30 am on Sundays for stamps and telegrams. The busiest time was Christmas with unwrapped, none too fresh, pheasants going through.

An important part of the work was licences, not only cars but also for dogs, armorial bearings and menservınts, all of which were applied for together on the same form! Female servants were tax free.

All the post would arrive from Southampton at 5 am each day. This was then sorted in the office behind the post office, and postmen

155

from surrounding villages as far afield as Droxford would collect the mail to deliver to their particular area.

At weekends I went home to Southampton and the train driver would wait for me when he saw me running round the millpond (now a road) to Bishop's Waltham station, which is now a roundabout. I would travel to Botley along a now non-existent railway and change there for Eastleigh and then change again for Southampton; 90 minutes for nine miles.

So much is gone from Bishop's Waltham but the post office is still there.'

## THE DOORSTEP DELIVERY

'The milkman and his family lived on a farm on the outer edge of Lindford village. In their early days they kept a dairy herd, milked the cows and delivered around the village by way of horse and flat-backed cart loaded with churns of milk, ladled out with pint measured jugs. This was a daily ritual and when we first saw the milkman on his rounds he was already a very old man. So regular was his routine that his equally old horse would stop and start without any command, taking time to amble along the road, stop whilst the milkman delivered his pints, then on again until the whole delivery was completed.

Mr Souter, the milkman, was a slightly built man but obviously tough. He wore a flat cap, always a check shirt, and riding breeches tucked into leather gaiters, and in winter he wore a warm jacket. He was always on time, probably due to the regular pace of the old horse, but in those almost timeless days this was not unusual.

Some time after we came to live in Lindford, bottled milk became the accepted way of delivery and the whole process was changed. Milk was collected in churns from the farm daily, taken to a depot, pasteurised, bottled and eventually milk deliveries were made back to the farm in crates. The crates were loaded on to the flat back of the cart and then milkman and horse made their way around the village leaving their bottles instead of jugs of delicious fresh, creamy milk. There was time to live in those days rather than the rush of today.'

'When I was a boy in the 1920s we lived in the newly built garden suburb of Bitterne Park, right on the edge of Southampton, adjoining open country. Our house in Manor Farm Road looked out on to water meadows grazed by Lord Swaythling's cattle.

Our milkman, Reg Saunders, had a small dairy and stable in the adjoining Dimond Road. Reg's brother delivered milk in a hand cart, calling out the traditional "Milko!" as he went. Reg served the more

*The milkmen of Eastleigh Dairies in the 1920s, showing the churn and the measures used to fill customers' jugs at the door.*

distant customers from his horse-drawn milk float. Both hand cart and float carried a milk churn from which metal pails with lids were filled for delivery to the various houses. This was in the days before milk bottles, let alone pasteurisation, and each household left out a jug covered with a muslin cloth for the milk to be ladled into with a metal measure, three of which were carried on the milk cart: half pint, pint and quart.

As the milk was not pasteurised it went sour very quickly and two deliveries a day were necessary. Reg drove his pony and float twice a day to Swaythling Farm, at the junction of Wide Lane and Mansbridge Road, to collect the milk once after the morning's milking and once after the afternoon's. In the summer my mother would scald the milk to try to prevent it souring.

Round about 1930 a revolution occurred: Mr Edmunds who farmed at Benhams Farm, Midanbury, started delivering milk in bottles – wider topped than today's with cardboard caps. We changed milkman: no more jugs to be put out.

Some time later Mr Edmunds obtained "accredited" status for his milk – a precursor of the Tuberculin Tested designation. This guaranteed a minimum standard of hygiene and bacterial content. His milk bottles had to be covered with a paper cap over the lip and sealed. This "Grade A" milk kept better but milk was still delivered twice a day right up to the war. By this time however, pasteurisation had become the norm and the twice daily delivery was no longer necessary.

By now Benhams Farm was no longer a farm. The cows had been sold; the land built over. Only the buildings remained as a milk depot for Alfred Brown's dairies and to provide stabling for the fleet of horse-drawn floats which remained until well after the war.'

'When I took over a small milk delivery business at East Woodhay in 1947 the milk was rationed – at times to only two pints per person per week. The milk was taken round the village in a churn in the back of a van, from which it was transferred to a lidded bucket which was taken to the customer's door, a standard half or one pint measure being used to ladle out the required amount into her personal jug.

I still smile when I recall one frosty morning – a lady came out of her house with a jug in each hand and on descending the steps towards me she slipped on the ice, fell and dropped both jugs which shattered to pieces. I felt concerned for the lady but her only exclamation was, "Oh, my poor jugs!"

As soon as I could after taking over the round I changed to the use of bottles. I collected milk from local farms twice a day and sometimes if supplies ran short made two deliveries. I had no refrigeration and the milk was not pasteurised (most customers preferred it that way!) As funds allowed I bought machines to help speed up the washing up and bottling.

It was most difficult to get delivery vehicles. Although the war was over there was not much available on the home market and my vans were always in need of repair. A good local garage was always ready to help. I actually waited over three years for the delivery of a new van.

Frosty weather brought problems – driving and walking on icy roads was extremely hazardous because the roads were not treated then.

I was fortunate to have supplies from good local farms and when the owner of the Guernsey herd began charging the premium to which he was entitled I wondered if my customers would be willing to pay another penny per pint. I need not have worried – most customers wanted rich creamy milk and were only too pleased to pay the extra penny. How times have changed!'

'Jim was apprenticed as a gentleman's outfitter to H. W. Collett, General Draper and Outfitter, Commerce House, Odiham on 24th April 1913. At that time Collett's occupied the whole of Commerce House and there was an inter-communicating doorway linking the two shops inside. The right hand side was the gentleman's outfitters where Charlie Hiscock was in charge. A ready-made suit could be bought for 15 shillings and sixpence, or for 30 shillings one could be measured and have a suit tailored by Gerrish, Ames and Simpkins in Basingstoke. Collett's were also the suppliers to the Robert Mays grammar school of red with yellow striped caps and ties. The left hand side sold a miscellany of merchandise – ribbons, lace, buttons and general haberdashery.

The stock included ladies' and children's ready-to-wear clothes – hats, shoes and slippers, socks and stockings, corsetry and dress material by the yard. Also blankets, coconut mats, bales of cloth including damask (to be made up into tablecloths). American cloth was a good sales line, as most cottagers used this daily as a tablecloth. Bales of sheeting – both bleached and unbleached for making into sheets. (Ready-made sheets and tablecloths were not available then.)

Against the wall in the right hand corner of the shop was a wooden cash desk. Lifting the lid revealed a wooden tray with hollowed out sections for the various coins. All assistants took cash and were required to give a receipt for each purchase even if it were only sixpence. The duplicates were filed in a Lamson Paragon folder and checked by Mr or Mrs Collett. Mr Collett was a good employer. He was a kind man, never lost his temper or became agitated. He would expect the staff to keep doing something when he was about, if only to dust the shoe boxes or straighten out the clothing fixtures. He would always expect them to be punctual at opening times, but not too anxious when closing time came. He served in the shop when required and always attended to special customers. Travellers called at regular intervals or by appointment producing samples or catalogues of their wares. Occasionally Mr and Mrs Collett went to London by train on Wednesdays to visit the wholesale warehouses.

Facing the door was a fixture used for displaying the latest fashions. This partially screened the area at the top of the still existing steps. Here was the Millinery Department where the latest styles could be fashioned to order. This was Mrs Collett's domain with her assistant Miss Jackson and, apart from choosing a hat, it was to here that Miss Boylett was summoned to measure lady customers for corsets and their dressmaking requirements. Miss Boylett was the Head Dressmaker and she and her staff of five girls made suits, coats, dresses, skirts and blouses in the workrooms upstairs behind the shop in what is now a separate cottage.

Miss Alice Goulding was employed as cook/housekeeper. She, Miss Jackson, Miss Boylett and Bob Culver the coachman all lived on the premises and slept in the bedrooms on the top floor of Commerce House.

Jim's days were long. He walked to the shop from his home at Whitehall but eventually saved enough money to buy a bicycle. From Monday to Friday the shop was open from 8 am to 8 pm, with Wednesday early closing. Saturday was even longer and Mr Collett would send Jim along the High Street about 10 pm to see if Monks were closed: while the butcher was open there was always a possibility of further trade. Shops did not close at lunch-time either. Jim was given a cooked lunch in the dining-room below the dressmaking rooms and in the afternoon a cup of tea and bread and butter, or a piece of cake. On Saturday evening if the shop wasn't too busy he would be given a break about 9 pm to go and have a cup of cocoa and a piece of jam tart in the kitchen behind the shop.

As well as serving in the shop his duties included sweeping, dusting and tidying the shop, and cleaning the windows. Every morning he put out a display of trousers, hats and hobnail boots in the entrance to, and outside, the gent's outfitting department. He also measured out the lino to customers' requirements. The lino was kept chained to racks in the archway which at that time had large wooden gates which were locked at night.

Merchandise arrived by rail at Winchfield and was delivered to the shop by the London & South Western horse-drawn waggon. The bleached and unbleached sheeting arrived wrapped in hessian which was stitched all round the sides with string in a looped-over stitch. Jim had to painstakingly unpick the string and save it for use in the shop. The hessian was then folded, the label reversed and readdressed to the sender. The sheeting then had to be rolled on to a wooden reel to make a bale for display in the shop.

Collett's also supplied all drapery requirements for funerals. When a made-to-measure gent's mourning order was received, Jim was dispatched to Chappels to hire a bicycle. He then pedalled to Basingstoke to give the order to John Mares in New Street since there was no telephone at Collett's at that time.

Collett's served all the surrounding villages. Through the archway and behind Commerce House there were stables and a hayloft and across the cobbled yard a coachhouse.

Bob Culver was the stable lad and coachman and he was responsible for looking after the two horses – Brig and Tommy. He also had to maintain the water supply to the kitchen. There was a storage tank over the sink in the coach-house and every morning Bob pumped water from the still existing well in the courtyard to fill it. The water then went under the courtyard in a lead pipe to a pump over the sink in the kitchen. Next to the sink in the coach-house was a two-seated privy – Odiham did not have main drainage or electricity at that time. Outside gas lamps illuminated the shop windows.

Three times a week Jim accompanied by Bob drove around the villages. The back of the trap drawn by Brig was filled with all the items ordered the previous week by customers when they visited the shop. Any space was filled with items which might sell well. Customers paid upwards of sixpence a week towards payment of the items they had already received. The customers that paid up promptly were tempted to purchase further goods before they had finished paying off existing items. These rounds took most of the day and Jim was given a tin containing sandwiches to sustain him.

Mr Collett did rounds with the trap drawn by Tommy – a lively two-year-old – on Mondays to Rye Common, Crookham, Dogmersfield etc and on Friday as far as Herriard.

After the outbreak of war in 1914 life at the draper's shop, as everywhere else, began to change. Charlie Hiscock was called up. This meant a rise for Jim. His seven shillings and sixpence a week was augmented by a commission of sixpence in the pound on his sales on his rounds. Then the army came to Odiham requisitioning horses and Tommy went to play his part. This prompted Mr Collett to buy a motor car to do his rounds and he was one of the first people in Odiham to acquire this new-fangled machine. The car was a Swift – a green open tourer with a shamrock on the bonnet – bought from the agents Chappels.

Then in October 1917 Jim too was called up, which began the second part of his varied and interesting career. Although his apprenticeship had been for five years, after demobilisation Jim could not face returning to Collett's. Mr Collett was very understanding and gave him a golden sovereign and a good reference.'

## TYRRELL AND GREEN

'In 1931 I left school at the age of 14 having always been good at crafts, needlework and arithmetic. I was fortunate to be recommended for an interview with Mrs Green of Tyrrell and Green in Southampton, and I was taken on to do a five year apprenticeship in the gown workroom. This was when Tyrrell and Green was a family

161

business, and both Mr and Mrs Green were often to be seen in the building.

We apprentices wore navy blue dresses and white aprons and we always worked with a qualified hand until we were fully qualified ourselves. We started with simple tasks and worked our way up to the fine stitching, tucking and beading and all the intricacies that went into the making of the very beautiful gowns of every description including wedding dresses. We worked from 8.30 am to 6 pm.

The workroom was very basic, containing large tables covered with a kind of dark coloured linoleum, treadle sewing machines and ironing tables. The irons were clipped onto the wall, there were no flexes to fall over. We never made a gown ourselves until we were qualified.

In those days the shop mostly catered for the upper class county customers who had accounts (this was unheard of for the general public). These account holders could have clothes sent to their own homes on approval.

When customers came to the shop, they were greeted by shop walkers – men in morning suits – who would usher them to the department they needed and they would sit whilst being served.

The Barova Restaurant was situated at the end of the building and had its own entrance. A uniformed gentleman would open car doors, often chauffeur driven. No parking problems, very few people had their own cars.

Later in the 1930s the shop was sold to John Barker and then, still in the 1930s to John Lewis who extended the building to include different departments. The shop was bombed in the early part of the Second World War. They took on a small shop near the Bargate and another very small one in Winchester behind the Buttercross.'

THE DOCTOR'S SURGERY

'Before the National Health Service started in 1948 doctors had their own dispensaries at their surgeries where most of the medicines prescribed for their patients were prepared by dispensing assistants. These were women who had trained in pharmacy to a recognised standard and passed an examination at the Society of Apothecaries in London. In practice the duties involved a good deal more than dispensing. One was expected to test urine and blood samples for a diversity of medical conditions; deal with accidents and emergencies when the doctors were out of the surgery; sterilise instruments and assist at minor operations. Book-keeping, filing, wages and general clerical work not to mention typing, were all part of the job.

Additionally it helped if one could unblock drains, smooth ruffled feathers and make a good cup of tea.

I was employed as dispenser/book-keeper in a partnership of four doctors whose practice was centred at Elingfield, Totton and spread in a broad strip from Ower in the north and Redbridge down the entire western side of Southampton Water to Calshot and Lepe. It included many of the adjacent New Forest villages, farms and gipsy encampments.

The surgery in the High Street was in one of the oldest houses in the village complete with its own ghost. The building had been divided into four consulting rooms, waiting room and dispensary on the ground floor. Upstairs was a spacious flat occupied by the junior partner and his young family.

The dispensary was, in fact, little more than a partitioned-off cubby-hole lined from floor to ceiling with shelf upon shelf of bottles, jars and packets of all shapes, sizes and colours. Dozens of Winchesters containing bulk liquids encroached on the floor space beneath. The working surfaces were little less cluttered. The minute dispensing bench was topped with an off-cut of ancient, brown patterned linoleum on which stood an antique set of apothecary's scales. Next to this a bunsen burner hissed under a heavily furred tin kettle which steamed on a tripod throughout every surgery, its contents used from time to time for cleaning syringes and making tea. As a gesture to modernisation a new, deep, white porcelain kitchen sink had been installed in the corner. This together with the bunsen burner was the focal point of the laboratory facilities. In another corner at the other end of the dispensing bench was an old wooden desk top bearing the Day Book at which the doctors

stood to enter every visit and consultation they made throughout the day. Prescriptions were also recorded in this book. They were then dispensed and handed to the patient. However, if they were to be collected later following a home visit, each item would be carefully wrapped in white paper, sealed with sealing wax and left outside the surgery door on a shelf in the porch.

All entries in the Day Book were transferred to the accounts ledgers and bills were sent out monthly or quarterly according to the amount of treatment received or the reliability of the patient to pay. Preparing the hand-written bills was a mammoth task and took hours of work after surgery hours. Consultations cost three shillings and sixpence to five shillings, often including any medicine that was prescribed. Home visits were from seven and sixpence to ten shillings. The charge for a confinement was from £10 to £20, depending on the family's status, which included attendance at the delivery and ante and post natal care. The level of charge for all treatment was always geared to the patient's ability to pay.

I joined the surgery in 1947, nine months before the Health Service started. Most drugs in those days were plant or mineral based and given time, worked. Sulpha drugs which had been of such great benefit to the troops in the war were also making an impact in civilian medicine. Penicillin would shortly follow but when it did the substance was so unstable that it could only be given by injection from crystals that were dissolved with sterile water at the time of use. Most of the prescriptions we dispensed were for indigestion and coughs. Tonics for general debility were popular and worked by stimulating the appetite. But a high proportion of patients suffered from stomach ulcers, TB, bronchitis and rheumatism due to bad living conditions. That applied to all classes of society. Houses were inadequately heated and the cold and dampness took its toll. Heavy smoking amongst the population did not help either.

For a number of years after the war, bottles were a problem. Fortunately we had a ready supply of recyclable ones from the dozens that were brought in each week containing urine samples for testing. They were mostly ketchup bottles which after sterilising were used for dispensing lotions. I think those patients who used old medicine bottles might not have done so had they realised how the system worked. Quantity was a matter of pride for some. The patient who filled a whisky bottle to the stopper may have been surprised to learn that it was stolen from the back seat of the doctor's car while he visited another patient. Though perhaps not as surprised as the thief. Whisky was in very short supply at the time.

There were two surgeries a day – Monday to Friday 8.30 am to 10.30 am and 5.30 pm to 7.30 pm. A morning surgery only was held on Saturdays. There was no appointment system. There was no need for one. The well off were seen at home and the rest could not afford the privilege. However, with the introduction of the National Health Service the two hour surgeries extended into sessions lasting up to four hours or more. Eventually two assistant doctors were added to the practice to help with the heavy workload.

The waiting room seated 15 to 18 people on straight-backed wooden chairs ranged around the walls. A low wooden bench ran up the middle of the room bearing a vast selection of mutilated magazines. There was just enough room to pick one's way through the jungle of feet either side of it. When all available seating accommodation was filled people stood wherever possible inside and the less fortunate queued outside in the cold. An elderly portable gas fire gasped out heat when required but comfort was not encouraged. The doctors felt that if the waiting room was made too comfortable even more people would come.

Among our patients were a number of New Forest gipsy families who lived out in the open forest in tarpaulin tents. They all had the same two or three surnames and often shared the same Christian names. As none of them could read or write and could only make their mark with a shaky cross, it caused no end of confusion in our filing system. On the rare occasions that gipsies came to the surgery they tended to get priority treatment. As soon as they left all the doors and windows had to be thrown open to ventilate the place. But I had great admiration for the womenfolk. They lived hard lives and never bothered a doctor unless it was absolutely essential, usually because of a sick child. They were always very polite and grateful for anything that was done for them. And they never forgot a kindness.

Minor operations such as the removal of cysts, teeth and tonsils were routinely performed in the surgery under anaesthetic when necessary. The opening of an abscess was a frequent occurrence. Personal hygiene was minimal and septic foci were commonplace as a result. Before the use of penicillin, the gathering would be lanced and drained to remove the accumulation of pus. The wound would then be dressed daily and cleaned with antiseptics until healed.

Disposable hypodermic syringes and needles were unheard of. Syringes were made of pyrex glass with metal fittings and could last a doctor years. Needles were used over and over again and only replaced when they became blunt and painful for the patient. They and all surgical instruments were sterilised by boiling in a pan of water.

The senior partner in the practice, Dr George Habgood, was also Medical Officer of Health for the New Forest. This was a part-time appointment and much of the routine non-medical work was done by Commander Brown, the Chief Sanitary Inspector of the New Forest District Council. However, Dr Habgood was responsible for smallpox vaccinations and diphtheria immunisation in the area. Regular clinics were held and detailed records kept in an official register. There were serious epidemics of poliomyelitis from time to time. These together with outbreaks of food poisoning and dysentery which mercifully were less frequent, necessitated extensive investigation to trace the source of infection and to isolate contacts. Appropriate samples would be brought to the surgery which I would then have to take to the Path lab at the Royal South Hants Hospital in Southampton on my bicycle, a round trip of about 15 miles.

Dr Habgood was also factory doctor for the district. This meant that if there was a serious accident at any of the local works he would be called to attend the casualties. However, if the patient could stand he would be brought to the surgery, usually at a time when all the doctors were out on their rounds. This was a situation the dispenser was expected to deal with. I quickly learned to get all the background details of the accident before uncovering the wound. That way I was at least partly prepared for some of the dreadful injuries I found.

There were no bleepers or mobile phones and contact with a doctor on his rounds could only be made by ringing round those few patients who had telephones. It was a problem and I always felt very badly if a patient died before I could locate a doctor. But as one of the doctors said to me, "If the patient is that near to death there is nothing I could do anyway." How different from the modern emergency response system and resuscitation techniques of today.

I left the practice to get married in 1952 at a time when the new wonder drugs called antibiotics were just coming into use. They were used very sparingly in life or death situations only. The move from organic to chemical compounds was rapidly changing the whole face of medicine. But the National Health Service was well established despite the initial suspicion and dislike of it by many doctors when it was first introduced.'

WORKING FOR THE GAS COMPANY

'I left Odiham grammar school when I was nearly 15 years old. I wanted to learn a trade and a vacancy for an apprentice fitter had occurred at the Gas Company.

In 1910 the Aldershot Gas, Water and District Lighting Company took over the Odiham Gas Company which had started in the London Road in 1847. Subsequently, a booster station was built in Fleet and the gasholder and works were removed from the London

Road site and replaced by a small showroom and workshop. Here I started work on 19th November 1921 at, I believe, ten shillings a week. The place was staffed by a resident inspector, a fitter apprentice and one casual labourer. I spent the first hour each day cleaning and polishing the showroom and then assisted the fitter on the district. We rode our own bicycles, for which we were paid a shilling, later increased to one shilling and sixpence per week. A fitter had to provide his own tools so I saved one shilling a week and bought them one at a time.

In 1922–23 we had the job of refitting the street lamps which had been taken down and stored in the workshop for the duration of the First World War. Most of the lampposts were still in position, but had to be painted and the lanterns reglazed and replaced where necessary. The lamps were originally fitted with upright burners, which had a long mantle suspended on a porcelain fork. The new ones had two inverted mantles and a super-heater, and they also had pilot lights which saved having to carry a torch around.

When the work was completed, the parish council wanted a lamplighter and I was asked to take it on at twelve shillings and sixpence a week, which I gladly did as it nearly doubled my wages! It was quite a tie to light the 27 lamps at half an hour after sunset and then to return to extinguish them at 10.15 pm every night, except for a short time in the summer. I used to cycle around with a stick which had a hook in the end to pull on the lamp. The snag came on a rough night when some of the pilot lights would be out. This meant standing on your bike and fitting a climbing iron around the lamppost and lighting the burner with a match. The town was well lit as some of the businesses had large outside lamps which were alight until nine or ten o'clock.

After two or three years, another apprentice, Leo Bradford, was started and we shared the lamplighting on alternate weeks. We cleaned the lamps in the company's time, which was charged to the parish council, but when the latter became short of money we were told to clean them in our own time, which we did on Saturday afternoons. This must have been the answer to inflation in the 1920s?

I can still remember the position of all the lamps starting from Western Cross through the High Street to the bottom of London Road to the canal bridge, and there were seven in The Bury and Stoney Alley, the latter being better lit than today.

In 1927 we laid gas on to Greywell. All the small houses were fitted for three lights and a cooker. This was carried out free of charge and included a pre-payment meter; the customers having to buy burners, globes and mantles at three shillings and ninepence each. Transport was scarce in those days, so we kept a few cookers in store and if an urgent case arose we would load tools and cooker on to a handcart and take it out and fit it, sometimes as far as Hook which would take up half a day. We had no tarmac for reinstating trenches, but had to make our own by mixing hot tar with granite chippings in the yard and taking it to the site on the truck.

I moved to Hartley Wintney as fitter in 1928 and in 1929 to Aldershot on maintenance.'

# WAR & PEACE

# THE GREAT WAR 1914–1918

**The First World War has left vivid memories for those who were children then, of rationing and shortages, Zeppelin raids and wounded soldiers, and most abidingly of all, of the sorrow brought to so many homes then and for so many years afterwards.**

## WHEN THE WAR BEGAN

'When the Great War began in 1914 the riverside village of Bursledon was a very quiet place. The shipbuilding industry ceased when the wooden men o'war were no longer needed by the navy, and strawberry growing had become the principal occupation. The lanes were free of traffic except for the occasional horse-drawn vehicle. Our house in an old orchard had no gas or electricity or piped water, but a deep well. We had paraffin lamps, a kitchen range which burned coal, and fireplaces which consumed logs. We had vegetables and many kinds of fruit. The shop/post office delivered groceries, and bread, milk and meat arrived at the door. We went by train to Southampton for special purchases and clothes. Our doctor came four miles by pony and trap when called, and a travelling chemist on a tricycle (like the later "Stop me and buy one" ice-cream salesmen) had a box of remedies. He wore a bowler hat. Tuberculosis was incurable, and pneumonia a killer with no drugs to treat it.

The young men went to war, and older men and some women into factories. Three of my mother's brothers were in France; one was killed on the Somme at 21. My father, in the Royal Naval Air Service, was at Calshot, the seaplane base. One of our neighbours, an RAMC doctor, walked daily to Netley hospital through the woods and fields, but he was killed soon after going to France, leaving a young wife and three small children. There were many such tragedies. I remember the men in hospital blue at Netley, some on crutches and some with empty sleeves. It was a terrible war. The rector called regularly on his parishioners who needed comfort as the death toll rose.'

## I WAS AT SCHOOL IN PORTSMOUTH

'It was during the First World War that I was attending a local school in Portsmouth. In those days a school had three sections – one for the infants and that was at the far end of the area. The big block had two storeys, the top one for the girls and the ground floor for the boys, ages seven to 14. Boys and girls were well separated in those days and they took it for granted. The boys had men teachers only and followed suitable subjects, while the girls were taught by women teachers for their appropriate lessons.

I enjoyed most lessons but especially cookery. My mother was very amused when I took home samples of custard with half water, and cakes with half butter and many other queer recipes introduced in war time.

We played netball after school hours and did strict drill for half an hour once a week, in the playground if dry.

At that time there were no bomb warnings in our area but London was the target, as my cousins soon realised. However, I did see a Zeppelin one night when my parents lifted me out of bed to gaze at the long silver cigar-shaped airship with a halo of bright lights sent up by sailors in the dockyard. No damage was done and the Zeppelin departed unharmed.

One school nearby had been made into a military hospital. We saw the trains bringing in the wounded soldiers and we felt very sad. At school every Friday we collected lovely apples in our waste-paper baskets and the best behaved girls carried them to the hospital and were allowed to take them to the wards.

After the war was over the hospital was returned to its former state and opened in 1919 and I became a student there. I often remembered how we used to hear the band passing our old school playing the Dead March as another soldier was being taken to the cemetery. It happened so often.

Rationing was introduced during that war and people had to be very quick and careful to queue at the shops as soon as they heard the food was there. Sometimes my mother sent me to the butcher's at 6 am to queue while she gave Dad his breakfast before he went to work. Then she came round and took my place while I went home to have my breakfast before going to school. A friend and I travelled round the town on Saturdays to try to get biscuits or jam or any other luxury we could find. Sometimes we were lucky.

What rejoicings we had when all the strife was done, and we were at peace once more. On 11th November at 11 am we all rushed home from school, full of joy that war was over at last.'

## PRISONERS AND RATIONING

'At the outbreak of the war everything at Hambledon changed. The young men were called up and the army officers came round to the farms and businesses and requisitioned many of the horses. Women took the places of the men who were called up both on the land and in business, food was severely rationed and every available piece of ground was used to grow food. Many ladies volunteered as nurses at the new military hospital which had just opened at Cosham, the Queen Alexandra.

In time German prisoners were brought over and they worked on the farms under supervision. The winter evenings were spent knitting socks, gloves and balaclavas in khaki for the troops and in general "keeping the home fires burning". No blackout or air raids then but we did see the first German Zeppelin that came over, lit up with searchlights and the guns firing at it. There was also great excitement when the first aeroplanes flew over and everyone stopped to look at them. War Savings were started at the school and we bought sixpenny stamps each week; a certificate was 15 shillings and sixpence which became £1 after five years. A soup kitchen was opened for the school children and for twopence one had a bowl of vegetable soup and a bowl of milk pudding. The wounded began to return home, many having lost a limb and had to be retrained for suitable work.

Autumn afternoons the schoolchildren were given time off lessons and the girls had to gather blackberries to make jam for the troops and the boys gathered horse chestnuts (conkers) which were used in some way for the war effort. After four years came the Armistice and then Peace Day and counting the cost. There were celebrations but for many, many years after, on 11th November everything and everyone stopped for two minutes at eleven o'clock to remember those who died and were maimed for their country.'

VIVID MEMORIES

'Park Prewett hospital in Sherborne St John, newly built as a mental hospital, was taken over by the Canadians for the care of their wounded. My mother, in order to supplement her army allowance, did washing for the nursing sisters. This meant a long walk every week to the hospital with me in my high black pram, covered with layers of stiff, starched aprons and caps, all pleated! At the hospital I well remember large galvanised baths filled with apricots, and seeing a sister in bed wearing a black nightgown! There were many men in hospital blue, and one day two gave me half crowns, one for each hand – a lot of money by today's standards.'

'I was eight when the war began. A large house in Rowledge (now Frensham Heights school) was loaned as a hospital and convoys of wounded soldiers would arrive there. Rowledge lies between Aldershot and Bordon Camp and we children used to go to the main road to watch the soldiers marching, bands playing, from one to the other. The rations for Bordon were collected from Aldershot in mule-drawn waggons, travelling up one day and back the next, stopping at the little bridge at the bottom of Wrecclesham Hill to water the animals.'

'At Greatham we were allowed to trap rabbits to supplement our diet, but not pheasants. On my way home one day I found two eggs and proudly took them home to my mother, only to be told by my father that they were pheasant's eggs and I must take them back at once.

George V and Queen Mary visited Longmoor Camp to see the Italian prisoners of war who were lodged there. I had a special blue dress with red and white braid on it for the occasion.'


THE SENSE OF RELIEF

'To me, Portsmouth during the First World War was a rather sad place, with families consisting of mum and the children. As Pompey was a naval town most of the husbands were at sea, and many of us did not recognise our dads when they returned after the war.

We lived in two rooms near St James' hospital where the war wounded were looked after. Some were allowed out for a while, many on crutches. They loved talking to us children, sometimes about their own families, teaching us to play cat's cradle, or watching as we played hopscotch or hoops, and the many variations of skipping. When Armistice was declared my mother ran up and down the garden with her precious brass fire-irons, using the kettle stand as a drum and the tongs as drumsticks. The neighbours came out with saucepans and a variety of spoons, ladles, etc to bang with. The noise was terrific, but even as a child I could feel the sense of relief. Some time later, with great jubilation, a huge bonfire with an effigy of Kaiser Bill on top, was burnt in the dried up bed of the old canal.'

'Schooldays were a two mile walk to our Church of England girls and infants school. Boys left at the age of seven to attend the boys school, a half mile away. Heating came from a slow coke-burning stove in the centre of the classroom. On some frosty mornings, our hands so cold we were unable to hold pens, we had to exercise by throwing our arms round our waists. We heard news of the First World War Armistice when Ella Fielder, our postmaster's daughter, returned from her lunch. Miss Hitchens, the headteacher, promptly found a long piece of rope which she tied to the school bell, and everyone pulled with great joy.

Peace celebrations took place at Bramble Hill, a large house in the village, in 1919. The Southampton Police Band, masses of races for young and old, and a super tea. Children were given Peace Mugs; mine is inscribed:

The Triumph
of
Right over Might
AD 1918

with photos of Lloyd George, Admiral Beatty and Marshall Foch.'

## THE MEMORIAL INSTITUTE

'After the war had ended large sums of money were collected throughout the towns and villages in the country to erect memorials to the fallen. In Overton most generous contributions poured in. After many meetings and much deliberation it was decided to erect a small stone cross in the churchyard bearing the names of the fallen (34) with the rest of the money going towards the cost of building a Memorial Institute. It was felt this would serve as a perpetual memory to those who had given their lives and would be of material benefit to those who survived and to the community in general.'

## THE ARMISTICE DAY WIDOW

'The telegram from the War Office arrived on Armistice Day 1918. Amidst all the rejoicing Lizzie was now a war widow with a son of seven to bring up. "Our poor Lizzie," said her sisters, who couldn't understand why Lizzie refused to wear black mourning clothes, something quite unheard of in those days.

A lady lodger arrived – a man was quite out of the question of course – and sewing alterations for the local draper and occasional cooking in large country houses kept her busy. Later, in school holidays, I visited her. She would "run up" a couple of dresses for me. She always seemed to have pretty material "kicking about". Perhaps she would "knock up" a few cakes, or we would "trot up" to the forest to collect firewood.

"Our poor Lizzie" never had any new furniture or changed a thing in her house. Her sisters wondered why. "I like to stay just the way it was when my Will went off to the war," she would say. People thought her rather odd.

As her only niece she confided in me, "Don't you dare tell your mother, she'll think I'm potty. Nobody believes me but I'm sure Will is still alive, perhaps injured or lost his memory. One day he'll come whistling down the hill to me. I wait at the gate every night at eight o'clock. That was the time we agreed to think of one another when we were apart."

No longer was she "our poor Lizzie". From her shabby home emerged a beautiful princess waiting for her prince to come. The romance, the tingling, awesome excitement as we waited, to a child so wonderful, always ending with, "Never mind, we'll wait again tomorrow." Eight o'clock was forever our secret.

Her son married and our poor Lizzie supplied over £600, a fortune in 1939, to have a house built for the newlyweds. "Wherever did she get so much money?" said my mother. "I don't know." But I told a white lie. "Our poor Lizzie" had told me she would never spend a penny of her war widow's pension on herself. She knew she wasn't a widow. Will would come back one day, of that she was certain.

She loved whist drives and dances, she met other men, she explained to me what bigamy meant. "I wish our poor Lizzie would remarry," said my mother, but I knew she never would.

She wasn't really ill, just old and tired. The doctor suggested a few days in hospital for a rest. She asked for me. I went that evening. "Please comb my hair and put my pretty bed jacket on for me," she asked. I looked at the clock. Lizzie smiled a tender, secret smile and whispered, "He is coming at last, my beloved Will, I always knew he would." But only she could see him, for after all the lonely years her soul was soaring to Heaven and she would be in his arms at last.'

# HARD TIMES

Between the wars came the hard times of the depression, which hit some areas of Hampshire with severity. It was common to see men tramping the roads in search of work, moving from one workhouse to the next on their route, and newcomers came to the county from the even worse affected North East.

## TRAMPING THE ROADS

'My childhood home at Havant in the 1920s and 1930s was only a few yards from the workhouse, or Union as it was generally known. As well as a few permanent inmates, the "casual ward" catered for tramps who could get free board and lodging for the night, but admission was not until 6 pm.

Opposite our house was an angle in a wall which gave a certain amount of shelter, especially if the weather was bad. Quite often Mother would see someone sheltering there, and he would be asked to share our tea. Next morning he would usually come back, and Mother would give him a bit of tea and sugar, and sixpence to help him on his way.

If the thought of the workhouse was abhorrent, the "Old House at Home" provided a dosshouse where one could stay for a few coppers a night. One unfortunate woman, with a small son, was stranded there for several weeks, her husband having been taken ill and in hospital. She visited us on several occasions and, indeed, shared our Christmas dinner. Eventually, her husband recovered and they went on their way. I've no idea how Mother got to know her, but I suspect that she came to the door selling pins and tapes, or perhaps lavender, because of course it was an offence to beg.

I hasten to say that a lot of these people were not the real old tramps, but men travelling the roads, genuinely in search of work.

It was said that "safe" houses were marked in some way, and it must have been true, for ours was the only house in a terrace of twelve that as far as I know was ever visited. One wasn't afraid to open the door to strangers in those days!'

## CHANGING TIMES

'The only industry badly affected by the depression at Abbotts Ann was Taskers – the Anna Valley Ironworks – where many villagers were employed. Some did lose their jobs and those who stayed found things hard, but business improved later in the decade and flourished during the war.

The biggest effect on Abbotts Ann came about through the formation of the Land Settlements on land to the north of the village. Unemployed miners from Durham were given ten acres and a pig, with a co-operative market to sell their produce from market gardening. These Northerners, despite great differences in accent and attitudes, soon adapted to their new environment and settled in remarkably well. They improved the social life of the village and a few still live here.'

## THE DEPRESSION HUNG ON

'In the Lee-on-Solent area, always notorious for its low wages, the depression hung on through the 1930s. But we were happy enough; if one's friends also lived in homes with zinc baths, gas mantles and outside toilets, why fret? Anyway, wasn't Gracie Fields telling us all to *Sing as we go*?

These were the days when pawnshops prospered, horse-and-cart merchants hauled perishables in conditions of dubious hygiene and local tradesmen stayed hopefully open until nine thirty each evening. Foggy winter nights brought loud chants from bell-clanging muffin men and hot-chestnut sellers, while many an enterprising lady would throw open her front parlour for the sale of delicious smelling home-made faggots and peas (to be supplied straight into the customer's own basin). Even modestly priced goodies such as these, however, were beyond the purse of those really down on their luck. Young ex-servicemen, trying to keep body and soul together hawking matches and bootlaces from door to door, could not afford them. Indeed, it is a fact that when the Second World War brought its rationing there were many who realised the irony of finding their entitlements something of a blessing – especially when the massive surge of warwork provided the means of paying for them!'

# THE SECOND WORLD WAR
# 1939–1945
# UNDER THE BOMBING

When war came again, Hampshire was in the front line, with Southampton and Portsmouth particular targets for German bombers. There are so many stories to tell of those days and nights of fear that these can only be a brief reminder. Other places suffered bombing too, and some had lucky escapes to tell of. Soldiers on the move, especially in the 1944 push for D-Day, were a familiar part of our lives too.

## A PRIME TARGET

'When the New Docks were built, which were declared open by HM King George V and Queen Mary, Southampton was a prosperous town into which sailed all the great liners carrying the rich and famous, and more to the point giving a great deal of employment and very large tips for the on-board stewards.

Southampton naturally became a prime target for the Luftwaffe and at the height of the blitz the siren would sound about six in the evening and we knew we were "for it". At the end of one particular raid the whole of Above Bar was just one big bonfire. When the siren went many people would get their car, motorbike or pushbike and ride out to the outskirts of Southampton to get away from the town, as one learned that first the Germans would ring the town with incendiaries and then drop their bombs inside the ring of fire. Strangely enough, none of the old walls of the Bargate were damaged.

Later, the Americans were in the town ready to embark for France, and they made something of an impact. The then Mayor of Southampton went to the docks to bid farewell to the millionth American to leave for the Continent. Unfortunately we heard that this young man was subsequently killed but the Mayor was invited to go to America after the war, as he had done a great deal for them when they were here, and he went to see the widow and took a doll for her little girl.

Southampton also received many of the Channel Islanders when

178

the islands were invaded, as, of course, the Channel Island boats had always sailed into Southampton regularly. Also we had several of the "escapees" from the islands, as inevitably some took a chance and escaped in small boats, taking a very great risk.'

'In October 1940 I was beginning my Finals year at Southampton University (then an external college of the University of London). The war had been in progress for a year, but until the previous summer it had barely touched our lives, apart from the scarcity of men students and the inconveniences of blackout and rationing. Now, though, after Dunkirk, the fall of France, and an uneasy summer vacation waiting for invasion, things were different. We had no shelters for our Hall of Residence, some committee having decided that we should sleep on the ground floor, "protected" by the three concrete floors above us. "Just what I'm frightened of," said our warden, whose responsibilities were hair-raising. We learned later that she had instructions, if the invading armies appeared, to stay in the Hall so as not to clutter up the roads with her students. "Hitler's soldiers won't be interested in a lot of girls," said the Principal. Really?

I kept a diary throughout the war, and this bears witness to the gradual increase in the air raids, which had already devastated London and other large cities. We prepared ourselves as best we could; we formed fire-fighting teams and practised with buckets of water and stirrup pumps, and some of us actually learned to fire an army rifle, taught by a susceptible young army lieutenant whom we teased unmercifully. Neither of these useful skills was ever, fortunately, put to the test.

Our turn came during the three weekends of 16th/17th and 23rd/24th November and (the worst) 1st/2nd December. I still remember, after over 50 years, the distinctive throb of the German bombers and the whistle/crunch of the bombs as they fell. They all seemed to straddle our Hall, though in fact the bombing was concentrated on the town and the docks, several miles away. Still, our windows were shattered, and houses around us were flattened. The last raid was the most frightening; most of London Road, Above Bar and the High Street disappeared, all the solid, handsome Georgian and Victorian buildings, and the whole maze of alley-ways, sinister pubs and strange ships' chandlers that made up the colourful area of the docks.

We were young and resilient, but we lay in our beds, or sometimes on the floor under them, and wondered if we would still be alive in the morning. We were, though, each time, and a certain stoic fatalism developed after a while. "Swept up glass," I noted on 24th November, "then did ironing." However, after the third

179

weekend we had all had enough. There was no electricity, gas or water, no trams or buses, no trains nearer than Winchester, no post, no telephone. The University closed and we were left to get home as best we could. I set off on my bicycle for Liss, where my mother happened to be staying with friends, and remember the blessed peace of the winter countryside, and my absurd doubts about my welcome, since I had not been able to let my mother know. To my surprise I was greeted like a long-lost heroine, for they had seen the flames and heard the bombs and until I came pedalling up the road did not know if I were alive or dead.'

'At first things were comparatively quiet over here but in 1940 all of our big cities were being bombed, London and Coventry getting the worst of it at first, but then we were getting our share in Southampton and getting worse all the time, their aim being the docks of course.

My sister had been evacuated to Dorset along with many others, but came home as she had previously won an art scholarship and started at the Art College in the Civic Centre at Southampton. On 5th November 1940 there was a daylight raid on the town and the Art School had a direct hit, killing one whole class of students and two teachers, my sister being one of the students. All of Southampton was shocked, and especially us, as these were the first children to be killed from the bombing; she was just 13 by then. My father knew nothing of this as he was away transporting troops all over the world and we never knew where.

At the end of November after enduring many sleepless nights and daylight raids, one of my mother's sisters said why didn't we go there for the weekend, which was in the country. We heard on the radio that Southampton had been hit very badly again at the weekend but didn't know until we arrived home on Monday morning that our house had been bombed to the ground. We began to wonder what would happen next.

Of course, we had to return to my aunt's and stayed with them for two or three months, when fortunately we managed to rent a house from someone who was moving away for the duration. You didn't get compensation for your home until after the war and then only the pre-war price. When people went anywhere from home the first things they took with them were insurance policies, ration books and anything of value, so apart from that we had to start all over again – furniture, clothes, everything in fact.'

# BOMBS OVER PORTSMOUTH

'We came from Scotland in March 1926, when I was 13½ years old. My father, a shipwright, transferred from the Rosyth dockyard to the Portsmouth dockyard. With the onset of war, we moved to Farlington to avoid the bombing. Most of the children were evacuated by now, my firstborn and my sister being sent to Winchester. The other two children were too young to leave home.

Before the youngest children went to school there had been air raids during the day. We had an air raid shelter sunk into our lawn, with earth piled over it giving added protection. When the siren sounded we went to the shelter. I took my knitting, trying to appear unconcerned, in spite of all the commotion from the anti-aircraft guns on Portsdown Hill (named Tin Pan Alley because it sounded like pots and pans smashing together), guns on Southsea Common, the sea forts, and warships nearby, plus the aerial battles above us. Bombs fell nearby, the blast bowed the leaded windows and damaged roof tiles.

In May 1942 I joined the Inland Revenue as a "temp" at Sunspan, a large house (above Auriol Drive, on the hill crest). My husband was also in the Inland Revenue, his office being in Southsea. Shortly he and the remaining staff joined us at Sunspan. The view from Sunspan was marvellous. On a clear day Chichester cathedral spire can be seen to the east, coming south across Hayling Island, Langstone Harbour, and to the west via Portsmouth and Southsea, Isle of Wight, Gosport and Southampton Water.

Part of our duties was to carry out a fortnightly fire watching. Meanwhile the children went to my parents, or stayed with friends of my parents, who lodged with us, after being bombed out of their house in Portsmouth.

We couldn't sleep very well when we were not on watch, sleeping in our clothes ready to respond immediately to any eventuality. On one occasion I called my husband to identify a light in the sky. Eventually we realised that it was a doodlebug, raised the alarm and donned our tin hats whilst running for the shelter. Since it was travelling at some 500 mph it overtook us, roaring overhead. (When it went quiet, you started to worry, because the engine had cut and it came down to earth with a bang.) We learnt that it came down at Wickham.

The house was full then, with us, the lodgers, and their two teenage daughters, who worked during the day. Our fathers worked together in the expense accounts of the dockyard, travelling by bus to work, dodging the bombs, diverting via the nearest shelter until the all clear sounded. Father's health suffered, and he could no longer work. In those days there was no unemployment or sickness benefit. It was the Works Panel who gave out a small benefit but there wasn't much to buy!

The first big blitz came in January 1942. The "crump" of the bombs and land mines, the crack of the guns, the characteristic chatter of the "pom poms" all added to the mayhem. Much damage and loss of life ensued. There were fires burning all around our vantage point at Sunspan.

It was during this period that Coventry was blitzed. The bombers flew over Portsmouth en route, flying along a radio beam pointing towards Coventry, awaiting the crossbeam to signal the release of the bombs. After similar raids, my husband cycled home, along to my parents, checking that all was well, returning to us to give the latest news.

We "did our bit" at home, being ready to deal with incendiary bombs, with the shovel, sand, and stirrup pump at the ready, accompanied by yells of "Put that light out" or words to that effect! Times were difficult, but we managed.'

'My home was in Portsmouth, but I was on holiday in Gloucestershire when war broke out. My two week stay with an aunt lengthened to four years, but only in term time. Thus I was at home for the worst two blitzes in January and March 1940.

One night I went with my parents to Fort Widley, one of Lord Palmerston's follies on top of Porchester Hill, overlooking Portsmouth. Here a friend of my father gave us safe, albeit damp, shelter in his mushroom-growing enterprise. During the raids that night, we stood at the entrance to the fort, viewing the fire bombs and gun flashes in the city below. It seemed to me, at that safe distance, more of a firework spectacle. My feelings were very different on the night of the big March blitz, for by then my parents had decided to take their chances at home and we spent the night in the Anderson shelter in the garden. That night a bomb rendered our house unsafe and my memories of those hours of bombing are of noise and fear and my constant repetition of "When will it stop?" My father, a veteran of the First World War, distressed my mother by making occasional dashes into the garden to watch the planes. After several of these he returned to us much shaken, his face bloodied by a fragment of shrapnel. It is sad to recall that shortly after we had moved to safe accommodation next morning, men with a horse and cart arrived and persuaded our neighbours that they had been sent to clear the house by my father. Most of our portable valuables were stolen, a not uncommon practice perpetrated by criminals.

Our new house had an indoor Morrison shelter, but my parents preferred to use the public shelters built in the nearby deserted grammar school grounds. The initial excitement of the evening routine, when we picked up our packed cases, our sandwiches, thermos flasks, hot water bottles and eiderdowns before going to the shelter when the alert sounded, quickly palled. It became a nuisance, especially when it was a false alarm. For my parents, who did this week after week it was an utterly wearying existence, which they gladly exchanged for a bed in an uncle's cottage in Rowlands Castle some twelve miles away. This despite the irregularity of the train service and a mile's walk along an unlit lane after a day's work.

One holiday when shopping in King's Road in Southsea, my sister and I were forced to lie in the gutter when a stray German fighter plane machine-gunned the area. As a 14 year old schoolgirl I was far more concerned for my dignity and the mud on my coat.'

'My greatest danger during the last air raids on Portsmouth came when, as a young assistant air raid warden, home on my school holidays, I was paired with a young sailor, home on leave!'

AIR RAID SHELTERS

'In the early days of the war public air raid shelters were hastily dug, usually in parks or school playing fields. These were often merely open trenches, zig-zagged to avoid blast and shrapnel ripping through the length of the trench, but useless except as cover from flying debris. Later, these were roofed over and covered with earth to make safer places of refuge.

Householders had also been advised to dig air raid shelters for themselves in their gardens and the government provided corrugated iron preformed sections, to be covered by the excavated earth, with sand bags to protect the entrances. These were virtually useless in Wellow, since most would have flooded, and few were dug, but later some Morrison shelters – steel table-height shelters which were for indoor use and kept the inhabitants safe if the house collapsed on them – were provided.

There was one large air raid shelter, on rather higher ground, which took "18 people and two dogs". Air raid alerts were frequent, with Southampton so close, but the village was relatively free from air attack. One German plane came down at Blackhill and a land mine fell on the post office at Ower, killing eight members of one family.'

183

# HOW LUCKY WE WERE

'I often think back to 1940 when I was living at Penrith Road, Basingstoke. In the August of that year I had intended to go to Cornwall for my holidays but my father advised me not to as the railway stations were being bombed so much at that time, so I decided to stay at home. On Friday 17th August I had arranged to meet my friend Winnie to go to the pictures. She was working at Murray's in London Street so we were going to meet at 5.30 pm in Church Square. However, on the morning of that day my friend Hilda's father called and said he and his wife were going to see Hilda in Newbury where she worked and asked if I would like to go with them. I went and saw Winnie and we arranged to go to the pictures the following evening. How very fortunate this was for us both.

At 5.30 pm on 17th August bombs fell in Church Square and several people were killed. The Methodist church was very badly hit and a lot of damage was done to St Michael's church. Bombs were also dropped the other side of the station but I do not think much damage was done there or anyone was killed.

Then in November of that year, I think it was Saturday 23rd November about 6.30 pm, the siren had sounded and my brother, who was a messenger for the air raid warden, had gone on duty. We heard a plane going over and my father said it sounded like a German plane; my mother came running in from the kitchen and said she could hear a bomb falling. The next minute it felt as if the walls were coming in towards us and we could hear the glass of the windows breaking and all the lights went out so we were in darkness. We had to leave the house and spend the night in an air raid shelter in Worting Road. The next morning we went back to the house to see what damage was done and found that most of the tiles were off the roof, and the back door was blown off and was resting against the dresser in the kitchen. The front door was at the bottom of the stairs, the fireplace in my bedroom was almost blown out and every window in the house had gone except the room we had all been in. We all felt this was a blessing.

We spent all that Sunday trying to clear up; many of the curtains were in shreds and a lot of the furniture was pitted with glass so for a long time we were finding bits of glass around. However, we were all so thankful that the family was safe.'

# WE HAD OUR SHARE

'The Bashley neighbourhood was organised early for Civil Defence and was a reception area for bombed out people from Southampton and Portsmouth. Troops arrived in the district in 1940, commencing with the 2nd Battalion Lancashire Fusiliers from Dunkirk and other battalions throughout the war. Then in 1944 came the troops prior to D-Day including Canadian heavy armour with their huge tanks roaring through the village on their way to the Forest.

One Sunday morning not long before the memorable day, General Montgomery, as he then was, visited Bashley with his staff and in a large field of Bashley Lodge (now Bashley caravan park) inspected the Canadian troops and gave them a "pep talk".

The area had its share of bombing and damage, one episode in particular when a German bomber in flames flew over Bashley towards the sea, chased by two Spitfires pouring bullets into it. The sound was horrific and the bullets hit houses down the lane, the village shop getting a number, ripping open tins of soup etc. Luckily it was dinner time and no one was killed as they were having their meal in the back room. The plane was brought down across the fields at Milford and four Germans are buried in Milford churchyard. Bombs were dropped near Blackleads Farm just east of Bashley Lodge and some at Ossemsby. Though some animals were killed, there were no human casualties.'


SAVED BY SABOTAGE?

'Did an act of sabotage save Lyndhurst from being blown off the map? Locals in Lyndhurst counted themselves extremely lucky on the afternoon of 14th August 1940 when they were deluged with bombs – none of which went off.

A German Stuka dive-bomber, flying at almost roof top level, hotly pursued by a Spitfire, dropped a stick of seven high explosive bombs which effectively straddled the whole village. One was dropped at the back of the Workman's Club, one in the High Street at the exit of what now is the car park, another in what was then the fire station (now Bow Windows Café) and the remainder in a line across the back of the Stag Hotel, Mailman's Arms, and the last one where the Meridien Garage now stands.

The only casualty was Richard Galton, then aged 16. He was on duty in the fire station control room and was knocked unconscious by flying debris when the bomb went straight through the roof and into the concrete floor alongside him.

To this day it is not certain why none of the bombs exploded. Rumours via the Bomb Disposal Squad suggested that the bombs had been made in Czechoslovakia and may well have been deliberately sabotaged by the forced labour inmates working in the munitions factory. If this is true, then, on that hot summer's day over 50 years ago, Richard and many other Lyndhurst people owed their lives to some unknown Eastern European man or woman.'

## SOLDIERS ON THE MOVE

'The long summer days of 1944 stretched before us, children went to school when possible and most households carried on their daily routine in as normal a manner as the Luftwaffe allowed. Food was rationed and most housewives had learnt to stretch their rations by using more flour and less eggs. However, there was hope in the air that Great Britain and her Allies would soon free the peoples that had suffered at the hands of German occupation.

In a small village on the south coast there was an air of expectation that something "big" was afoot. No villager dared to voice an opinion and Mr Winston Churchill was unusually reticent as to the next move the Allies would be undertaking and this helped to fuel the speculation.

My family household awoke to a rumbling noise and waited to hear the piercing wailing of the sirens that warned us to take to the air raid shelters because Jerry was about to bomb us yet again. However, minutes passed and no siren sounded. Still the rumbling continued and through the bedroom windows, open due to the humid summer night, the distinct smell of tar pervaded. My grandmother exclaimed, "I can smell burning tar and that droning noise could be vehicles travelling on the Southampton Road." My uncle replied, "This could be it!" We learnt early the next day that troops were on the move, we assumed to converge on Southampton. A smoke screen had been sent up to camouflage the troop movements and hence the pungent smell of tar we had all experienced. On reflection it must have worked as I recall no bombing of these valiant convoys.

During this eventful period, that seemed so prolonged to an eleven year old girl, dark-faced soldiers in camouflage battledress streaming past my village became a familiar sight. My family and many others baked large chunks of bread pudding and poured endless cups of tea to keep the boys rolling. They accepted our frugal offerings with cheeky smiles and I received many a kiss on the cheek from our brave warriors, often not much more than boys themselves.

How many of that fighting force returned to these shores? I do not know, but I do know that we should never forget that they fought for our right to be free and this should never be taken for granted. The smell of burning tar will always transport me in memory back to those long hot days when convoy after convoy slowly and deliberately moved through Hampshire on a quest that changed the future for me and my generation with hope for a free world.'

'My husband and I and two small children were living in Southsea just before D-Day. My husband, an Engineer Officer RN, had an unusual job training a small Naval party to go across the Channel to start opening up ports and repairing damaged ships and installations as quickly as possible, directly they were recaptured from the Germans. There were just five of these parties, each of which had to be totally self sufficient, and my husband had to discover the best places to train them in anything from field cookery to the best way of recognising and coping with booby-trap explosives, apart from specialist lorry driving and other technical skills. Most important was their ability to work together as a self contained group; one or two had to be replaced on this account.'

'Part way along the Ride between Stansted House and Rowlands Castle stands a wooden cross, a memorial to a Canadian, Flying Officer J. G. Clermonts of 175 Squadron, whose life ended when his plane crashed into the Hampshire countryside. There used to be an airfield at Funtington and as children we were well used to hearing the drone of approaching and receding planes. We hardly glanced up on that day in May 1944, as three Typhoons passed over the garden where we played. Suddenly the sound changed, one Typhoon shooting upwards into the clear sky, the engine trailing fire, then falling with screaming speed to crash behind Woodberry Lane. There was a second of silence, a tremendous thud and a great column of dense black smoke. No enemy action, "just one of those things that happen".

The woods around Rowlands Castle were, for quite some time during 1944, the camouflaged camping ground for the troops preparing for embarkation for the D-Day landings. To this day there are the dugout hollows and brick foundations of cookhouses, as well as bomb craters, to be found "off the beaten track" and one can imagine how the woods, quiet now, once reverberated to the sounds of thousands of men preparing for action.

The day of embarkation arrived and word spread that the King was coming to inspect the troops. All who could do so gathered around Redhill and Whichers Gate, where hundreds of trucks were assembled, filling every available space under trees and on the verges. The soldiers had been forbidden to leave their vehicles and local children had often been given pennies to buy sweets and cigarettes for them.

At a later date the King's Stone was erected by Lady Martin of Redhill House as a memorial to those who had fallen and a reminder of the day when the King had visited Rowlands Castle to bid farewell to his troops.'

'My husband was a gardener at Winchester College and we lived within the college walls. I remember the river Itchen being used for raft practice in preparation for D-Day. General Eisenhower visited the college when there were Americans stationed in the grounds, and General Montgomery was a regular visitor at the headmaster's house. An old tramp often used to sleep in the college boathouse and was furious to find the soldiers were storing their rafts there, so he burnt candles there at night to try to make them believe it was haunted.'

'For 40 years my husband and I had a newsagent's and general store in Trinity Street, Fareham. We opened at 5 am and closed at 8 pm. One morning during the war we were startled to see an enormous tank parked outside the shop. In fact, the tanks were nose to tail all through the town. The soldiers were mostly Canadian and many tents were erected in the local park for their living quarters. During the time they were there we made friends with many of them but one in particular was Jack, with whom we often shared our rations. He gave us a letter to post to Canada should he not return. As suddenly as they arrived, all the tanks left overnight and the town seemed very empty. Jack did finally come back to us and he then returned to Canada. I often wonder if he remembers our little corner shop.'

## A SAD MEMENTO

'The late Mary Carter, who was landlady of the Five Bells in Buriton, recounted this poignant memory at a Village Association meeting. She recalled how a troop of Canadian soldiers were camped on the outskirts of the village for several weeks and became familiar faces in the Five Bells.

One night two of the men explained that they had run out of money, but could they leave a wallet and watch as security and settle when they were paid? Mary agreed to this, but was a little disconcerted when the camp was struck the next day and the men departed, never to return to Buriton.

After a while she felt that the watch and wallet should be returned to the men; particularly the wallet which contained photographs and letters which were obviously treasured. She wrote to the Canadian Embassy and received a reply denying all knowledge of the men.

At the time nothing was reported of the Dieppe Raid and it was years later when the facts were published that she realised that these young Canadians had taken part in that ill-fated raid and did not survive to return to Buriton.

She kept the watch and wallet; hoping that one day someone would return to collect them, but no one came. A sad memento of those lads who stayed briefly in Buriton.'

# A CHILD'S WAR

**Children soon came to see war as a normal part of life and to accept its restrictions and inconveniences, but there were moments of terror and sadness for us all.**

## A CHILD'S VIEW OF THE BLITZ

'I started school on 4th September 1939, the day after war began. It was a small private school close to my home in Farlington, a suburb of Portsmouth. At first we had no air raid shelters so we were simply sent home whenever the siren sounded. As I ran up the road I would meet my mother running down, and together we would sit under the table until the all clear sounded.

Farlington had its first bad raid on 10th April 1941 when a land mine fell in the road next to mine. I was awoken by a rushing noise like a hurricane and the next moment the ceiling fell in and broken glass came flying on to my bed. As the dust settled I realised that the small twinkling lights above me were the stars shining through a hole in the roof!

Next day as my mother, crying silently, attempted to set her home to rights, I wandered along the road. I saw a piece of paper flapping about and recognised the Easter card made by me with such care. I picked it up and saw the crumpled silver paper cross and torn crepe paper daffodils. Suddenly the full impact of the last few hours seemed to hit me and it was then that I stood and wept.

However, someone in the next road was having a much worse time. She was a teenage girl, later to become my sister-in-law, who had cycled from Petersfield where she had been evacuated with the Portsmouth high school. To her horror, she found her home in ruins and did not know if her family had survived or were under the rubble. No one could answer her questions, and sick with fear, she set off to cycle back to Petersfield. On the way she decided to call on her mother's friend who lived about a mile away. To her great relief she found that her mother and brothers had taken refuge there, having been made homeless.

When we returned to school after Easter there were several missing faces and I wanted to cry for my lost friends. I didn't dare to cry as children were expected to carry on as if nothing had happened, just like adults. No one ever thought we might need counselling either.

189

*Collecting scrap iron at Catherington for the war effort was just one way children could feel they were helping. Nothing was wasted, from scrap iron to paper.*

Life was not all gloom however, and a week after the blitz our brick-built shelter was erected. This was as good as a Wendy house to me and I played Mothers and Fathers with my friends, using the bunk beds and folding chairs as if they had been specially provided for play. The flat top of the shelter made an ideal bird table and every day I climbed the step-ladder to place food on the top.

The school shelters were grim, damp places, and the teachers must have been hard pressed to keep us occupied when the raids were long lasting. We couldn't do any written work there so we practised our tables and spellings and learnt the many verses of long poems and songs. I made my first acquaintance with classical literature as the teachers read stories such as *The Wind in the Willows* and *Black Beauty*.

Sometimes when we were in the middle of the weekly class test, I would long for an air raid to cause a diversion. Then I would think of the people who might be hurt and feel guilty!

In spite of all these traumatic experiences most of us grew up unscathed. Such is the resilience of childhood!'

## MORE EXCITED THAN FRIGHTENED

'I spent a happy childhood in a small street near the dockyard in Portsmouth. At the outbreak of war in 1939, I was sent to my aunt in Wales – and by the time I came back to Portsmouth two years later things were very different. My family had moved out to one of the outlying areas and this was a wise move because the area around the dockyard had been flattened by bombing. Barrage balloons floated overhead and batteries of anti-aircraft guns were located in all of the parks. Air raids occurred almost every night when we would all rush out to the Anderson shelter in the garden. This was a corrugated iron structure big enough to house an average family and was partially sunk beneath the surface of the garden with earth heaped on top for additional protection. I remember ours as being damp and smelly but good for playing "house" in during the day time. People who did not have shelters for any reason went into cupboards under the stairs of their houses or to large brick-built public shelters. If one of these received a direct hit from a bomb (which happened in Portsmouth on several occasions) the loss of life was considerable.

I suppose to us children it did not seem too bad a life – we were more excited than frightened by the bombing and gunfire – but for adults it must have been a terrible time. My mother, who was a widow, would set out for work each day not knowing if her factory would still be standing after a night raid (during which she might well have been taking her turn at "fire-watching").

191

During the days we children occupied ourselves hunting shrapnel (metal pieces from the shattered cases of bombs and anti-aircraft shells) that had come down in the streets or parks, and watching dogfights between Spitfires and Luftwaffe planes overhead! What we really missed were sweets, chocolate and fruit although sometimes we could make home-made toffee if we could get some sugar – and eat fruit like apples that we could grow ourselves. Most people dug up their lawns to grow vegetables and fruit. They also kept chickens and rabbits to provide a few eggs and some meat for special occasions.

Perhaps my most vivid memory of the later war years was of the V1 flying bombs or "doodlebugs". We would listen to their characteristically throbbing engine note and hope that it wouldn't cut out because they then fell immediately to earth and exploded. The RAF fighter pilots became skilled at tipping the V1s over with their wing-tips when they were still out over the sea or over open countryside. I remember being in bed one morning when a V1's engine cut out seemingly overhead. My mother immediately flung the bedclothes right over my head – much good that would have done! – but fortunately the doodlebug did not fall nearby.

When VE (Victory in Europe) day finally arrived we had a tea party in the street. In spite of food rationing, which continued for years after the war, we had a tea that I still remember.'

## MACHINE GUNNED FROM THE AIR

'Ministry of Defence officials from the local military camp (Bordon and Longmoor) called one day to demand that our bungalow and chicken house roofs should be painted black. This was to make sure that they could not be seen from the air. Apparently the Germans could have used their white reflections to pinpoint the camps for their bombing raids.

Getting to school was hazardous. Once, while waiting on the open platform at Liphook for a train to take us to Petersfield, we were machine gunned by a German plane. No one was hurt but the bullet holes in the nearby pub doors remained for years.'

## MANY HOURS IN THE SHELTER

'In August 1939 my mother and I together with other pupils and teachers from Bitterne Manor school in Southampton were evacuated to Corfe Mullen in Dorset. We were taken by train to Wimborne where we assembled in a hall to be allocated to homes. We were billeted in the Old Mill Restaurant at Corfe Mullen together with

Miss Hammond, one of the teachers. While there we listened to the radio and heard the news of the outbreak of war broadcast by the Prime Minister, Mr Neville Chamberlain. We stayed there for just about two weeks but as they did not want her as a helper, Mother decided to return home to Southampton and my father came to fetch us in his Austin 7 saloon car. Miss Hammond also returned with us as she was not needed to teach since the local school already had sufficient teachers. Our first sight of Southampton was the barrage balloons.

After the outbreak of war, the schools in Southampton were not functioning for some months but eventually I started going to Bitterne Park senior school in Manor Farm Road for half a day. During the Battle of Britain we spent a lot of time in the shelters, some of which were reinforced corridors in the school building, where we had oral lessons until the all clear sounded when we were sent home. I remember the day when the Super Marine works at Woolston was bombed. We had been sent home following the all clear from a previous raid and just got into the shelter at home when the Super Marine raid started.

During the months of the blitz my parents and I spent many hours down in the Anderson air raid shelter. Every night we would go down into the shelter at 6 pm and remain there until 7 am the following morning in order to get some sleep. My mother invited other neighbours to join us for company and so friendships developed. My father and a neighbour, Mr Cox, did fire guard duty one night a week on different nights and on those nights each family used the other one's shelter so that each man knew that the other was looking after his family. One night a land mine fell on Bitterne Manor House and when we came out of our shelters we were amazed to see that dogs released from a quarantine kennels by the blast were gobbling up meat from the damaged cold room of Tom Jolley's butcher's shop. One of the neighbours who was an ex-colonial type had come out to see what had happened dressed in a pith helmet and a silk dressing gown, which caused a great deal of laughter.

We had great faith in our Anderson shelters and there was a wonderful spirit of comradeship in those dark days and people really did their best to help one another. Food rationing was a matter of concern among housewives and many ingenious recipes were invented to make the food go round. Despite the shortages the nation kept very healthy. I remember my father making a Dutch oven from some sheet metal so that it could be put on the open coal fire to cook the Sunday lunch when Southampton gas works was out of action after bombing.'

'As a child of ten when war was declared, I had no idea that my repertoire of songs would increase as a result.

At first we did not attend our new grammar school as we had to wait for the shelters to be built, and so we collected homework weekly. The frequency of the air raids meant we spent many of our school hours down in the shelters sitting on long benches facing each other and singing songs. I learned, amongst others, Handel's *Did You Not See My Lady* and, at the other end of the scale, *There's a Hole In My Bucket*. There was a bucket with a seat behind a curtain at the end of the shelter and our singing increased in volume whenever one of our schoolmates needed to visit that end. It wasn't long before we had tables down the middle and some lighting available and we got used to taking our exercise books down with us in order to carry on with our proper education!'

## INTO THE DITCH

'One of my most vivid memories is of when we were living at Wyck. One afternoon on our walk home from school the sirens went. The older children grabbed our hands and rushed us along, but before long we heard the German planes coming our way, so everyone jumped into the ditch, trying to hide as best as they could. I can still see one of the mothers coming along as fast as she could on her bike to make sure we were all right – she ended up in the ditch with us. After the all clear we hurried home and the next day went to the fields to see the craters left by the bombs that dropped that day.'

## SLEEP WAS DIFFICULT

'We lived in Bedhampton, part of Havant, and two miles from the boundary of the City of Portsmouth.

Portsmouth was an "evacuation area", from which children were evacuated to safer parts of the county. Petersfield, to where I travelled daily to the Petersfield high school, was a "reception area", to which evacuees were sent. We had to share our school with a London girls school, Battersea Central School. The nearby (boys) Churchers College shared its premises with the Emanuel School, Wandsworth. Bedhampton and Havant were known as "neutral areas".

We saw the sky lit up during the Portsmouth blitzes and had air raid damage of our own – the bungalows next door but one and next door but two to us respectively were each half-destroyed when a high explosive bomb landed between them. We had to leave our house for six weeks when an unexploded bomb landed in the field at the bottom of our garden. It was safely dealt with by the army, eventually.

In the woods opposite our house were stationed anti-aircraft guns. Sleep was difficult and many nights were spent in our Anderson shelter in the garden. In Basingstoke, my grandmother slept in an indoor Morrison shelter. When she died in January 1948, the *Hants and Berks Gazette* reported her as the oldest inhabitant of Basingstoke; she was aged 96 years five months.

During air raid warnings at Petersfield we at school went into the cellar. In September 1940 I was walking home along my road when a roof-top raider shot bullets at me, the companion walking with me pushed me into a ditch and the bullets fell short of us. I shall always remember the plane bearing the swastika, and the pilot. A merciful deliverance. On walking further up the road we saw an ambulance outside a house near my home. A lady had gone to her door and had been fatally shot. Her name is on the roll of honour in St Thomas' church at Bedhampton. That German plane was later shot down by our anti-aircraft defences.

When I was aged 18, I volunteered to man the Civil Defence local report centre on one night a week. When an air raid warning sounded, we had to telephone all the area's air raid warden's posts to tell them to get all their personnel in. We received all details of bombs having dropped, and, at the all clear siren, we had to telephone all the wardens again to tell them that "all personnel can be dismissed".

Nine days after the invasion we in southern England were attacked by unmanned V1 and V2 aircraft, which became known as "doodle-bugs". They appeared to buzz, then the noise would stop, and then they would crash and explode. Buildings were destroyed and lives lost in "Hitler's last attack". These buzz bombs were launched from France. During the days immediately before and after D-Day, southern England was divided into zones, and one could not pass from one to another without good reason. For instance, we at Bedhampton could visit Portsmouth to the west, but not Chichester to the east, over the Sussex border. Fortunately this particular restriction did not last long.'


LIFE IN THE NEW FOREST

'My father was in the navy so we only saw him on his short, infrequent leaves. Home was with my grandmother, mother, brother, sister and me, with Nanny and a living-in cook and her daughter (they had been bombed out of Portsmouth). Granny also employed a daily and a full time gardener over military age. He grew all our fruit and vegetables and was a member of the Home Guard.

We kept ducks, geese, hens, rabbits and bees. Many people kept a house cow and a few followers. The cow would graze the Forest by day and come home each evening to be milked and to a snug bracken bed in the byre, but as their milk dried off they tended to be distracted and not come home so every cow wore a bell producing a lovely sound I greatly miss today. All cow owners churned their butter, which was rationed; butter and cream were exchanged for eggs, honey etc. A lot of time in the Christmas holidays was spent cutting blind holly to feed the rabbits. Our breeding doe quite often escaped and had half-wild brown young instead of the grey pelts my mother made into gloves (clothes were also rationed). An unpopular job was going down the garden at dusk in all weathers to shut up the free range poultry; if they were forgotten the fox always had them and on one horrid occasion a badger was discovered trapped in the henhouse having slaughtered all the hens. Dredge corn was grown on land not ploughed for many years. It was harvested with a horse-drawn reaper and binder and we went gleaning to collect any left-over grain to feed the hens.

Enterprising neighbours gave wonderful parties, feeding their guests with moorhen soup and roast swan, but at a more austere children's party the host announced, "There is one slice of bread and butter for everyone and one chocolate biscuit for each child."

We rode a lot, on one occasion being stopped from going up an enclosure track because of an unexploded bomb, but on another track we found a German parachute hung up in a tree. There were a number of firing ranges with notices saying "Keep off when the red flag flies." There were nine airfields in and around the Forest and tanks manoeuvred all over the moors; the tracks can still be seen whenever the heather is burnt. Before D-Day there were tents under all the trees round the village and vehicles lined the road wherever there was any cover from air reconnaissance. In spite of the blackout and all the troops no one locked their doors and we children rode our ponies and bicycles, without adult escort, often coming home when it was getting dark.

Gymkhanas were held to raise funds for Red Cross parcels for POWs. The Pony Society show was the high spot, combined with the flower show held in a marquee in the Manor Park. Everyone went, largely to meet friends they seldom saw. We always went to see the stallion show, driving seven miles each way in the pony cart. We also went by pony cart to bathe on the one beach open, among the anti-invasion barbed wire and tank traps. Despite the war, I had a wonderful childhood.'

## SCHOOL AND WAR IN BURITON

'My first days at school coincided with the outbreak of war. Previously the older children had gone to Petersfield, but there was no room there now and consequently the village school at Buriton was overcrowded, for besides the older pupils there were many hop pickers' children. Families came every September from Portsmouth for the hop picking. They camped in primitive huts at Pitcroft Lane. However, with the onset of war the women and children settled there permanently and were joined by the men at weekends.

The youngest and older children remained in the main building, but the middle class was taught by Miss Digby in the WI hall. Facilities were very limited – a blackboard, desks, and an enormous cupboard. This stood some way from the wall, so that one of the hop pickers' boys, who was always in trouble, could get behind and refuse to come out. The cupboard was so wide that Miss Digby could not reach him.

We were not allowed to come to school without our gas masks. Oh, how I hated that suffocating, rubbery mask, so I was frequently sent home for mine. Two bombs fell on the village and one lunch time an enemy plane flew over, firing down on the High Street. Fortunately there were no casualties. When the doodlebugs started coming we were told that we must not watch them, but as soon as we heard one we had to run straight into school and crouch under our desks with our hands over our heads, until we heard the explosion.

Army convoys were routed through the village, particularly on the lead up to D-Day, using the tree-shaded lanes instead of the A3 so they would not be detected. The heavy roar of the tanks could be heard long before they reached the village. This terrified me and I would shelter behind the chapel wall. The convoys often camped in a field opposite the drive to Buriton House, where large oaks provided cover. When the Americans came they were generous with sweets and chocolate and wanted our mothers to make tea for them.

The ringing of church bells was to be a warning of invasion and when they rang out to celebrate victory I thought this was the dreaded invasion and instead of rejoicing I ran home terrified.'

## LIFE IN ALDERSHOT

'When war was declared in September 1939, a great many changes came about. The Municipal Gardens at Aldershot was an early casualty, losing its gates, railings and old guns from the First World War for smelting to help the war effort. Only recently I learned that the metal from this source proved to be of no use for making weaponry and was subsequently dumped off the Isle of Dogs.

The air raid siren was sounded from the fire station. As we lived so close, it was deafening as well as frightening. At gas mask fittings my baby brother was placed in an egg-shaped mask, large enough to take him completely, and which my mother was taught to hand-pump to provide his air. I remember her crying as she sought to get to grips with this new contraption, no doubt all the while worrying for the safety of her children. Thankfully the masks never had to be used.

We schoolchildren, pushing a municipal barrow, and accompanied by a teacher, would set off for Dolly Hill, now Rowhills nature reserve, to collect cones and tree branches to help with the fuel supply, anything to get out of school! I remember a very tall chimney near our playing field being toppled as it would have provided a marker for enemy aircraft. It was also close to the place where the air raid wardens practised putting out fires. My father became a warden with the ARP (Air Raid Precautions), and carried a card which bore these immortal words, "The man who shows you this card is an air raid warden. Lie down on the floor and do what he says." No wonder my father did so many extra duties . . .

Our large town house was filled from basement (where I was born) to attic with relatives home on leave and music hall stars from the Aldershot Hippodrome, billeted on my parents by the Ministry. We had an actor who had played opposite Vic Oliver in some film or other, a ginger-haired trombonist of 80 years from Ivy Benson's All Girl Band (and could she blow a mean note), plus a troupe of tap-dancers. I was determined to join them when I grew up.

My mother made valiant attempts at bottling all kinds of foods in her Kilner jars and did battle with dried egg recipes. She also made turnip cake. One of my aunts had a go at making goat's milk cheese; a smelly ball of the stuff hung dripping from the kitchen ceiling into a bowl beneath. I don't know whether it got eaten, certainly not by me.

Pocket money was spent at Mrs Malone's shop near the school. Our pennies were exchanged for pear drops, hundreds and thousands and sherbet dabs by this wonderfully kind old lady with heavily rouged cheeks who had all the patience in the world for her young customers. I remember her with great affection.

There was also the baker's shop, Clarkes, where my mother would send me to buy a loaf hot out of the oven; this would be wrapped in a sheet of white paper. They owned an enormous ginger cat who could often be found sleeping by the cakes in the window and sometimes he would lie fully stretched in a box of Shippam's pastes. Imagine what a furore that would cause today. My Aunt Brenda made hats and posies out of odd pieces of felt, and very good they were too, whilst Uncle Roy planted sunflowers against the fence in our back garden in order to harvest the seeds for cooking. Every day he inspected their growth and very soon the heads were above the fence. Imagine his dismay when one morning he discovered that every head had been snatched, all that remained were the stalks. He never repeated the exercise.

My friend Heather and I often slept in her Anderson shelter and enjoyed midnight feasts all unbeknown to her parents. It was all a great game. However, a bomb did fall on The Oaks school in Eggars Hill, Aldershot and one pupil was killed, with several others injured. There was much damage. The blast blew out windows in the art room at the Aldershot county high school where I was a pupil. I was in the room when it happened and recall our teacher telling us to get down under the desks. Apart from being showered with glass we were all right, a lucky escape.'

## COLLECTING THINGS

'Once a poster was put up in class at St Mary Bourne showing the birds whose eggs we could collect as they stole the farmers' grain. The boys were hugely delighted and collected eggs with abandon but that autumn my mother and I walked across Morestead Gallops and every stem and stalk was covered with chrysallises and the noise the moths made eating their way out was unbelievable. Needless to say, next year the poster was taken down.

We collected blackberries for the WI to make into jam, acorns to feed the pigs and, just once, rosehips to make syrup for babies. Did we really make as much as that? Twopence a pound?'

## CASUALTIES OF WAR

'It was one of those lovely soft spring days which tell us that winter is at last over, with the countryside showing a haze of green shoots and everything looking tranquil and peaceful. The reality was far from this. The date was 6th April 1944, when the countryside around Littleton, in the centre of Hampshire, was teeming with troops and military armour, both British and American, preparing for D-Day which was to be exactly two months later.

As it was the first day of the Easter school holidays, we boys of the village were a bit like young colts who had just been let out into fresh spring pastures. One of the great interests for village boys in those days was bird nesting, so with this in mind, some of the boys decided to go to Farley Mount – a local beauty spot. We had been warned at school not to go there because the American troops were using it for tank training. However, boys will be boys, and five of us, three Johns, one Bill, and a Peter, set off on three bicycles.

Once there, we had started to explore when one of the younger boys picked up an unexploded grenade. The older boys shouted at him to put it down. The warning was too late, the grenade exploded killing two boys, seriously injuring one, and less seriously injuring another.

Fifty years later I can still remember the effect on a close knit village community. One of the boys killed was an only son, the other boy killed also had a brother seriously injured. The other injured boy was my cousin.

As my father was the local nurseryman and florist we had to help him well into the night preparing wreaths and flowers for the funeral. This was a very sad occasion with the two small coffins carried up the church path between walls of flowers held by the village children. All I can recall from the service was the parson telling us that our bodies were only the tents in which we lived. The boys were laid to rest in the tranquil village cemetery among the daffodils on a lovely spring day. They were the victims of war just as much as any soldier killed in action; they grew not old as we that are left grow old.'

# THE EVACUEES

**For some children, evacuation from the dangers of bombing led to a happy new life in the country, for others it was a traumatic and unhappy time away from their families.**

A TRAUMATIC TIME

'I was watching the Armistice parade on the television and my mind went back to August 1939. The start of a very traumatic time for two small girls aged five and twelve years.

It all started during the previous month when our parents were told it would be safer and therefore better for us to be evacuated from Southampton if a war was to start between Britain and Germany. We, being my sister and I and our two brothers aged seven and ten years, met with all the other parents and children involved, at Shirley Warren school two weeks before the fateful day, to mark our belongings. Into a carrier bag went a change of underwear, a pair of socks, a skirt and jumper. Gas masks were issued to us all, the babies had funny red ones which we all called Mickey Mouse.

On 2nd September we again arrived at the school. This was a Saturday; it was raining hard. We went by bus to Southampton central station. We were not told where we were going. Whilst waiting on the platform we were given a sandwich, biscuits, chocolate and a small bottle of milk, all this went into our carrier bag. The train arrived and we all scrambled in. We were off. It should have produced excitement but all around the mothers and children looked frightened. Can you imagine a train loaded with children and a few mothers, not knowing where they were off to or how long before they would be able to come back? Maybe thinking of those they had left at home, the little ones probably too scared to think. My mum came with us to see us settled.

We arrived at the station and were told, this is Bournemouth. It was still raining! We were ushered into more buses and taken to a school. It was not until the next day that we were told it was Malmesbury Road school at Springbourne.

On arrival at the school we all went into a hall to wait – to wait for what, none of us knew. Everyone was very quiet, the occasional cough or snuffle, just waiting. A lady would come into the hall, call a name or two and off they would go. My two brothers went first and then my mum with our baby sister. We were now all alone. Mum left with orders for me to "take care of Zena and I will see you in the morning." We sat and waited. Eventually everyone else had been called and we were the only two left. We began to think we had been forgotten. "Cough," said Zena, "they might hear." Cough I did and they heard. "My, there's still two here, I thought we had placed them all," said a lady who came into the hall.

We soon realised they had nowhere for us to go. We were taken to a car and driven around the streets. The lady was knocking on doors asking people to take us in. It was getting late, about eight o'clock, and still raining very hard. It seemed to us that nobody wanted us. The lady tried once more. "Sorry," this person said (who turned out later to be Aunt Polly), "I can't take them, I have my old mum to look after, but I am sure my sister will. She lives in the next street." Off we went. I can remember vividly sitting in that car with Zena, clutching a carrier bag, a gas mask and feeling very cold and tired and a lady looking into the car window and saying, "I didn't really want evacuees but poor little mites, I'll take them for now and maybe you will find them a place by Monday." Mrs Mead was her name and that Monday never came, we were still with her a year later and she was wonderful to us.

After a good night's sleep we were returned to the school. It was Sunday 3rd September 1939.

Seeing Mum again when we all met in the school hall was very upsetting. We were there to await a special news report that was being broadcast at eleven o'clock. I remember thinking if there is a war we have to stay here in Bournemouth, separate from the rest of the family, if not, home tomorrow. As I think back I remember the silence, the strained faces, the tension in that hall.

Eleven o'clock – Mr Chamberlain gave his now famous speech, we were at war with Germany. We would be staying.

Everyone was crying, mums and children alike. We were two very sad little girls as we realised Mum would be going away again and we would not see her for about a month. We felt very alone.

We returned to Mrs Mead, met her two daughters and then went to tea with Aunt Polly, who we soon both loved. We saw our two brothers and our previous school companions at Malmesbury Road school. But we were not taught there. At first we had lessons on the beach, until it was too cold. Miss Jacks, a lovely teacher, often carried Zena on her shoulders whilst we were beachcombing, as she was about the smallest and youngest evacuee with us at that time. Then a school was found for us all in Boscombe, St John's hall. We shared this hall with Bassett Green school of Southampton, on an alternate basis of morning and afternoon.

During this time our brothers were not very happy with their billet. They were with two very elderly unmarried ladies who did not know what to expect of two normal boisterous boys. One can only say that they did their best. Anyhow, they were moved and were very happy in their new place. I expect the elderly ladies were as relieved as they were! We spent many a happy month with the people of Bournemouth. We stayed for a year, returning to Southampton for the school holidays.

September 1940 arrived, Mrs Mead was always very pleased to see us and we went back to St John's school. The first day back at school was clear and very cold and we were playing in the school playground. Someone shouted, "Get down." The playground and the children playing there were machine gunned, but luckily no one was hurt. Another time my sister and I were playing in the street and again we were machine gunned. Mum and Dad heard about all this on the wireless and arrived next day to take us home. They said we would be just as safe in Southampton as in Bournemouth.

I have never forgotten my stay in Bournemouth, especially Mrs Mead who was very kind to us and treated us just as she did her own girls. May God bless her and look after her wherever she is today.'

## FORMAL AND INFORMAL

'When children were removed from industrial towns and the vulnerable south coast in 1939, Alverstoke Roman Catholic primary school was evacuated to Wellow. Mr and Mrs Rogers were responsible for finding accommodation for children of both sexes between six and ten years old. People were asked to take in these children and Embley (once the home of Florence Nightingale and not then a school) took 20 – a magnificent contribution to solving the problem. (Billeting officers requested help, but wartime regulations required householders in safe areas to take in evacuees unless they could cite good reasons for refusing.)

The headmistress, Mrs Thomas, and another teacher lodged with Mr and Mrs Rogers, who also gave shelter to two boys. Inevitably some children settled and some did not. Some children were soon taken home by their parents, at first unconvinced by the threat of air raids. Other children enjoyed the novelty of the countryside and Mr Rogers even took his two boys pheasant shooting.

The government paid the hosts a small sum each week to provide for the evacuees' food and care. In the case of the headmistress this amounted to 19 shillings, though less was paid for children. Mrs Rogers would give the boys sandwiches for lunch at school but Mrs Thomas came back for a cooked meal at midday and then shared in the cooked evening meal with the boys. It is a tribute to Mrs Rogers' housekeeping that she could provide this sort of food during wartime rationing, though it was somewhat easier in the countryside than in towns. Rabbits and wild game, in the nature of things, could not be rationed and many country gardens were large enough to keep chicken and even goats.

Every other Sunday the parents would come out by coach from Southampton and stop at the Red Rover. They would save their sweet rations for their children, often causing discomfort to both landladies and children.

When the air raids started, there was also an informal evacuation scheme, with adults and children taking buses out of Southampton to avoid the nightly raids and returning to their homes and work each morning. The buses were parked overnight in Wellow – they too were evacuees, removed from the danger of bombs and fires. Wellow was not the only village to provide nightly shelter of this kind – many made their way to Melchet Court and other places within easy reach of Southampton. Villagers made an attempt to provide some sort of hot food for their guests, who slept in barns, halls and in whatever shelter was available.'

## IT WAS WONDERFUL

'It was 1941. Southampton had been severely bombed and two houses demolished in our road in Shirley. The town is so close to the docks, which stretch along the banks of the rivers Test and Itchen right into the town and were the prime target for the bombers. All the surrounding areas were very vulnerable. My father, who was in the army and posted to the north of England at that time, persuaded my mother to take me out of town to live. She chanced to tell one of our local shopkeepers, who said that she was living in temporary accommodation in West Wellow. She gave my mother the name of a farmer who might take us in.

Such a move was not easy for my mother, who was town born and bred, but we took the trip to Hamdown Farm and met Mr Parsons and his daughter Ursula. Apparently they had already been asked to take evacuees from the town, so we moved to Wellow and stayed for four years. I remember my mother saying that she did not know which she was the more frightened of – the bombs in Southampton or the cows in the field which she had to walk through to get to Whinwhistle Road! For me, as a toddler, growing up in the country was wonderful. We were so lucky to find such friendly people to stay with. I gained adopted aunties and uncles, and Mr Parsons was "Grandad" to me as soon as I could talk. His grandchildren lived just down the road at Warners Farm, so there was always someone for me to play with.

I was too young to remember much of those four years, yet still the friendships have continued. I spent many a happy holiday in Wellow during my school years, and made my home there for 15 years. It was like coming home.'

## A SERIES OF DIGS

'In the spring of 1940 my family moved to Gosport when my father, who was in the Fleet Air Arm, was appointed to Lee-on-Solent Naval Air Station. One of the first tasks was to find schools for us three girls. Gosport grammar school had already been evacuated to Eastleigh which was thought to be safer from German invasion than

Gosport. So my elder sister and I, aged 15 and 13 years respectively, were to be sent away to Eastleigh and my younger sister, aged nine years and rather delicate, was dressed up in a very fancy uniform with blue and silver striped blazer and sent to the local private school.

During my four years in Eastleigh I was placed in a series of "digs". These were arranged by the wife of one of the schoolmasters. The foster parents on the whole were very worthy people who put themselves to endless trouble to make us feel at home. But it was pot luck as to the success of the digs. Four of my contemporaries were the envy of all of us because they had struck lucky in a large house with a butler.

My sister and I were not so fortunate. Our first billet had an unhappy couple who spent most of their time cursing and swearing at each other, and after a while we plucked up enough courage to ask to be moved. The woman then locked us out so that we couldn't get our belongings after school, so, not to be outdone we managed to gain entry by the French windows, retrieve our belongings and carry them to the next billet. We were then accused of breaking and entering and stealing (our own belongings). However, this all blew over and we settled into the next billet, where we had to mind our Ps and Qs as the wife was very houseproud. We were given our tea – a plate of bread and margarine – sitting on the kitchen doorstep and whenever possible did our homework out in the garden. We survived this for about a year before we were asked to move.

The third billet had already been badly damaged by bombs and rebuilt, leaving our new foster mother naturally somewhat nervous of air raids. Since we were only five miles from Southampton and less than a stone's throw from a busy railway junction, this was understandable. Every night for months we were taken to the nearest underground concrete air raid shelter dressed in our nightclothes and given a piece of matting to sit on. Our foster mother dozed in a deck chair until she decided she'd had enough and took us back to bed – air raids or no air raids. My parents could never understand why we always seemed to have colds.

At the end of two years my sister left school to take a job as a teleprinter operator until going to college. I was left on my own quite happily until the master of the house reappeared. I don't recall the circumstances, I only remember that he came in drunk most evenings and proceeded to knock his wife about. I was helpless to do anything and became nervous for my own skin and asked to leave. You may wonder why I didn't report all this to my parents. There were two reasons. One was the "blue and silver blazers", and the second that the answer to any sort of complaint was, "Don't you know there's a war on?" My fourth billet was a dream. I lived with a very kindly retired couple whose sole stipulation was that I went away at weekends. This was my intention anyway. I stayed there until I left school in 1944 to go to college.

I had a relatively easy time at school. We shared a building with a local school and our hours were staggered so that we didn't see much of the other school. Organisation must have been a nightmare for the staff – many of whom were retired and recalled because of the war, to replace younger staff who had gone to fight. My particular friend and I, to our shame, led them a merry dance. I felt sorry for my sister who was constantly being asked to "do something about your young sister."

Getting about was a difficulty at first until we persuaded my father to come to Eastleigh for the day and buy bicycles for us. We each chose a secondhand cycle for £2 each, with five shillings added to mine for a new saddle. Father wisely made us pay half the cost each from our Post Office savings, knowing that we were more likely to look after them. From then on we were mobile and life became much easier.

Going home for weekends was naturally discouraged. On Fridays after school many of the pupils would catch the train to Fareham, then change to a bus to Gosport. This cost half a crown which was rather more than my shilling a week pocket money. As soon as we had the bicycles, having learnt to ride them in a few evenings, we set off on the Friday for Gosport. We had noted roughly the route from our school atlas but hadn't realised the difficulty in finding our way when all signposts had been removed. And some of the people we asked, refused to tell us the way in case we were German spies! And us in school gymslips! My mother nearly had a fit when we wobbled into the garden at Gosport having taken about four hours. We ate our supper standing up! Within a few weeks, many of the rest of the school joined us in cycling home at weekends. We became expert at finding the best route and reduced the time to one and a half hours. The school's reply to this was to make us go to school on Saturday mornings. Our answer to this was to cycle home and stay until Monday morning and go straight to school. I remember having to mend a puncture and I arrived late for a history class. I explained that I'd had a puncture and was told by the master that I didn't look very deflated!

Gosport suffered badly from air raids and we often were afraid of what we would find. Sometimes we would hear on the grapevine of some particular area that had been bombed. Once a large bakery was bombed and we took two large loaves each in our bicycle baskets. We also would buy fruit from the farms we passed on the way. Many were the times we would have to jump off our bikes into the nearest ditch when German fighter planes came too close. Often we would stop and watch the dogfights and cheer when a German came down in flames. I don't remember being afraid of being killed. The nearest we ever came to being injured was in Eastleigh when the railway junction was being strafed. We were sitting on our beds and saw the German plane flying low at roof level with guns blazing. Our windows smashed onto our beds and a heavy mirror was thrown off the mantlepiece. We absolutely flew downstairs!

Food was in short supply although some of the major foods such as bread and fish were not. Our foster parents kept our ration books of course, but we had midday dinner at school. This cost fivepence and was obviously subsidised. One day a week the meal consisted of thick soup and a slice of bread. Often the steamed puddings, known as "stodge", were sweetened with grated carrot. Most of our pocket money was spent on food. My favourite best-value-for-money item was an enormous round of scone for twopence halfpenny. It kept me going nicely between dinner and tea. My mother had the almost impossible task of feeding two extra mouths at weekends and food hunting became my Saturday morning job. I would take my young sister on our bikes into Gosport and join the queues for food. I would give her some money and instructions not to speak to me but follow behind and do the same as I did. In this way we would double our allowance of unrationed foods such as cakes, fish, sausages etc. We became expert shoppers.

The authorities closed their eyes to our going back to Gosport for the holidays – though these were much shorter than nowadays. During the summer holidays lots of us went potato picking to help with the war effort. We were paid fourpence an hour and worked very long hours. I remember a large, fat foreman who used to watch us like a hawk and shout at us to, "Pick 'em up clean, m'dears." For the first few days we would be exhausted at the end of the day, but soon we were playing tennis after a day's toil. One of the rewards was extra rations. I remember having an enormous ration of cheese – meant for our midday sandwiches on the farm. We also had an extra soap ration, but I don't think this meant much to me.

My time as an evacuee in Hampshire came to an abrupt end when I was offered a place in a college in London at the age of 17 years – and started my course just as the German doodlebugs arrived over the capital!'

# IN CHARGE OF EVACUEES

'It was September 1942 when I was appointed to be in charge of 80 junior evacuees aged eight to eleven years, from Portsmouth high school, now living in the lovely country house of Hinton Ampner. The next three years were some of the most demanding and happy ones in my life.

Some children were homesick at the beginning of term, but soon forgot this with so many others around them. In fact, the numbers were an advantage as all had to learn to live together and realise that the few rules laid down were for a purpose.

Springtime was also lambing time and at the bottom of the field where they played, was the shepherd and his hut. It was a thrill for many to be able to see the new-born lambs and the care given to them – something beyond their imaginations should they have remained in the city.

There was no "going home" at weekends or half term, so something special was always arranged for the latter – maybe in summer it was a sports afternoon or, in the autumn, a treasure hunt laid by one of the mistresses on duty. Another great pleasure was a Saturday picnic when the housekeeper made up separate lunches for each child and off to the pond, where newts could be seen. This included an unrehearsed nature lesson besides lots of fun and pleasure.

Air raid warnings were telephoned to the house and we had our share of raids and doodlebugs. In these circumstances, the girls knew exactly what to do and did it.

Christmas term had quite a highlight – Mr Dutton, the owner of the property, gave a tree, which stood in the hall and on the last Saturday of term, a nativity play was performed. This was excellently produced by the English mistress, a helper and a music teacher.

Cooking for a crowd was easier than for one on rations and our housekeeper was excellent. After meals, teams of six girls plus a mistress did the washing up.

At the end of the spring term 1945, we said goodbye to Hinton with some regrets and I took 18 children back to Southsea as boarders that term.

One Saturday, on returning from an afternoon on a farm at Cowplain, the girls suddenly saw all the lights of Portsmouth twinkling below them. It is difficult to put into words the reactions of those youngsters who had grown up with darkness all around them after daylight hours.'

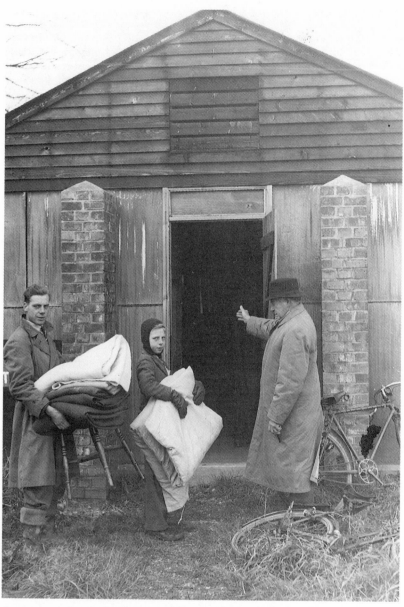

*So many people were bombed out of Gosport that finding homes for them proved a headache for local billeting officers. At Wickham some had to stay in poultry houses.*

## INTO POULTRY HOUSES

'My father was chief billeting officer at Wickham and his responsibility was to find room for families whose Gosport homes had been bombed. He scoured all the neighbouring houses and put evacuees in them. It got to the stage where some families with small children had nowhere to go, so they put them in poultry houses. To begin with it was just a reception area and the people were passed on, but towards the end of the war they had to be accommodated somehow. Because they had their own lifestyle they were sometimes difficult to house and a lot of the local rather genteel ladies found it hard having them as lodgers.'

# DOING OUR BIT

**We all did our bit for the war effort, from joining the Home Guard or the air raid wardens, to helping our towns and villages prepare for war and possible invasion. Many people were involved in the making of munitions or aircraft such as the Spitfire, which although production continued in other areas, was a Hampshire-based project.**

## TWYFORD HOME GUARD

'Twyford formed their Home Guard platoon early in the war. Called the Local Defence Volunteers, their uniform was a khaki armband with the letters LDV. This name was soon changed to the Home Guard and they wore khaki denim overalls which were later replaced by serge battledress uniforms. They were armed with any weapons they could find, from shotguns to souvenir revolvers from the First World War. One man pushed his heavy, old revolver, loaded, into his trouser pocket without checking the safety catch. The trigger caught on his pocket and fired. Miraculously the bullet went down his trouser leg, through his boot, passed between his first two toes and ended up in the ground without doing any harm.

The Home Guard drilled in the parish hall, practised on their rifle range off the Hazeley Road and learned to use hand grenades and spigot mortars on Hazeley Down. Soldiers from the regular army came to train with them and they were moulded into an efficient unit. They patrolled various strategic points in the village every night. They slept at the telephone exchange at Shawford, the golf club near the Hockley crossroads and at the far end of the golf course. Six men were on duty at each post, two on patrol and four resting. The golf course patrol were looking for parachutists. One night the men resting heard the patrol calling for help. They followed the correct procedure and silently surrounded the caller, ready to capture any lurking parachutists. They found that one of the patrol had thrust his foot deep into a rabbit hole and was stuck. They had to dig him out with their bayonets.

One night in the early 1940s the church bells rang. This was, of course, the warning for an invasion. All the local Home Guard platoons were mobilised immediately. They remained, armed, on standby for two whole days. There was no confirmation of an invasion, nobody really knew why the bells had been rung. There were sinister whispered tales of bodies washed up along the coast. Nobody is sure what actually happened.

On another occasion a German plane crashed on Hazeley Down. Sergeant Best, of the Home Guard, took three of his men, rushed up there in a truck and disarmed the crew. They all took the threat of invasion very seriously indeed. Several elderly members felt they would be a liability in active combat. They asked that, in the event of invasion, they could have a rifle each and a few rounds of ammunition so that they could hide beside the road and "make sure I take a few of the blighters with me when I go." One man even made a hole in his garden wall so that he would have a clear view up and down the road and could pick off some of the advancing troops. Their passionate sincerity is moving even when retold today.

In 1945 the Home Guard was disbanded but some of them were recalled in 1951 when Russia was seen as a threat. Four men from Twyford joined the Winchester platoon. They were to be trained as guerrillas and, in the event of invasion, would go underground to train other young men in guerrilla warfare. Their secret arms dumps and food caches were carefully planned. The Home Guard finally ceased to exist in 1957.'


A TOWN PREPARES

'At Odiham, street shelters, built of brick, above ground, with reinforced concrete roofs, appeared in several places. A few of these survive today, for example in Crown Fields and on Cemetery Hill, although others, such as those on Gospel Green in the High Street and outside the almshouses, were removed many years ago.

A couple of years before the war, a fire siren had been placed on the tower of the fire station, which was adjacent to the parish room. This was now used as an air raid warning, operated by an on/off switch in the police station. The local police force – normally a sergeant and two or three constables – was augmented by calling on the spare-time services of men who had previously volunteered as Special Constables. They took their turn in manning the police station and patrolling the area on foot or on bicycle. Mr Baker, the manager at Dicker's grocery store, became Inspector for the whole area, with Mr Holmes, science master at the grammar school, as Sergeant.

To augment the local volunteer fire brigade, Odiham had a part time unit of the national Auxiliary Fire Service. This enabled the fire station to be manned full time, and the men and women on duty used the parish room as their rest room. Since the AFS had its own new vehicle and trailer pump, the old fire station was no longer adequate. Fortunately, the former Thames Valley bus garage in Alton Road was available, and the two fire engines and their trailer pumps could be properly housed there. Eventually, the teams were amalgamated under the National Fire Service, with central control of their functions, under which the AFS staff were required to serve full time, wherever they were needed, away from home if necessary.

The ambulance and medical services were centred on the old Buryfields school, where the first aid post was run jointly by the Red Cross and St John Ambulance Brigade. The local ambulance vehicle was garaged at the hospital, in what later became the out-patients building. For most of the war, Dr Widdowson was the only full time local doctor, as his partner Dr Harward had joined the forces: eventually the doctor's car was one of very few private vehicles to be seen on the roads, as most non-essential users lost their meagre petrol ration and had to lay-up their cars "for the duration".

Odiham had its team of volunteer air raid wardens, who maintained a duty roster, and were based initially at Western House, and later at the Conservative Club behind The Bell in the Bury. Mr Dauncey, mathematics master at the grammar school, was Head Warden.

Most of the early wartime changes had been planned well in advance, but the fall of France in 1940 brought a threat of invasion and air attacks from bases much closer to Britain. The formation of the Local Defence Volunteers – later the Home Guard – was aided by the resources of drill rifles and other equipment belonging to the grammar school cadet corps, so that Odiham never had the legendary "pikes and cutlasses" phase before proper weapons could be issued.

The headquarters of the LDV was established on the ground floor of the Assembly Rooms in King Street.

Defensive works were rapidly built throughout the Odiham district. The town lay close to the "tank trap" – a continuous deep ditch, stretching for many meandering miles, and coming nearest to Odiham near the point where the present electricity pylons cross the Winchfield road. (It was filled in after a relatively short existence.) Defence in depth was provided by numerous brick and concrete pill boxes, mostly built with small loopholes for rifles, though a few, at strategic points, were of a larger type with wide apertures and mountings for anti-tank or heavy machine guns. Many of these have since been destroyed, though they were strongly built, and one lying in the open fields between the Firs and Crown Fields had to be blown up. More conventional methods were used to remove others, such as one at the bottom of the Firs road.

Road blocks were built, consisting of concrete "dragons' teeth" either side of the carriageway. When necessary the gap could be closed either by barbed wire coiled on wooden frames or by cylindrical concrete blocks rolled into the road and linked by a steel hawser. One set of dragons' teeth, obstructing the footpath beside 125 High Street, was responsible for injuries to an air raid warden who fell over them in the blackout. Other road blocks (eg at the bottom of King Street), involved rows of holes, normally blocked with wooden plugs, to take lengths of girder, railway line or mines.'

## MAKING SPITFIRES

'Spitfire – the very name still brings a thrill to my friend and I, because we worked in Newbury for Vickers Armstrong helping to make this superb little plane. The original factory was bombed out from Woolston in Southampton, so they took over every available garage and building to start again.

My friend, who was about 19 years old, volunteered to be trained to work in an engineering firm as soon as the war started, and was sent away to be trained. We found ourselves working in the same factory after I had been called up to do war work in 1941. She had already become very proficient, and worked with a small gang turning out 40 pilot seats a week. This job was highly skilled and men's lives depended on the accuracy of the work. She went on to become a shop steward, then was voted to become a representative on the joint production committee, quite a feat for a woman in those days. She had great integrity, and fought fairly for the rights of the girls working alongside men.

I went into the assembly section where I learned to make all kinds of things reading from a blueprint. I was very quick, earning quite a lot of bonus money. Our hours were from eight to eight, day and night shifts, and we were paid £3 a week. I was made a chargehand when they built a larger factory, and had as many as 100 girls to look after, most of them part time workers. I grew to like these women from all walks of life.

Two friends from one parish, East Woodhay, we succeeded in a man's world knowing that lives depended on our skill. We would not have missed the opportunity for the world, knowing that we were doing our bit alongside the men – apart from the pay!'


SWINGING THE COMPASS

'Born in 1903, my father grew up with an interest in and fascination for aircraft. At the age of 23 he joined the Royal Air Force where he was trained as an aircraft engineer and came into contact with many of the early aircraft. He remained in the RAF for twelve years and in 1938, he went to work as an aircraft fitter at Super Marine (to become Vickers Armstrong) at Woolston in Southampton where the Spitfire was in production. His experience of working with aircraft in the RAF resulted in his transfer to the Eastleigh factory at the airport, being one of the few people at that time who knew how to "swing a compass".

Swinging a compass is, I believe, a method of checking, calibrating and correcting the aeroplane's compass. It involves positioning the aeroplane on a concrete pad marked out with 16 points of the compass. These pads were situated some distance from the hangars and a Spitfire would be taxied to the pad. The aeroplane would be moved around by lifting the tail to each point and the compass within the cockpit then checked and corrected.

During 1938 and 1939 production of the Spitfire was at fever pitch; war was coming and Britain was unprepared. However, I can well remember the feeling of pride even at the age of seven when seeing the Spitfire being hurled across the sky in a series of acrobatic feats, and thinking, "My daddy made that!"

A special treat at this time was a visit to the airport at Eastleigh. A small strip of land had been fenced off near to the factory where the employees' families were able to sit and watch the comings and goings. It was a long walk from Bishopstoke to the airport but well worth it to enjoy a picnic and sometimes see my father taking a Spitfire to a compass pad or seeing one of the test pilots taking the plane to the sky.

Those days were to end, of course, when the war became reality. I remember my father cycling to work armed with a rifle, tin hat and gas mask; working long hours and using any spare time training in the Home Guard and fire watching, not to mention digging up the garden to make an air raid shelter.

The Spitfire, too, was putting its acrobatic prowess to good use as the battle for our way of life was fought high in the skies over southern Britain.

Then there were the air raids. I think that the factory at Woolston was bombed, for my father always said he was lucky to have been moved to Eastleigh.

One day he had taxied a Spitfire to one of the compass pads and was swinging the compass. He heard the approach of aircraft. He looked up towards the sound. There had been no warning, no siren. He saw the bomb doors open and what he described as a "string of sausages falling from the sky". He thought that his end had come and stood up in the cockpit unable to move. The bombs fell on the air raid shelter of the nearby factory of Cunliffe Owen; many were killed in this air raid. My father taxied the Spitfire to the safety of the hangar and lived to tell the tale.'

# THE WOMEN'S LAND ARMY

**Women who did not want to work in munitions or the services, could volunteer for the Land Army. Many did so, having no idea of the kind of life they would lead, and went on to love the farming life. With the men called up to fight, keeping the country fed was essential to the war effort.**

## I WOULDN'T HAVE MISSED IT

'I joined the WLA in 1941 after hairdressing for five and a half years. I worked on a farm one and a half miles from my home at St Mary Bourne until my parents moved, then I lived in at the farm.

The farmer, not having had a land girl before, didn't seem to know what to give me to do, so as it was potato harvest I went potato picking. This went on for three weeks, first with a lot of helpers from the village and then on my own.

After that was over he taught me to hand milk which was much more interesting, then I learned to drive the tractor and use the many different implements, the plough being my favourite. I was sent to fields well away from the farm with the dog and a gun (in case I saw a rabbit).

In the summer when it was very hot, being fair skinned, I wore long-sleeved shirts, long trousers and a hat. I quite envied the girls who came later with the threshing gang. They mostly wore shorts and short-sleeved shirts and were very brown.

The jobs were very varied, haymaking, harvesting, milking, calf rearing etc, and of course the inevitable potato picking.

We had old fashioned cow sheds with mangers when I first went to the farm. Later on we got new sheds and milking machines, but with the old sheds, on a cold frosty or snowy moonlit morning as I was putting out the cows' rations, I could imagine the baby Jesus lying in the manger. It was never the same with the new sheds, the atmosphere was gone.

I remember one night being woken by the sound of a doodlebug engine. I could see the flame from its tail and then the engine stopped which meant that it would drop within a mile and it dropped in a field on the next farm.

I enjoyed my life on the farm but after four years I saw an advertisement for Milk Recorders which meant visiting different farms each day weighing the milk and taking butterfat samples. The farmer didn't want me to leave but said he wouldn't stand in my way if I wished to apply for it, I would be replaced anyway, so I applied and did get the job. This meant I had to get a car and learn to drive which I did, my first car being a 1933 Austin 10.

It was a very interesting job, visiting one farm in the afternoon, doing the books in the evening and going to the same farm the next morning. It meant getting up very early in the morning, sometimes having to drive 16 miles to a farm for a 4.30 am milking. When it was very cold, frosty or snowy, I filled a hot water bottle and had it on my lap with a blanket (no car heaters in those days).

I also had to earmark the cows, which meant clamping their ears in a machine and putting in numbers. It was an awful crunching noise (the farmer said it didn't hurt them!)

They were happy days and looking back I wouldn't have missed them.'

FARMING WAS IN MY BLOOD

'Hampshire was a lovely county to grow up in during the 1920s and 1930s. Especially in the friendly little village of Crookham in the northern corner of the county. Leaving school at the age of

216

14 I worked in a local nursery, tending maidenhair ferns that were sent to London to be used in bouquets etc. At the commencement of war most of the fern was dug up to make way for market garden produce.

Feeling the urge to do more for my country I volunteered for the Women's Land Army, as being born on a farm and spending the early years of my life living there, farming was in my blood.

In 1941 when I was 17 years old I applied for a position only to be told that the enrolment age was 18. Determined to achieve my ambition I obtained work on a local farm. To my delight after six months I was allowed to become an official member of the Land Army.

Rising with the lark it was often moonlight when I started work. On my first day I was given a white jacket and a three-legged stool and asked to help with the milking. On the farm where I had lived we did not keep dairy cows and so I was rather nervous about it, but I thoroughly enjoyed it and was told by the farmer that I had made a good job of it. Next the wood had to be chopped to stoke the boiler to provide hot water for washing the dairy utensils. Washing down the cowsheds came next after the cows had been turned out into the field. Feeding and watering the massive, but friendly bull was my next task.

Feeding the hens and collecting their eggs was always an enjoyable task. In those days eggs really were free range. It was like hide-and-seek to find them in the most inaccessible places. Rearing young calves and teaching them to drink from a bucket by letting them suck the fingers could mean getting soaked with milk if they butted the bucket too hard.

Haymaking and harvesting was hard work but enjoyable. Neighbouring farmers shared their workers, making sure that the crops were gathered in on time. Double summertime meant that work often continued until 10 pm.

One of the perks of working on the land was the extra cheese ration allowed for agricultural workers.

Enjoying the work helped me as I rarely remember being over-tired. During the hoeing and potato and swede harvesting local women were employed as extra labour.

In my memory most days seemed fine and sunny during the summer months, while the cowshed was warm in the winter. Milk was sold from the farmhouse door, costing a few coppers a pint. Villagers came with jugs or small cans to collect it.

There was much harmony and friendship among the village people. My life in the Land Army holds many happy memories.'

*Land girls, led by the band, march through Winchester in 1943 as part of a recruiting rally. Many girls chose to work on the land rather than go into munitions or the services.*

## I GREW UP

'Although I did not spend my childhood in Hampshire I think I can claim to have grown up in that county. I joined the Women's Land Army in 1943 at the age of 17 and I believe I grew up in the three years I was in that illustrious band.

I came from the North East to a farm near Hambledon, and remained there for three months while the farmer decided that the metamorphosis into a 17 year old city girl of the 30 year old experienced milk-hand he required was more than he could bear and we parted amicably enough. I was redirected to Petersfield to a hostel which contained 20 girls, plus warden and kitchen staff. From the first I absolutely adored being there.

Petersfield was great. We lived in a big house by the lake. Each morning at about seven thirty a shooting brake – remember them? – called for us and took us to our respective farms. It could not hold us all so if you were lucky you would be on the second load. That meant, of course, second load home in the afternoon. There might be four girls hoeing at one farm, and six threshing somewhere else.

218

Others might be sorting potatoes, sizing them and bagging them. We thought nothing of carrying a hundredweight bag on our backs. In later life we remembered it, though. According to the time of year we did haymaking, harvesting, planting cabbages and picking up potatoes. We became strong and brown.

In the evenings there was the Home from Home canteen in a drill hall near the Red Lion. There we met the opposite sex in the person of soldiers from Longmoor camp (REs), Bordon (Canadians), Air Force lads from Telegraph Hill, sailors recuperating at Laydene, French sailors recuperating at Steep House and REMEs who were in Petersfield itself. Later there were Americans stationed all over the countryside, Tichborne, Bighton, Ropley etc.

As 1944 wore on, the roads were being widened, we did not know why. Then the verges became filled with lorries containing troops who lived in their lorries.

On D-Day itself, three of us girls who had finished threshing a rick in one of the fields on the West Meon Hutt crossroads were allowed home when it was finished at just after 11 am. We sat on our sandwich tins and just watched in amazement the tanks rolling down the road from Alton towards Bishop's Waltham and eventually, Portsmouth or Southampton; and from the Winchester direction joining the queue. We knew what it meant.

The next day, we could hardly work for watching the sky with hundreds of planes going over with supplies, Dakotas, I think. They were apparently wing tip to wing tip, in layers. An extraordinary sight. On the Saturday of that week when we rolled round to the town hall for the dance, there were no men. Hampshire had been emptied.

The day peace in Europe was declared, I was in the Regal picture house. The news was flashed up on the screen. I didn't know whether to get my one and ninepence worth or go out and find someone to celebrate with. In the end many of us ended up in the Red Lion. Yes, I think I "grew up" in Petersfield.'

IT BECAME PART OF MY LIFE

'Joining the Women's Land Army seemed much more attractive to me than any of the armed services. The application form asked if I had any specific area of interest and I wrote I would like to work with poultry. That must have been a popular response because I was subsequently asked if I would accept threshing and field work in Odiham – a place I had never heard of. Anyway, I said "yes". In due course my uniform arrived and on the specified day I set off by train from my home near Dorking, dressed up in my new khaki-coloured dungarees, biscuit-coloured shirt, beige, stiff felt hat and heavy brogue shoes. It was a very warm day so my green pullover was in my suitcase.

All the new recruits had to meet at an appointed time at Woking and from there we all went by special train to Land Army head-quarters in Winchester. Here we were able to exchange any garment that didn't fit and we attended a lecture explaining our future role in the Land Army. We were also given the address of where we would be billeted and the name of the girl we would be sharing with. We were then taken to our billets by lorry and there was a great chatter as we got to know our new mates.

There were five of us left on the lorry when it reached Odiham and turned into West Street. Two sisters were taken to Mrs "Wobby" Farmer, one girl to Mrs Hall, and Lillian Todd and I to Mrs Hope. It was all very strange but after being shown our bedroom and deciding who was going to have which bed, we unpacked our belongings and began to feel more at home. We were paid between one pound two shillings and sixpence and one pound five shillings a week, and we paid one pound and two shillings for our board and keep. The following day we reported to Mr Thomas at Palace Gate Farm. After a chat we were each given a hoe and taken to a vast field, now largely covered by the houses of Buffins Road and the Kings Firs estate, and shown how to thin out mangels. That was 22nd June 1942 and the start of a prolonged heat wave. I don't know how we survived working all day in fields in that heat. One girl fainted several times and we all suffered from sunburn on our arms and neck, and our hair in the front, not protected by our scarves tied turban fashion over our heads, turned blonde.

We had each been allotted a bicycle and after only a few weeks we were sent to Murrel Green Farm to work with the threshing machine. We visited all the local farms – Hillside, Rye Common, Down and Mr Darnell at Adams in North Warnborough Street as well as farms as far out as Long Sutton, Well and Upton Grey.

Initially we were given forks to clear away the cavings – the straw and chaff which built up around the bottom of the threshing machine. At first we nearly got buried but soon learnt to start heaping this up a good distance away from the machine! We had to wear goggles to protect our eyes and at the end of the day we were completely covered in dust and if the crop was barley, the awls were embedded in our socks and sweaters. Beans and peas were the worst to thresh for dust.

From that dusty, dirty job we were soon promoted to band cutter and feeder of the machine. This involved cutting the string which bound the sheaf of corn and feeding it into the thresher. Lillian and

I took turns and unfortunately on one occasion we got out of rhythm and instead of me cutting the string I cut my friend's fingers.

I think in all we spent some ten months travelling around with the threshing machine. The corn ricks had to have wire netting put round them before threshing could begin, to trap the rats. As we got to the bottom of the rick there would be dozens of them jumping over our feet. We were armed with sticks and this was the most dreadful task – hitting and killing the rats.

On one occasion when pitching corn I suddenly felt something a bit odd around my middle. My deepest fear was that a mouse had run up my trouser leg! Clutching my clothes tightly my mate Lillian peeped in the placket of my dungarees and I read her lips, "It's a mouse," and I started shouting for help! Les Green, one of the farm workers came and squeezed and suffocated the mouse and Lillian managed to retrieve it. A few days later the same thing happened to her and after that we copied the men and tied string around each leg and started a new female fashion.

By now the other three girls had moved on and when Mr Thomas's son Ken asked us if we would like to work for him doing general farm work we jumped at the chance. Permission was sought and granted from Winchester and then we worked at Potbridge, Scotland and occasionally Snatchangers farms.

Italian and Polish POWs who were based at Winchfield helped with hoeing and field work but they were always kept well apart from the local labour force.

As well as hoeing, dung spreading, haymaking and rick building, we were taught by George Adair (who also lived in West Street) how to thatch ricks. We started off thatching the tops of the round silos and received great praise when they were subsequently opened and not a drop of wet had got in.

We also had a long spell helping out in the dairy and with the milk round. The milk cart was drawn by a lovely pony named Polly. Andy Wilson drove the milk van; Lillian and I especially enjoyed the ride out to Hillside with him. We were out with the milk float when we heard the news that the war was over. So we decorated Polly and the cart with orange blossom picked from a drive at Hatchwood Hill and continued our round in great style.

We didn't enjoy helping with the silage. Mr Thomas had the first cutter blower and molasses was mixed with the grass. Wearing macs and sou'westers we girls had to get inside the silo with the aid of a ladder and flatten the silage by stamping around to level it as it came out of the spout and all over us. A bit of a sticky mess! On one occasion it had overheated and Mr Thomas asked us to climb in and turn it over to help cool it. The fumes made us feel ill and we had to hang our heads over the top for air. We complained to Mr Thomas and he let us get out; I think we had hangovers afterwards!

Cutting the kale which stood some four feet tall in the winter for animal feed was not much fun either – especially when it was covered with snow and ice!

The local land girls had to report periodically to Mrs Guy Slater at The Close; she was very hospitable and sometimes invited us for supper. All in all we worked very hard doing all the general farm work but it was a very happy time. We enjoyed going to the Regal cinema on Dunleys Hill in the evenings and we were also invited to dances at RAF Odiham. My mate Lillian would sing and hum all the Glenn Miller tunes and we often would sneak into a barn during our dinner hour and dance – just the two of us. Mr Thomas surprised us on one occasion. "Now I know what you girls get up to," he said, "but I'll turn a blind eye because you are excellent workers." Some praise indeed and we felt really chuffed.'

## THE RAT CATCHERS GANG

'My mother and sister and I came to live in the tiny village of East Stratton, about seven miles from Winchester, at the end of 1939. My sister was employed by Barings Bank who had been evacuated to the large country house of Lord Northbrook. As we were Londoners born and bred it was certainly something of a cultural shock to live in this tiny village of mainly thatched houses. We were lucky to be able to rent a cottage from the then Lord Northbrook who owned the whole village.

I joined the Land Army and at first worked on a small mixed farm nearby. The pigs were fed by boiling up all the waste food that could be collected from the army camps. The Americans' food was the best. Sometimes we would find whole unopened packets of biscuits and tins of fish, which of course we took home. I strained my back lifting heavy pails of pig-swill over the sty walls so had to change to a lighter job, which was rat catching – actually it was rat poisoning!

Each gang was made up of four people – a man in charge, who drove the small van, and three land girls. We drove to farms all over Hampshire, with a dustbin in the back full of white powder. The first two days the powder was made up of flour and sugar with which we fed the rats, with tablespoons tied on to long poles to reach down their holes. Then on the third day we added powdered Warfarin, a tasteless poison, to the flour which proved very successful.

I also joined the village fire brigade! The fire engine was an ancient wooden hand-pushed and pulled contraption, which was found in

*The ratcatchers' gang display their catch! Farms all over Hampshire called on their services.*

an outhouse belonging to the "big house in the park", and had not been used for years. It had a large water container in the middle with a hosepipe attached and two wooden arms each side which had to be pumped up and down to draw the water up when the hosepipe was put down a well. In theory this was fine, but the very first time we had it out to practise, and about six of us pushed it down the village street, we found to our dismay that the hosepipe was far too short to reach the water down the well! Actually we were very lucky in that not once did we have any incendiaries fall on the village although there was quite a clutch once fell on some fields nearby. But, if there had been, can you imagine us all frantically winding up buckets of water by hand from the village wells while the thatched roofs burned merrily away!

I never went back to London. After the war I married the leader of our rat catchers gang, who went back to his rightful job as gamekeeper to Lord Rank.'

# LIFE GOES ON

**Whatever happened, life had to go on. Couples got married, families had to be fed and clothed, and we still wanted to be entertained and busy, especially if we were doing something for the war effort at the same time.**

OUR SPARE TIME

'Memories of the war evoke smells and sounds. I can never smell old damp buildings without remembering the underground shelter my father built in our back garden. We put pieces of carpet on the dirt floor and stuck candles on the wall to make it more habitable but this terrible fusty smell pervaded everything and eventually we abandoned it for a Morrison shelter which you erected indoors. This shelter resembled a large cage. The top was of strong sheet panels, the sides were thick steel mesh. My mother had to forgo her precious front room as it took up nearly all the floor space but it was infinitely preferable to going into the bowels of the earth when the siren sounded.

Basingstoke was regarded as a safe haven from the bombing. Consequently we had a large influx of evacuees from Portsmouth. This curtailed our education and it meant we had part time schooling, attending the school mornings only.

Our spare time was soon put to good use though. In the summer months we picked tomatoes and carnations at the local nurseries, and in the winter we worked with land girls, harvesting potatoes, swedes and turnips. This was backbreaking work and oh so cold!

Food rationing meant you were always hungry. There was no junk food to fill you up and usually it was a slice of bread with a small scraping of margarine or precious dripping. Being brought up in the war stood me in good stead for years later when my husband was to be made redundant and unemployed for six months.

Old sayings were bandied about such as "Waste not, want not", "Make do and mend" and a new one, "Dig for Victory".

Everyone was encouraged to dig up their flower beds and lawns and plant vegetables. Our neighbours kept ducks and chicken in their small back garden and nobody complained when the cockerel crowed at an unearthly hour in case it jeopardised their chances of a few fresh eggs. A real luxury was when my mother obtained a rabbit from her friend in the country. This provided two good meals with the added bonus of sevenpence from the rag and bone man for the skin. Everybody queued for everything. Sometimes there were little luxuries – bananas or elastic, and word would go round the town like wildfire which shop was selling them and I was sent post-haste to join the queue.

I came home from school one day with a note from the school nurse informing my mother I had head lice. This horrified my mother who had been a nurse in the 1918 war and so began the evening ritual over a spread out newspaper and my head was raked through with a metal comb and then washed in a strong carbolic solution.

Looking back to the 1940s, I realise how lucky we were. The enemy was not really interested in our sleepy market town and we had very few bombs dropped here but it still seemed a great adventure to my sister and me.'


WAR AND THE VILLAGE

'I moved to Liss in 1939, a village closely connected with the army. When the Second World War broke out, families had to move out of married quarters and many were billeted in the village, some of them moving in with their parents as they were village girls. Later there were evacuees from Battersea and Portsmouth. An empty house was taken over as a canteen to provide the children's lunches. Working there I got to know some of the army "mums" and we remained friends for many years.

I was also involved with the army in a quite different way. We lived on an estate which was entirely self sufficient. Part of my husband's job was to maintain the electrical installation in which the turbine was powered by the river Rother which ran through the grounds. This provided our electricity and also pumped water from a very deep well into our reservoir.

When the owner's duties took them abroad we were taken over by the War Department and about 30 permanent staff from the Royal Berkshire Regiment moved in. We were also lent to the Norwegian Government for use as a secret special training school. Men who had escaped to England were trained before going back to prepare for the invasion. I often wonder how many survived. They were grand men, always cheerful, but knowing that on their return if they were caught they would be shot.

In those days the military railway ran from Longmoor Camp to Liss so there was always a good attendance at dances, whist drives etc and some of us would be invited to entertainments in the Kitchener

Theatre in the camp. Now the railway has gone as also has the camp church with its lovely memorial windows and the school. The camp is now used only for training courses and is cut in half by the new A3 bypass. The lovely beech trees which sheltered the extra huts have been felled. How times have changed!'

'"This country is now at war with Germany." Neville Chamberlain's words echoed round our living-room and it was a very serious occasion, I realised that, even though I was only seven years old. One of the neighbours broke down and cried. They were sat around our wireless set with my parents, my three brothers and myself, because not everyone had a wireless set in 1939.

My parents ran a small village shop in Sandleheath. My father delivered paraffin, hardware, soap powder, candles etc to the surrounding villages. I don't know how my mother coped with all she had to do, she made pounds of jam to sell in the shop. As the war progressed we had convoys of soldiers passing through the village and she made pies, pasties and sausage rolls to sell to them. She was also involved in organising socials in aid of the Red Cross and the war effort, so her life was very busy, especially as she had the added worry of rationing and the points system to contend with.

We were always exhorted to "Dig for Victory". My father had always grown most of our vegetables as we had a large garden but he decided to keep more livestock. He had always kept hens but now he built a pigsty and installed several pigs and he started bee-keeping. Eventually he had 40 rabbits as well, which we sold to a local butcher for food. It was up to my youngest brother and myself to collect food for all these rabbits – much to our disgust we had to collect a large sackful every day!

A searchlight camp was built just up the road from us and suddenly our sleepy village became quite busy.

We had a dog that *always* slept in the middle of the road outside the shop. All the locals knew that they had to drive round him (not that there were many cars around anyway) because he would not move. Unfortunately he wouldn't move for the army either, be it lorries or tanks he stayed put. There were many confrontations which always ended up with one of us going out and forcibly removing him.

Later in the war, the Americans arrived. They took over the two large houses in the village and caused quite a stir.'

## STARTING MARRIED LIFE

'I was married in 1941; just before the wedding we had to replace our new furniture since that already purchased was destroyed by enemy action while still in the shop at Portsmouth.

Since my husband worked at the AEW Haslar we rented a house in Alverstoke which had been repaired after an incendiary bomb had damaged the roof. The house overlooked the creek and had two rooms above stairs and two downstairs. The kitchen, which was one of the downstairs rooms, included a bath since its inclusion became a late building requirement while the house was still under construction. We spent our nights in a make-shift bed downstairs, but we were eventually driven out by the noise of a new gun battery at Stokes Bay.

We moved to Fareham where our bungalow backed onto HMS *Daedelus*. During enemy action we could hear from our street brick shelter activity from within the base – whistle calls, loudspeaker instructions etc.

In 1942 my first child was born in St Mary's Hospital, Portsmouth. I was in there for three or four weeks during which air raids were particularly severe. On these occasions the babies were wheeled in their cots to the centre aisle of the ward which was considered the safest place.

One very bad night during a raid we were allowed to have our babies in bed with us. Soon after, the ward was evacuated to the ground floor, and a fire crew carried us lock, stock and baby to a lower side ward.'

## SHOPPING AND FOOD

'Despite rationing and having to register at your chosen grocer's, throughout the war a sales representative from the grocer called on my mother each week to take her order, tell her of any special items available, and the order was delivered the following day.

We only shopped for meat, fish, bread and greengrocery. We were fortunate in having a large apple and pear tree in the garden and each year the fruit was bottled. We also grew a few of our own vegetables, but had a weekly travelling greengrocer who traded from a horse-drawn cart.

Milk was supplied by a local man who bottled in a small complex in the next road. It was delivered in quart, pint or half pint bottles.

Bread came from a local baker. I can remember when "National bread" came, neither white nor brown! Good Friday was always special as it was the only day on which one could buy hot cross

*A guard of honour formed by land girls greeted Joe and Betty Rudd after their marriage at Wickham in 1942. Betty could not get a bridal veil because 'there's a war on', but the baker did manage a wedding cake using soya flour.*

buns and we used to go to the bakery in the morning to buy them still warm.

When we could get eggs they were preserved in waterglass. We were not allowed sugar in tea as it was saved for jam making and cakes. Our family used to mix butter and margarine, half and half, to make it more palatable. Our cheese ration we used to have once a month and eat in one meal!

I can remember one year having an extra fortnight's holiday in October so that schoolchildren could help with the potato picking. This was the first money I ever earned.

Obtaining sufficient coal was sometimes a problem. We rarely had a fire in the front room, and sometimes we would sit in the kitchen of an evening where we had an anthracite boiler. The boiler heated our hot water so often I would do school homework in the bathroom as that was a warm area with the airing cupboard. We started the winter with a supply of logs for the open fires. We had open fireplaces in the bedrooms, but these were only lit if someone was very ill.'

## PIGS AND CHICKENS

'When I lived in Bedhampton, Havant during the war, we had only two doctors in the area, the other two having been called up to the forces. They were overloaded with work and a few elderly doctors living in the area gave them occasional help during their retirement.

One of the two regular doctors kept pigs and on the let-down dicky seat of his car, he had secured two dustbins, in which he collected patients' scraps when on his rounds!

When anyone kept a pig or pigs, during the war, not only did they have to forfeit some of their bacon ration, but when the pigs were ready for slaughter half of the pigs or pig(!) had to be sold to the Ministry of Food.

Likewise, when anyone kept chickens, some of the egg ration had to be forfeited, if the householder wished to supplement the chickens' diet of scraps with a ration of meal, called "balance meal".

Every week the national newspapers published "Food Facts", giving details of any rations increase, economical recipes etc. We were told we were the best fed nation in Europe and this I believe.'

'My husband's great aunt Lottie lived in Totton and he tells me she was the epitome of a real countrywoman: apple cheeked and of ample proportions. In about 1942 he was taken to visit her. She lived in a semi-detached house with an orchard behind in which she kept chickens and she also had a permit allowing her to keep two pigs, who lived in sties. They were fed on waste food and anything else available. One pig was kept for pork and the other for preserving. He well remembers the two halves of the second pig hanging up on either side of the fire to be cured by the smoke.'


PENNY LOLLIES

'We had to boost trade at our little shop in Fareham because so many items were rationed, and so during 1943 we decided to make penny ice lollies. A fridge had to be bought and we wondered if we would ever recoup the £30 it cost! Fate was kind to us because we had a very hot summer. The lollies became famous among schoolchildren and while it was hard work it was fun making them and more than paid for the fridge. All these years later I still get stopped in the street from time to time by someone who remembers the penny lollies.'


MADE TO LAST

'My earliest recollection before the war is having to wear a coat with matching bonnet and button-up leggings, which I hated. Then with the coming of the war and clothing coupons I was saved from these garments.

I can remember coupons being saved up carefully for essentials. Clothes were darned and patched to make them last; I can even remember lisle stockings being patched!

All jumpers etc were hand-knitted and presumably were all wool. Wool was bought in skeins and had to be wound by hand. Until I was ten I always had a liberty bodice – complete with rubber buttons – as well as a vest and often two pairs of knickers for warmth. All girls seemed to wear pixie hoods in winter, usually with matching gloves or mitts.

My mother suffered severely from chilblains and needed to wear sheepskin bootees in winter. These became very precious and she lived in constant dread one pair would wear out before she could get another.

Another problem I remember was household linen. Coupons for this were in short supply and our sheets were patched and "sides to middle" so that the last ounce of wear was extracted. Also I remember some of our curtains being patched where the sun had affected them.

Fully fashioned silk stockings were very precious – and nylons brought over by American personnel like gold dust. Stockings were made to last by having them invisibly mended at the cleaners.

After the war there were a lot of weddings. My mother still had a wedding veil, which was lent out on many occasions. I went to a lot

of church services and saw that veil make its way down the aisle yet
again!'

WOMEN'S CONTRIBUTION

'From 1939 to 1945 the members of Hampshire's Women's Institutes
worked tirelessly in support of the national war effort. They applied
their talents and skills to the demands of wartime Britain with
ingenuity and determination.

In the early days members assisted, with other organisations, in
the billeting of evacuee children. Some WI halls were used as central
canteens in which the children were served meals. In others, rest
centres were set up by members for the use of visiting mothers most
of whom had endured long journeys to see their children. Later,
following the heavy bombing raids on Southampton and Portsmouth,
institutes outside the blitzed towns collected clothing, blankets
and bandages for the victims and helped to arrange temporary
accommodation in safe areas.

WI halls, like others in the community, were in great demand for
civil defence units such as the Home Guard and ARP posts. Some
were requisitioned by the army for military use and not returned
to the management committees until the end of the war. The loss
of use of these halls, whether WI or village halls, caused many
problems for institutes who had to find alternative accommodation
for their activities. In some instances, where institutes were located
in militarily sensitive areas, they had to be closed down altogether
for the duration of hostilities.

Despite the problems, the shortages and the restrictions, the
members of Hampshire's WIs quickly organised their resources
to the benefit of both the civilian population and the men in the
armed forces. Knitting parties were set up to knit "comforts", as they
were known, for the troops. Such items as socks, gloves, scarves
and balaclavas were made throughout the war years and beyond.
When the war in Europe ended in 1945 the work continued and
thousands of items of clothing and blankets were sent for the relief
of the destitute people on the continent.

"Make do and mend" was one of the popular slogans of the
time and WI members attending classes organised by the County
Federation soon became masters of the art. Slippers were made out
of old felt hats for the use of hospital patients, including wounded
servicemen. Aprons and "luncheon satchels" were made out of
hessian for use by the Women's Land Army. The alteration and
updating of old clothing for women and children was a constant
and well-practised skill. Members, it seemed, would turn their

hands to anything. When an appeal was made for baskets for potato lifting, a number of them eagerly volunteered to learn the craft. One institute organised classes for men and women in the village under the direction of a skilled craftsman and well over 100 baskets were made to meet the immediate demand.

By far the largest contribution to the war effort made by Hampshire WIs was the preservation of fruit and the canning of surplus vegetables. Jam making centres were set up at members' homes, often in garages, where the women pooled resources to produce vast quantities of preserves for general distribution. In 1940 alone 109 centres were set up in Hampshire which produced over 37 tons of jam and nearly three tons of bottled fruit. This enterprise, which continued throughout the war and was repeated by WIs throughout the country, must have made a very significant contribution to the nation's food supplies. In fact the achievement was formally acknowledged by Lord Woolton, the Minister of Food, who wrote to institutes thanking them for their hard work.

Another important project was "The Pie Scheme" set up by the government to supplement the diet of agricultural workers in the country. Many WIs became involved with the distribution of these pies which contained two ounces of meat and were sold at fourpence each – one per person. One institute records selling 30,000 pies in ten months in 1943.

Institutes throughout the county collected rosehips each year which were sent to Eli Lilley in Basingstoke to process into rosehip syrup, a valuable vitamin supplement for babies and young children. Each institute was paid by weight for the hips sent which was a welcome addition to their funds.

As D-Day approached in 1944 and troop concentrations in Hampshire increased, members turned their attention to providing leisure facilities and practical help for service personnel. Dances and whist drives were organised and one institute joined with other village organisations to run a games room and canteen nightly for American GIs camped in the vicinity. Many members opened their homes to overseas troops and friendships were forged that last to this day. On a more mundane level, several institutes responded to an appeal to mend soldiers' uniforms and darn socks.

Whatever needed to be done WI members were ready and willing to take up the challenge. Most of the work was organised locally by institute committees in response to local or national needs. It touched on every aspect of daily civilian life and did much to improve the lives of those enduring the debilitating shortages in wartime Britain. And it was accomplished by women who not only had homes to run and children to rear in the absence of husbands but many of whom belonged to other organisations as well. It was a remarkable achievement.'

## A VOLUNTARY ENSA

'When I became 18 during the war, like everyone else, I became liable for service in the armed forces, or one could opt for the police force. I chose the latter so that I could continue living at home with my parents and joined Portsmouth City Police. The WAPC wore uniforms which were very similar to those worn today by women police, except we wore black ties and soft-topped caps like those worn by the WAAF and ATS. We had no powers of arrest other than those that any citizen could make, our main purpose was to take over secretarial, administration and driving jobs usually done by male constables and so release them for service with the armed forces. I enjoyed my work with them and after a spell at headquarters, I was posted to a division and attached to the CID, which I loved. I remained in the police force until I married in 1946.

My mother had an excellent voice and bubbly personality and had entertained in a semi-professional capacity and nothing would suffice but that she "entertained the troops". She set about organising a group of entertainers, myself included (I sang ballads) and formed a voluntary ENSA. We were vetted by the powers that be and pronounced as suitable entertainment for the forces. So I found myself in any off-duty periods meeting up with others and going off to give a show. We entertained at garrison theatres with fully equipped stages, lights, sound and dressing rooms and, at the other end of the scale, at tiny gun sites where the "curtains" were army blankets, the "lights" candles stuck in cut-out empty food tins and the "stage" a few planks of wood resting on raised bricks! But what appreciative audiences there were – wonderful! Perhaps the most unusual venues were the sea forts in the Solent, Spitsands, Horsands and Nomans. We used to set off on a Sunday afternoon in a small motorboat and sometimes it was very rough, but even those members who were not good sailors would not have dreamed of staying behind. We would climb up the side of the fort, not looking down, give our show, have tea and then make our way back to the harbour. The forts were fascinating and rather reminded me of a giant swiss roll. In all we gave about 1,000 shows.

By 1943 there was the feeling that perhaps the tide had turned in our favour and the end of the war was almost in sight. There was still some way to go but the optimism and hope could not be denied. I lived just over the brow of Portsdown Hill and by late spring of 1944, the road where I lived and all the others in the area were awash with army vehicles of all shapes and sizes, armoured cars, lorries, smaller cars etc. The drivers and crews of these vehicles slept in, on, or under them and there was not a house in the road which didn't welcome in the boys to have baths and shaves and to share our food with them. This continued for a few weeks and one morning I woke to the sound of aircraft. I went into the garden and the sky was filled with hundreds and hundreds of aircraft – the invasion was about to begin and the road outside was empty of vehicles. We were happy to have been part of it.'

## GOOD ENOUGH FOR THE PALLY

'In the war the ladies of Church Crookham organised a tea dance in the village hall every week for the soldiers manning the two guns and searchlights in the area, as they were on duty at night guarding us. All of us young girls were more or less instructed to go. We had a wind-up gramophone to dance to and the sight of those soldiers in battle-dress and hob-nailed boots advancing towards you was sometimes rather daunting, especially if they weren't very good dancers.

One who was a particularly good dancer taught us girls several good tips – "'Ow to 'old yer 'ed proper," etc. He said he'd make us good enough dancers to go to the Pally at 'Ammersmiff up in "the smoke". Unfortunately we moved away so I don't know if any of the girls ever did get to the 'Ammersmiff Pally.'

234

# HIGH DAYS & HOLIDAYS

# WE MADE OUR OWN ENTERTAINMENT

**Dances, whist drives, sports, concerts – the amount of entertainment we managed to make for ourselves in the days before television (and before radio!) was astonishing, even in the smallest of villages. Men's clubs thrived, and from the 1920s the women of the village also found new outlets and enjoyment in the rapidly growing Women's Institutes.**

HOME-MADE ENTERTAINMENT

'Entertainment was all home-made at Four Marks in the 1920s, with dances and "sixpenny hops" where our own village band played until 2 am, the lancers and quadrilles being particularly popular. There were also social evenings, whist drives, concerts, billiards and an annual pantomime. Every occasion was fully supported. There was a local orchestra and operettas were performed. From 1920 there were tennis, cricket and football clubs, debating and dramatic societies, spelling bees, Guides, Scouts and a very popular ladies' choir.'

'There were many dances in local village halls and ballroom dancing classes were popular to help us learn all the steps. We would cycle to dances with our long dress packed in an attaché case on the back of the bike and change in the cloakroom.

Cadnam had a brass band and entered competitions. They also played on the village green in summer and at local fêtes.'

'Before the Second World War Sway had a tennis court which, for a fee, villagers could use. Old Time, Flannel, Fancy Dress, New Year's Eve and end of season Football Club dances were in great demand, as were the village hops. Men and boys played football and cricket, and the men were happy to go to the Working Men's Club, which was strictly men only. There were whist drives and Band of Hope meetings, where we had magic lantern shows. We cycled to Hordle Cliff to swim and also cycled to the cinemas at Lymington and New Milton.'

*A charabanc outing from Whitchurch in August 1929. Ideal for parties, charabancs were popular vehicles for that rare day out.*

## FOR MEN AND WOMEN

'Men played cricket and football, in teams then drawn entirely from village inhabitants. After the 1914–18 war, ex-servicemen's social clubs were set up, usually by public subscription. Almost every village had its band and after band practice (which is thirsty work) the men repaired to the village pub to play darts, skittles and shove-halfpenny. No self-respecting woman would be seen in a public house but as a special treat, the family might sit outside and be regaled with crisps (salt in a little twist of blue paper) and fizzy lemonade. Less fortunate children would languish outside until closing time or until Father (and in some cases Mother) had drunk that week's wages. For those who liked a drink but did not care to be seen in the pub, there was the "bottle and jug".

It will be seen that there was very little for women and so the Women's Institute (many formed in the 1920s) was a lifeline.'

'My growing up in Fair Oak village had quite a lot to do with the WI. I was twelve years old when it was founded in January 1918. The war was still dragging on with all its miseries and apart from the Mothers Union there was nothing in the village to cater for women's interests outside the home. In fact over 100 joined that first year and on the first committee were my mother and my mother-in-law to be.

Soon all sorts of activities were under way, both for grown-ups and us children. The very first Christmas, when the war had just ended, we were given a wonderful party. In subsequent years these parties improved as supplies became more plentiful, each child receiving a present. I particularly remember one organiser, Mrs Denham. Every year she made several trips into Southampton to buy the presents and I was invited to her house to help sort them out and to label them, after which I stayed to tea. On one of these occasions I had birthday cake. On the day of the party Mr Denham brought the prizes to the hall in his wheelbarrow.

Altogether we were very well catered for by the WI. We were given dancing classes, folk and ballroom, in the early evening before the grown-ups arrived, and we were taught to play tennis on the vicarage court, a privilege bestowed by the then President, the vicar's wife. We older children were also allowed to attend the classes organised for the adult members so we became involved in plays and the choral society which won the shield in a county competition in its first year. Cheese-making classes were of particular interest to me as we kept goats. There were also rush-work classes at which several ladies made hats; the vicar's wife made mats for the vicarage stairs as she couldn't afford carpets; and I made tool baskets for my father who was the local carpenter, wheelwright and undertaker.'

## THE VILLAGE HOP

'The local village hop was always held on a Saturday night. My parents took me for the first time when I was 15. From then on, I was hooked on dancing!

The Second World War was nearly at an end and, at that time, the evening was just a social occasion. Games were played and during

the interval there was a raffle. Refreshments consisted of either tea or coffee together with sandwiches. Sausage rolls were a luxury. Just before midnight (the gaiety could not continue into the early hours of Sunday morning) the last waltz was played. The tunes – *Who's Taking you Home Tonight* and *Goodnight Ladies* echoed through the hall.

After the war we moved to Heath End. The Yanks had gone home and many of our boys had come back from overseas. There were plenty of dances around but my girlfriends and I would cycle to Farnborough. The army dances seemed much better organised than civilian ones. There was a Master of Ceremonies on duty, there were plenty of partners, and the bands were good.

Sometimes well known bands played. This meant that most of the floor was taken up by foot-tapping couples standing watching the orchestra. Little room was left for the more serious occupation of actually dancing which I wanted to do. The quickstep and the waltz were my favourites. If ever I was a "wallflower" for the first half of the evening I would get on my bike and go home!

Older, but still in my teens, my mother persuaded me to go with her to an Old Time Dance. This was great fun and clubs sprang up in many country areas. Village halls rang to the recorded sound of Sydney Thompson and his Music. Everyone enjoyed the music and dancing, even though there was still only coffee and sandwiches for the evening break. Progressive dances made sure that all age groups mixed and, in contrast to modern dancing, the Old Time was relaxed and friendly. It didn't matter if you couldn't do the steps, you just followed the people in front. If they did it right you were all right. If not, well, it didn't really matter.

Each week there was a short teaching session when a new dance would be learnt and once every few months a coach would be hired to take members to a ball. Clubs took it in turns to arrange a grand affair with a live orchestra. The ladies wore long dresses and the men evening suits. Tickets consisted of printed programmes listing all the dances for the evening. There would be the Lancers, the Mississippi Dip and the Gay Gordons to enjoy. Each dance finished with a curtsey from the ladies and a bow from the gentlemen who always escorted their partners back to their seats. I made many friends at Old Time Dances, one of whom I married in Bramshott Church, in 1950.'

## THE FIRST RADIOS

'I remember watching my father make little wireless sets in the 1920s, which fitted into a twelve-cube Oxo tin. I helped him find the tiny screws which dropped on the floor, and at other times to hold small cylinders which he wound wire round to make coils. My mother was probably the first person in Woolton Hill to own her own wireless set, which she listened to with earphones on her head while she did her knitting. Later we had a crystal set, which we adjusted with the "cat's whisker" to hear more clearly. Many years later, my father met Logie Baird, the man who brought television into our lives.'

# ROYAL OCCASIONS

**Jubilees and coronations provide many happy memories of town and village celebrations across Hampshire.**

### JUBILEE AND CORONATION IN THE 1930s

'I remember being marched to the Walled Meadow at Andover on two occasions in the 1930s. The first was for George V's Jubilee in 1935 and the second time was for George VI's Coronation in May 1937. We sang patriotic songs, then marched back through the town to the Drill Hall, where we were given a tea and a commemoration mug each time to take home.'

'For Coronation Day in 1937 my sister and I, like so many young girls, had special dresses made. Ours were white cotton with red and blue chain stitch worked round the hems, sleeves, collar and belt; we loved them. The military arranged a day for all Farnborough schoolchildren at the Army Command sports ground. In the morning and afternoon games, sports and activities were held and then we were all taken to the barracks for tea. It was a grand spread with each child taking home the special coronation china mug he or she had used. We were also given a coronation book by the Farnborough District Council.'

### CELEBRATIONS AT TWYFORD 1953

'Twyford's celebrations for the coronation of Queen Elizabeth II started with a service in the church. The vicar then led a procession, headed by the choir, down to the crossroads in the middle of the village. Here the oldest man in the village, and a young woman who shared a birthday with the Queen, planted a commemorative cherry tree on the bank overlooking the crossroads.

Later in the day there was a grand carnival parade. Led by the Twyford village band, a procession of floats paraded round the village. Most of these floats were mounted on the backs of lorries from the Allbrook Gravel Works. Every organisation in the village, Girl Guides, Mothers Union, and many more, decorated their float and rode on it in full costume. Everyone was in fancy dress. Two village men dressed up as tramps and wheeled a gramophone along on a push-chair. There was a splendid coronation cake, iced and decorated. This was part of the parade; it sat on a table top, complete with decorated cloth, fixed over a child's pram. It was pushed along by Mrs Bull, imposing in a white dress and tall chef's hat, and pulled by four young lads dressed as pages in tabards decorated with the royal arms.

The parade finished in a field along the Hazeley Road where there were sports and races for everyone and a splendid tea where the cake was cut and eaten.'

## PENNINGTON'S SPECIAL DAY

'June 2nd 1953 was to be a very special day in our village. The coronation of our young queen, Elizabeth II, was taking place in London. We, who were not lucky enough to see the spectacle live and not fortunate enough to own a TV set, were going to celebrate too. The Mayor was going to present commemorative mugs to the children. A bunch of very excited youngsters gathered in the village square; fortunately traffic was almost non-existent then. How many mugs came to grief on the way home I wonder? The highlight of the day was yet to come. Mothers had been busy baking and jelly making. Tables were being carried out of the houses and set up in the street, tablecloths appeared as if by magic and the tables were soon groaning with goodies and almost as quickly cleared again by hungry youngsters. Balloons and paper hats were very much in evidence and the "three hearty cheers" for our new Queen would have raised the roof.

Meanwhile, on the Lymington sports ground, many of our husbands, members of local village cricket teams, were battling for the Coronation Cup.

More excitement after the street party as participants gathered for the highlight of the evening, the Carnival Parade. A colourful collection of decorated floats interspersed with many and varied characters on foot, money buckets clanking, kept time to several marching bands. As the procession wound its way through the cheering, flag waving crowd, an extra loud cheer greeted Pennington Cricket Club, firmly ensconced on the leading float and holding aloft their prize for the day, the Coronation Cup.

What an exciting day, little feet were lagging and small heads nodding. Back home to bed after a day to remember. Needless to say the cricketers staggered home very much later having well and truly christened their trophy, which still resides in Pennington Social Club – waiting for the next coronation perhaps?'

STILL TREASURED

'At the time of the coronation in 1953 I was eight years old, and won second prize for my coronation scrapbook in an event organised for children at Farringdon. We were all taken to London to see the decorations, and to a cinema afterwards to see the film of the event. On the day itself we watched the ceremony on a television set in the village hall. An oak was planted by the church lychgate, we had a grand tea and sports and were each presented with a mug, which I still treasure today. The day ended with a bonfire and fireworks.'

# ALL THROUGH THE YEAR

**There were celebrations and activities to be looked forward to all the year through, such as famous fairs like the Overton Sheep Fair, Hospital Sunday or Club Day, and seasonal delights such as May Day. Many of these events have gone from our calendars, but each one was eagerly anticipated when we had few other holidays to look forward to.**

FESTIVALS AND OUTINGS

'The progress of the year was marked by festivals and outings. On Whit Sunday the Twyford men's clubs – Oddfellows, Foresters and the Friendly Society – paraded their banners. Led by the village brass band, they marched from Shawford Down round the village,

*The Queen driving through Odiham in 1953 on her way to the RAF station.*
*People had waited for hours to cheer her on her way in Coronation year.*

collecting a following of children on the way, and finished up with a service in the church.

On May Day the girls from the village school chose their May Queen and two attendants. Dressed in their best summer dresses they walked up to Twyford Lodge to dance round the maypole. After that Mrs Peach gave them tea in the garden, sandwiches and buns carried round in clothes baskets. Both girls and boys belonged to the Band of Hope which was run by the Methodist chapel. In the summer they had an outing to Boscombe or Bournemouth by coach. Miss Hull ran two separate Bible classes for the church boys and girls. Some girls paid a penny every Saturday to learn cross stitch at Waterworks House.

On August Bank Holiday many families took a picnic to Shawford Down. Friends came out from Eastleigh on the train to join them. While the adults chatted the children played games and organised impromptu races.

On 11th November, Armistice Day, the ex-servicemen paraded,

led by a band, and a local dignitary took the salute outside The Bugle. At 11 am on that day the hooter sounded and everybody stopped to keep two minutes' silence to remember those killed in the war. Cars stopped in the street, women stood quietly at home, work stopped everywhere.

On Empire Day the schoolchildren marched round the playground and saluted the Union Jack to show their loyalty to King and Empire.

There were weekly amusements for all. From November onwards there were regular Thursday evening whist drives, run by a different organisation each week. At the Fur and Feather Drive the prizes were rabbits, pheasants and chickens. Miss Hull and Miss Trask ran regular country dancing sessions. There was usually a dance in the village hall on Saturday nights and Old Time dancing on Fridays.

The village summer fête was held at The Elms. A favourite attraction was Living Whist. Fifty-two young women, wearing tabards representing a pack of cards, went through a complicated march routine to shuffle and deal, ending up in four corners with their backs to the centre. The four players then played a game of whist calling out the cards they were playing so that the cards could march to the centre. The rules were those of ordinary whist.

The Women's Institute provided an interest for the women. In addition to monthly meetings they ran dressmaking classes and a choir. The choir went as far as Southampton to take part in a festival. Some of the best needlewomen in the village worked for the Yew Tree Industry. This was a cottage industry producing counted thread embroidery on household linen. It was patronised by many rich households, and sample boxes were sent nationwide. Even Queen Mary bought some of their work.'

## TITCHFIELD'S HOSPITAL SUNDAY

'Hospital Sunday was celebrated at the time of St Luke's Day. There was a gathering in the Square of all the Friendly Societies, Oddfellows, Foresters and others, wearing the colours of their club. Titchfield at that time had a very good fife and drum band and they would be in attendance, and all would follow the band and march to the church for a special service. An exciting occasion for the village people.

The rear drummer of the band was short and fat and could barely see over his drum. They would play outside various public houses to get subscriptions for the band's upkeep. Of course they received a certain amount of liquid refreshment and the drummer, being very partial to a few glasses, over-indulged once and fell into his drum! He was quite often seen walking through the village with a bucket of lime-wash on his head and swinging a brush, which meant someone was going to have the "little house" at the end of the garden "done out".

In addition, he was also Titchfield's town crier, and a very imposing figure he was in knee breeches, white stockings and buckled shoes. He wore a blue coat with lace at the neck and sleeves and a three-cornered hat. He had a strong carrying voice and had to announce in each street such things as lost and found items, political meetings and smoking concerts.'

## SPECIAL DAYS

'I lived in Rowledge, a small village right on the border of Hampshire and Surrey, where the county boundary runs through the centre of the village. A deep ditch just inside the Alice Holt Forest ran along the edge of the school playground and the churchyard. This was believed to be where men of the two counties fought, giving rise to the original name of Rough Ditch. Fairs were held at the recreation ground at Holt Pound, also cricket matches and this was the original "Oval".

A well known village name was Parratt, and later I had the fun of scoring a cricket match between the village and a team of "birds" – ten Parratts and one Swan.

Special days at school included Empire Day, when the Union flag was raised and we all gathered round to sing the Empire song, the rest of the day being a half holiday. At the village fête each year we danced round the maypole in our crisp white dresses.'

## OVERTON SHEEP FAIR

'For many years before the First World War, and for some years after, there was a large and famous sheep fair held in Overton on 18th July each year. It was one of the highlights of village life. More than 30,000 sheep and lambs would arrive from a very wide area, driven considerable distances. They were penned in fields nearby. Stalls and various games' booths lined Winchester Street, and roundabouts and swinging boats were a great feature of the event. When young in the 1920s we lived on the route to the Fairclose and the first bleat was our signal to be up and out to help or hinder the drovers on the last lap. The fair was a holiday for everyone.'

# ODIHAM FAIRS AND FÊTES

'Whit Monday and August Bank Holiday in the early 1900s were outstanding dates as they were the occasions when Odiham enjoyed fêtes organised by the Hampshire and General Friendly Society of the Order of Oddfellows.

The first named society was founded in 1825 and its head office was, and still is, at Winchester. Branches were opened in all parts of Hampshire and the Isle of Wight, and that at Odiham was one of the earliest. Here, the agent and secretary, was Mr S. H. Clinker, remembered especially for his famous moustache. His office and residence were in the High Street. To assist the agent there was a chairman, vice chairman and committee members and these occupied themselves on a voluntary basis with collecting monthly subscriptions, visiting the sick and when the time came round, acting as stewards at the fêtes held on Whit Monday.

The members – the committee – adorned themselves with blue sashes, mustered in the High Street and then, headed by their banner and the Odiham Oaks Band (conductor Mr Tommy Parnell) or the Hook Silver Prize Band, would march to the parish church for a short service. Following this, all would adjourn to either a meadow at the rear of Palace Gate Farm, or to one on the south side of Farnham Road – where Archery Fields now is.

A large marquee had been erected in the meadow wherein all kinds of liquor was obtainable (a local publican would have been granted an "occasional licence" to sell intoxicants) and suitable lunch food was also available. There were also plenty of chairs, forms or bales of hay or straw on which to sit. The band would play during the afternoon and evening. The stewards organised races for the children and in addition there were swinging boats and other side shows. One great attraction was bowling for a live pig. The prize was on show enclosed in a pen made of hurdles, so that the competitors could see if it was worth "having a go". After tea, a highlight of the fête was the pillow fight. A wooden scaffold pole had been mounted on two trestles about five feet from the ground, and the local stalwarts (mostly young men) would be invited to sit on the pole, and, armed with a pillow stuffed with straw or hay, attempt to knock each other off. Sometimes one quickly succeeded and another competitor would mount the pole in an endeavour to dislodge the reigning champion.

Another test of skill, and a disregard for the state of one's trousers, was the greasy pole. A wooden scaffold pole, inserted firmly in the ground and spread with grease, was there to be climbed by any man willing to try. (Women did not appear to want to try their skill.) The

246

*Urging on their favourites of the Kings Arms tug of war team, Odiham celebrates the Oddfellows fête in 1955.*

competitors were cheered on by the crowd – very few got many feet up the pole.

Later in the evening there was an outdoor cinematograph show. The films usually included shots of the villain placing the bound body of the beautiful young girl upon the railway to await death. An alternative attraction, when the fête was held at the rear of Hatchwoods House, was a display by the local fire brigade who would stage a mock fire and then, by means of their manually operated pumps and water from the nearby Fisher's stream, extinguish the blaze. The strange thing is that it always seemed to be lovely fine weather when the fêtes took place – the same applying to August Bank Holiday.

The Oddfellows, whose agent was Mr Forder, put on a much more elaborate show. After the march to church, also complete with sashes, banners and band, and following the service, the members would adjourn to the Farnham Road meadow where there would be a competition to determine the best cart horses. These beautiful animals, from farms all round Odiham, would be lined up. Their tails and manes were adorned with ribbon and straw plaiting whilst rosettes were fastened to their heads. Their proud carters paraded them round the ring for inspection and judging.

After lunch and refreshment in the large marquee there was horse jumping in the arena. This was followed by races and other attractions for the children and later the skills of pillow fights and greasy pole – as described earlier – would take place. The band had been entertaining the crowds during the afternoon and evening – when dancing commenced.

In later years, in the summer at the Oddfellows fête, several unforgettable characters played their part – Young Billy Marshal, although aged 70 so-called because his father was also named Billy, and his dog called Sal; the sub-mariner, Charlie Ruddock, never at a loss for a good yarn; and Stan Musselle, who lost a leg in the war.

The Mid-Lent Fair was held annually in the Bury. The main attraction, the roundabouts, were erected at the side opposite to the church and nearer to the telephone exchange, now a private house (Little Court). A traction engine puffed away, the smell of hot metal and steam filling the air, and all the parts so well-made and maintained working smoothly. The rousing music added to the excitement as it came from the fairground organ, with the various figures all appearing to contribute. The smell and excitement was memorable, toffee apples produced on the spot, not hygienically wrapped, but hot and sticky. The stalls were not very different from today's, with cuddly toys and cheap trinkets to be won. On the far side near the stocks was the coconut shy. A row of four swingboats each worked by ropes, held by the two children riding in them, was popular. Then came the war and this excitement in the Bury never returned, the fair being transferred to the recreation ground, and the Mid-Lent date becoming only a memory.'

# CHRISTMAS PAST

Christmas has always been a time of special joy and of magic. Presents were often much cheaper and simpler in our childhood, but none the less enjoyable for that, and in some villages Christmas meant a visit to the 'big house'.

## A WONDERFUL DAY

'I was born in 1916 at Griggs Green, near Liphook. Christmas was a wonderful time. It began on Christmas Eve when my father put up the tree. The house was decorated with holly and mistletoe and it was very difficult to get to sleep that night. We woke very early to see what Father Christmas had brought us. One year we had large hand-painted wooden ducks which we could pull along, and another memorable year we both had a canopied doll's bed with mattress, blankets, lace trimmed sheets and pillowcases with a small feather eiderdown and beautiful lace bedspread matching the lace canopy. We were a small community of mostly adults so we had many presents from friends and neighbours.

After breakfast we dressed for church in our very best clothes; all our dresses were hand-made with bodices trimmed with lace and ribbon insertions. Our little tin church was at the edge of Weavers Down, about five minutes' walk away and we had helped decorate it two days before Christmas.

I can still remember the faces of the vicar, Revd Polhampton, and his curate Revd Taylor and I loved all the church services but never understood a word they were saying. Miss Pike played the harmonium which she later taught me to play; I already played the piano. After the service we had to be on our very best behaviour as the vicar and curate joined us for coffee and as it was a special occasion we children were allowed a very weak cup of coffee also.

There were usually just the four of us for Christmas dinner when we had either one of our own geese, or roast pork or a pheasant, all with sausagemeat and stuffing and home-grown vegetables. Afterwards there was Christmas pudding and trifle. Isabel and I would then clear the table which Mother would reset for later high tea while Father made up all the fires.

Family and friends arrived for high tea just before dark and at about six o'clock we sat down to more food – cold gammon, tongue, various cheeses, farmhouse butter and homemade bread, followed by scones, jam and cream and mince pies. In place of honour was the Christmas cake, iced and decorated by my mother and surrounded by Christmas crackers. Tea seemed to go on for hours as aunts and uncles ate so much, it was hard for them to want to or be able to leave the table. It was also very hard for Isabel and me as we had to be seen but not heard until we could finally leave the table. All too soon Mother would say, "Off to bed both of you", and so would end a wonderful day.'

## PARTIES AT HINTON AMPNER

'As a small child in the 1920s I was taken by my parents (my father being an estate carpenter) to the parties at Hinton Ampner House. I remember the old house with its dark panels, tea in the servants' hall, and carols around the brightly lit tree in the front hall with presents around the bottom for the children. Mr Ralph Dutton and the rector would be standing either side of the tree with a wet sponge on a cane to extinguish the candles as they burnt down.

Mr Dutton's mother, dressed in an ornately embroidered evening gown, would call our names and give us our presents from the tree.

The three Miss Duttons, holding flat flower baskets, suitably decorated, full of oranges, apples, crackers and sweets (often net bags of chocolate money) would give one of each to every child upon leaving. My mother always received a beautifully iced cake, decorated with coloured marzipan sweets, made by Dumpers of Winchester.

Then came the war years when the house was occupied by the Portsmouth high school – we would be invited to watch their nativity plays and listen to the carols performed by the school orchestra and choir.

For three years after the war my family and I lived at Hinton House. Food was rationed so the Christmas party was catered for by a Miss Batty who lived at Lawrence the newsagent's in Alresford. The children were given a new half crown each instead of presents.

It was at this time that Mr Dutton decided to arrange for a children's entertainer to come. After finishing tea in the dining-room, the chairs were quickly moved by the staff through the double doors into the drawing-room while the carols were being sung around the tree in the hall, then the children would be led into the drawing-room.

The children that attended Hinton Ampner school were all brought to the party by coach and I must not forget Mrs Cross who kept many of the small children happy in her kitchen and who prepared those delicious teas through so many years.'

## A MAGICAL TIME

'Christmas began for us as children (and the grown-ups as well!) in Overton in the 1930s when the Bazaar in the basement of Hide's drapery store opened in December. The excitement of going down the wooden twisting stairs to the Bazaar was almost too great to be borne! It had its own evocative smell, a mixture of mothballs and damp and the mysterious Christmas aroma. If I shut my eyes I can smell it now! We counted our money, carefully saved up for Christmas, and searched the shelves for presents to buy. There were books and toys, puzzles, paints and coloured pencils, balloons and marbles, and all sorts of exciting things. There were candle holders and candles and shiny baubles for the Christmas tree, and boxes of Christmas crackers. It was a magical place.

Before the war, at Christmas, children of the staff of the "big house", Southington House, were invited to tea in the servants' hall. After tea we gathered round the Christmas tree in the front hall and everyone was given a present by Father Christmas (Sir Bertram Portal), and then we sang carols. The carol I remember most clearly is *Like silver lamps in a distant shrine*.

## 'HAPPY DAYS'

'Christmas was a happy time at Overton. The parish church choir led the carol singing round the houses, finishing at the hospital. In the afternoon of Christmas Eve, Father Christmas, known as "Happy Days", accompanied by Jack Reid the blacksmith, suitably attired on his pony and cart and ringing his bell, would give sweets to the children.

On Boxing Day a great attraction was the meet of the Hampshire Hunt in the High Street.'

251

# Index